THE POLITICS OF
PARENTING

THE POLITICS OF
PARENTING

by

William B. Irvine

PARAGON HOUSE
St. Paul, Minnesota

Published in the United States of America by

Paragon House
2285 University Avenue West
St. Paul, Minnesota 55114

Library of Congress Cataloging-in-Publication Data

Irvine, William Braxton, 1952-
  The politics of parenting / by William B. Irvine.
    p. cm.
Includes bibliographical references.
  ISBN 1-55778-818-9 (pbk.)
  1. Parenting--Government policy. 2. Parent and child--Government
policy. 3. Child rearing--Government policy. I. Title.
  HQ755.8 .I783 2002
  649'.1--dc21
                            2003000335

10 9 8 7 6 5 4 3 2 1

For current information about all releases from Paragon House,
    visit the web site at http://www.paragonhouse.com

To VaVa

We have not the strength to follow our reason all the way.

—La Rochefoucauld, *Maxims*

CONTENTS

PROLOGUE

This book is in a sense a companion volume to my *Doing Right by Children: Reflections on the Nature of Childhood and the Obligations of Parenthood.* In that book, I was concerned with the *ethical* issues involved in parenting. I asked questions like, What's the proper goal of parenting? and, What do parents owe their children? I deliberately sidestepped the *political* issues involved in parenting: the government[1] remained in the background throughout my discussions. My intent was to use moral suasion to convince readers that they ought to take the responsibilities of parenthood far more seriously than many people do, that they ought to put the interests of their children ahead of their own interests, and that if they cannot do this, they have no business becoming parents in the first place.

In the present book, moral suasion falls by the wayside. In its place I introduce the iron fist of government and inquire into what role, if any, government has in *forcing* people to do right by their children. In some cases this might mean not allowing people to have children in the first place; in other cases it might mean allowing people to give birth to children but forcing them to turn their babies over to other, more-qualified parents; and in yet other cases it might mean allowing people to have and raise children but carefully monitoring and regulating the behavior of these parents.

The reader should not infer from these remarks that I am a friend of big government or a fan of governmental coercion. Quite the contrary. My politics are best described as libertarian. As such, I am sympathetic to almost any proposal to shrink the size and power of government. I think that most of the things the government attempts to do, it does poorly, and that the government has almost no business interfering with people's lifestyle choices as long as those choices do not harm others. Nevertheless, in much of this book I will be considering a stronger role for government with respect to the family.

This might seem paradoxical, and if children were the property of their parents—theirs to do with as they please—it would be paradoxical. The thing to realize is that I do not consider children to be the property of their parents, at least not in the same sense as a car or home might be their property. Furthermore, I do not regard parents' decisions about how to treat their children as being mere "lifestyle choices." After all, such decisions *can* harm others—namely, their children. For these reasons, advocacy of a stronger role for government with respect to the family is not, as it might first seem, inconsistent with the tenets of libertarianism.

In a perfect world we wouldn't need to force people to look out for the best interests of their children; they would do so willingly. In our less-than-perfect world, though, there are individuals who are unmoved by moral considerations; unless government gets involved, they are unlikely to do right by their children.

To be sure, most Americans are perfectly willing to allow *some* governmental interference with parental prerogatives. We acquiesce when the government stops parents from beating children or forces parents to educate, feed, and inoculate their children. Thus, for most Americans the question is not *whether* government should interfere with parental prerogatives, but *how* and *to what extent* it should interfere. My goal in the remainder of this book is to consider and provide partial answers to these last questions.

To facilitate my discussions I will break the question of the extent to which the government should be allowed to interfere with the parent/child relationship into three narrower questions: Who should be allowed to procreate? Who should be allowed to raise children? and, To what extent should the government regulate the behavior of parents? Let us take a closer look at these questions.

Who should be allowed (by the government) to procreate? In our society almost everyone who possesses the biological ability to make a child is allowed to procreate. People with genetic defects are allowed to procreate. People on welfare are not only allowed to procreate, but for many decades were encouraged to do so: by having children, they could increase the size of their welfare payments. Convicted child abusers and pederasts are allowed to procreate. Even when we strip an individual of most of his rights by putting him in prison, we don't necessarily strip him of his right to procreate. Indeed, thanks to conjugal visitation rights, many prisoners have fathered children while behind bars.

It needn't be this way. Indeed, in America it hasn't always been this way. A century ago the average American thought it entirely appropriate for the government to play an active role in preventing certain individuals from having children. To our forebears, the argument for government-enforced eugenic measures was obvious. There are, they reasoned, certain individuals to whom, because of their genetic makeup, no one would want to be born. To allow these individuals to procreate is to ignore the interests of children. Supreme Court Justice Oliver Wendell Holmes, in his 1927 defense of forced sterilizations, summarized the thinking of his time in no uncertain terms: "Three generations of imbeciles are enough."

There is another issue that arises when we ask, Who should be allowed to procreate? Some would argue that the government should interfere with people's procreative choices, not because these people are unfit to procreate, but because of a population problem. Thus, if a government worries that it has or will have too many citizens, it might take steps to prevent its citizens from having children or place limits on the number of children they can have; and conversely, if a government worries that it has or will have too few citizens, it might take steps to encourage citizens to procreate.

In Part One of this book, I will take up the question of who should be allowed to procreate. In Chapters 1 and 2, I will examine the history of eugenics and the arguments that can be developed for and against it. In Chapter 3, I will examine the eugenic issues that might arise when biotechnological breakthroughs give parents the power to "design" their offspring. Finally, in Chapters 4 and 5, I will consider the government's role in developing policies to influence the rate at which a country's population is growing.

Who should be allowed (by the government) to raise children? Once we have determined who shall be allowed to procreate, we must determine who shall be allowed to raise the children brought into existence. In our culture the assumption is that a child's biological parents should be allowed to raise him, but we can imagine other practices. Indeed, some have suggested that we should license parents—that only people meeting certain qualifications should be allowed to parent. To obtain a license, people should have, among other things, a certain financial wherewithal, a certain level of education, and a stable home life. If a man and woman have a baby without a license, they will not be allowed to raise the child they created; instead, it will be taken from them at birth and turned over to an adoptive couple that does possess a parent's license.

In Part Two of this book I take up the question of who should be allowed to raise children. In Chapter 6, I consider the argument—offered by the advocates of Children's Liberation—that children should not be raised by anyone, since to "raise" them is to violate their rights. I also discuss the view that the state and its hired nannies rather than particular couples ought to raise children. In Chapter 7, I examine the proposal that parents be licensed. In Chapter 8, I consider the issues that arise when determining who should be allowed to adopt. Finally, in Chapter 9, I analyze cases in which disputes arise over who shall act as a child's parents, including cases in which children are accidentally switched at birth and cases in which children sue to "divorce" their parents.

How should the government regulate parental behavior? Regardless of how we settle the question of who should be allowed to raise children, we are faced with the additional question of whether and to what extent the government, after allowing a couple to raise a child, should interfere with how they raise it. The government can, to begin with, take a laissez-faire approach to parenting and give parents an utterly free hand in determining how they raise their children. Few would favor such an approach, however, since it would entail that if parents want to beat their child, the government should stand back and let them.

Once we declare our willingness to let the government interfere with parental behavior, we are faced with the question of what limits should be placed on such interference. In Part Three of this book, I will examine the proper scope of governmental interference. In Chapter 10, I examine several of the debates that have arisen concerning governmental regulation of parental behavior, including the question of whether Christian Scientists should have to take their ailing children to physicians, whether Amish children should be forced to attend high school, and whether parents should be allowed to spank their children. In Chapter 11, I take up the topic of divorce. In its choice of divorce laws, the state is regulating parental behavior that can have a profound impact on the well-being of children.

It would be easy to devote an entire book to single aspects of the politics of parenting—to eugenics, population control, or the licensing of parents, for example. In this book, however, my goal is breadth, not depth. I want to cover a whole series of issues in the politics of parenting, showing how they interrelate. I also want to show how our views on the politics of parenting would change if we rejected the *ownership model* of parenting in favor of the *stewardship model*.[2] These two models of parenting embody two different viewpoints with respect to the moral obligations of parenthood. According to the ownership model, children are a form of property. As such, it is not the duty of parents to make sacrifices on behalf of their children; to the contrary, owner-parents will happily exploit their children in order to accomplish their own goals. According to the stewardship model, on the other hand, parents do not own their children but instead should act as stewards on behalf of their children. In this capacity, they have a duty to look out for their children's interests. They will routinely make sacrifices on behalf of their children.

For most of the history of mankind, the ownership model has been the dominant model of parenting. Around 1700 the stewardship model began to grow in popularity and by 1950 had displaced the ownership model in many developed nations, including the United States. Parents no longer sent their children off to work in factories, as owner-parents used to do; instead they sent them to school, where they learned things that would help them develop and carry out their own life plans. Mothers gave up their career prospects in the belief that the interests of their children were best served if they stayed at home and were full-time caregivers. Couples that found themselves in loveless marriages stayed together "for the sake of the children." In the 1960s, though, the popularity of the stewardship model started to wane as adults grew ever less willing to make sacrifices on behalf of children. Divorce became commonplace, as did out-of-wedlock pregnancy. Women turned their babies over to day-care centers and reentered the workforce. The quality of life of America's children, after centuries of improvement, started to decline.

One's choice of a model of parenting will significantly color one's views on the government's role with respect to the parent/child relationship. An owner-parent is likely to accept uncritically the view that everyone has a right to reproduce and the view that, having reproduced, everyone has a right to (try to) raise the child he or she brought into existence. A steward-parent will be concerned with the well-being of children and will therefore be much more willing to entertain the idea that there are people who should not be allowed to procreate and people who should not be allowed to raise children. Furthermore, a steward-parent will not be reluctant, in a country with an ever-growing number of owner-parents, to invoke the power of government to force parents to do right by the children in their care. This parent will remind us that if the steward-parents of the past hadn't invoked the power of government, it is conceivable that children would still be spending their childhoods laboring in coal mines.

It should by now be apparent that in my discussion of the politics of parenting I am not interested in defending the status quo. To the contrary, I will, for the most part, defend viewpoints that are unpopular or even radical. I will venture boldly into areas in which intellectual taboos commonly curtail thought and discussion. In the next two chapters, for example, I will undertake something that few in these politically correct times would attempt—a sympathetic reevaluation of eugenics. In Chapter 7, I advocate that we license parents and put up for adoption the babies of women who have them without a license. In Chapter 8, I argue that women should be allowed to sell their babies.

Some readers will be shocked by such proposals. They will regard them as not merely implausible, but as wrongheaded, perverse, or even profoundly immoral. They will be tempted to dismiss my proposals out of hand. Readers are hereby encouraged not to give in to this temptation. What they will find, if they look at my arguments for greater governmental interference with the parent/child relationship, is that although my proposals may seem radical, the arguments I offer in defense of these proposals are themselves utterly conventional.

One of my favorite argumentative techniques, in the following pages, is to point out inconsistencies in our views regarding the rights and responsibilities of parents. Consider, for example, my proposal that we license parents. The reader might be tempted to dismiss this proposal as one that only the most unenlightened of totalitarian governments would consider implementing. In thinking this, the reader is oblivious to the fact that in America today—the land of the free and the home of the brave—we *do* license parents. More precisely, we license anyone who lacks the biological ability to make a baby but wishes to become a parent through adoption. We make adoptive parents demonstrate their fitness before we let them anywhere near a child. All the licensing proposal recommends is that we end the double standard and treat biological parents the same as we treat adoptive parents.

Two arguments that keep recurring in the discussions that follow are anything but radical. The first—the argument from "negative externalities"—is based on the principle that the government is justified in preventing or regulating behavior that harms other individuals. The second—the argument from "universalizability"—is based on the principle that the government is justified in preventing or regulating behavior that, if engaged in by one person, harms no one but would be harmful if lots of people engaged in it. These principles are widely accepted and have been used to justify a number of governmental roles. I am simply applying them to the politics of parenting.

Some readers will be tempted to take refuge in the thought that "everyone knows" that the positions I defend are wrong—that "everyone knows," for example, that eugenics has been discredited. The problem is that what "everyone knows" tends to change from generation to generation. In the 1920s virtually every American "knew" that the government had a role to play in preventing genetically unfit individuals from reproducing. Furthermore, we should recognize that in the same way as we are disgusted by our great-grandparents' eugenic endeavors, our own great-grandchildren might look back on our abhorrence of eugenics as a symptom of muddleheadedness. It is the height of intellectual conceit to think, as each generation does, that at last we have arrived at the truth with respect to our social beliefs and that future generations will venerate us.

Generations usually don't arrive at their views on the politics of parenting as the result of long, careful thought. Rather, their views are a reflection of what feels good to them at the time. This book will attempt to look beyond what feels good and instead reason our way through some of the issues central to the politics of parenting. Furthermore, when a generation declares a certain view to be intellectually taboo, it isn't because the view in question has been refuted. What has happened, more likely, is that the generation suspects—indeed, fears—that the view is correct. By declaring it to be taboo, they remove it from the realm of polite conversation and thereby lessen the chance that they will have to defend their own beliefs: better no thought at all than troubling thought.

Readers who don't like the direction my arguments take, are encouraged to look at things not from the point of view of parents, but from the point of view of children. For me the interests of children are at least as important as the interests of their parents. The children, after all, did not ask to be born, did not ask to be born to these particular parents, and did not ask to be raised by them. In creating children, parents create a substantial body of obligations for themselves. It is, I shall argue, appropriate for the government to take steps to ensure that parents fulfill these obligations.

Thus, readers who feel like dismissing out of hand my argument for eugenics are encouraged to complete the following sentence: "I think two mentally retarded parents should be allowed to reproduce and bring into the world a dozen mentally retarded children because...." And readers who feel like dismissing out of hand my argument for licensing parents are encouraged to complete the following sentence: "I think an unmarried, drug-addicted, fourteen-year-old prostitute with a history of child abuse should be allowed to raise the children she brings into the world because...." Readers who find it easy to complete these sentences probably advocate the ownership model of parenting and therefore believe that fulfillment of parental whims counts for more than the well-being of children.

I, on the other hand, am a staunch advocate of the stewardship model of parenting. As such, I am suspicious of "reproductive rights." I believe that there are people to whom, because of their genetic makeup, no one would want to be born. Why, then, do we allow these people to reproduce? I also believe that there are people by whom, because of their indifference to or hatred of children, no one would want to be parented. Why, then, do we defend the "right" of these people to parent the children they bring into the world? This much is clear: if we take seriously the interests of children—if we think these interests count for more than the whims of their parents—we will question many of our society's beliefs about reproductive and parental rights.

PART ONE

WHO SHOULD BE ALLOWED TO PROCREATE?

CHAPTER 1

A BRIEF HISTORY OF EUGENICS

Eugenic programs attempt to improve our species by influencing people's reproductive activities. These programs can take many forms. There are, to begin with, *positive* and *negative* eugenic programs. Positive programs encourage the propagation of "good genes," while negative programs discourage the propagation of "bad genes." We can also distinguish between *voluntary* and *involuntary* eugenic programs. In voluntary programs people are given incentives to participate; in involuntary programs they are punished if they fail to participate, or they are physically forced to participate. People have a tendency to associate eugenics with programs of involuntary negative eugenics. They tend to think, more precisely, of Hitler's attempt to eliminate the Jews. This, however, is just one form—indeed, the least attractive form—that eugenic programs can take. We must be careful to keep this in mind in our thinking about eugenics.

In America today, eugenics is to a considerable extent a forbidden topic, but this hasn't always been the case. There was a time—roughly between 1905 and 1930—when a number of thoughtful Americans advocated a eugenic role for government. Many of the measures they advocated were enacted into law. America has since done an about-face with respect to eugenics. The average modern American can be described as adamantly anti-eugenics.

My goal in reexamining eugenics in this and the following chapter is quite modest. I am not advocating a radical eugenic role for government; instead I am arguing that Americans have gone too far in their abandonment of eugenics. In particular, our ancestors' advocacy of a modest eugenic role for government was evidence not of their moral bankruptcy, but of their concern for the well-being of children. If we share their concern for children, we will certainly want to prevent *some* couples from reproducing.

Plato's Proposal

Greek philosopher Plato (427-347 B.C.) was an early and important advocate of eugenics. In *The Republic,* Plato offers his views on the family, but in an incidental fashion. His principal concern is with justice—more precisely, he asks what it means for a man to be just. He argues that a good way to find out what justice is in a man is to find out what justice is in a city: since the city is bigger than the man, the justice that exists there should be easier to grasp. (It is, by the way, important for the reader to keep in mind that by "city," Plato had in mind the city-state, which was then the largest political unit in his part of the world.) This is why Plato, in the course of inquiring about the nature of justice, finds himself giving a detailed description of the ideal city and of parent/child relations in that city.

Plato argues that the interests of the citizens of the ideal city will best be served if their rights are subsumed to the well-being of the city. Thus, Plato sees nothing wrong with government censorship: "Our rulers," he declares, "will probably have to make considerable use of lies and deceit for the good of their subjects." He also sees nothing wrong with dissolution of the family. In Chapter 6 we will examine Plato's suggestion that the state rather than parents should raise children. In the present chapter, though, we will focus our attention on Plato's willingness to interfere with (what we today would take to be) people's right to reproduce and right to select the person with whom they reproduce.

Plato argues that for the best interests of the species—and the ideal city—to be served, eugenic measures must be taken: "The best men must have intercourse with the best women as frequently as possible, and the opposite is true of the very inferior men and women; the offspring of the former must be reared, but not the offspring of the latter, if our herd is to be of the highest possible quality." He also argues that this program of eugenics must be kept a secret from the people affected by it.

How can a government engage in a covert program of eugenics? By means of what Plato calls "clever lots": the rulers of the city will decide—taking into account the possibility of war and disease, and keeping in mind the resources available to the city—how many marriages shall take place. The men and women chosen for the privilege of marriage will not be allowed to select each other, but will be assigned a mate by a lottery that is "fixed" so as to guarantee that the best men marry the best women and the worst men marry the worst women. By resorting to such a deception, Plato tells us, "the inferior man…will blame chance but not the rulers." For Plato, it is more important that the city have a genetically healthy population than that people have the right to choose a mate.[1]

Above I have used the word "marriage," the same word as Plato used. It is clear, however, that his notion of marriage differs from our own. "Sexual union" would be a good term for what Plato has in mind, since the people who were married by means of the fixed lottery would not live alone together and would not even stay married for longer than it took the woman to get pregnant. As Plato puts it, "All these women shall be wives in common to all the men, and not one of them shall live privately with any man.…" Instead, the men and women will live together in common dwellings. The love that arises in a marriage is expected to be erotic and temporary, not romantic and lasting.

This view of things is, to be sure, a radical departure from current American views, to say nothing of contemporary Athenian views, on marriage and reproduction. It is important to keep in mind, though, that Plato was not some power-drunk dictator or crude bigot. He was arguably one of the most civilized men ever to walk the earth, living in what arguably was one of the most civilized cultures ever to exist. He was thoughtful—indeed, thoughtful to a fault—and it seemed obvious to him that if what you care about is the good of your society, you will be willing to undertake some fairly aggressive eugenic measures.

The government Plato describes will clearly have considerable power, and readers might worry that this power would be abused. More generally, readers might worry that a government powerful enough to undertake eugenic measures will invariably grow more powerful and that the eugenic measures it undertakes will grow ever harsher. Rest assured that this possibility will be considered in detail in the next chapter in my examination of what I call the Slippery Slope Argument against eugenics.

Eugenics in America

After Darwin published his *Origin of Species* in 1859, interest in eugenics grew. People had long known that in animals, desirable and undesirable traits are handed down from one generation to another. Through skillful animal husbandry a farmer could increase the number of desirable and decrease the number of undesirable traits so the animals in each generation would be more desirable than those of previous generations. Darwin did much to make people see humans not as a breed apart, but as animals subject to all the forces of nature. In his *Descent of Man* Darwin went on to point out that interfering with the forces of nature can have grave consequences: "We civilised men...do our utmost to check the process of elimination; we build asylums for the imbecile, the maimed, and the sick; we institute poor-laws; and our medical men exert their utmost skill to save the life of every one to the last moment.... Thus the weak members of civilised societies propagate their kind. No one who has attended to the breeding of domestic animals will doubt that this must be highly injurious to the race of man." A growing number of people became convinced that in the same way as the reproductive activities of a herd require some degree of interference if the herd is to remain healthy, so do the reproductive activities of humans.

Before eugenic measures could be meaningfully undertaken, though, an important question had to be answered: which characteristics of man can be inherited? For if a trait is not heritable, then no amount of interference with reproduction can make the trait any more or less widespread. It was clear that such things as eye color and skin color are passed down from parents to children. But what about mentality and tendencies to engage in criminal behavior? Early research led to some very interesting answers to these questions.

In 1874, Richard L. Dugdale began to study the "Juke" family and traced its family tree back to Max, a colonial frontiersman. In his search, Dugdale came across 709 Jukes or persons married to Jukes; of these, 18 had kept brothels, 128 had been prostitutes, over 200 had been on relief, and at least 76 had been convicted criminals. Dugdale calculated that the Jukes' depravity had cost the public (through relief, medical care, arrests and imprisonment, and so forth) the princely sum of $1,308,000.

Dugdale was careful to point to the depraved environment in which Juke children were raised—rather than their genes—as the principal cause of their adult depravity. Consequently, his recommendations were distinctly noneugenic in their scope: he suggested that the children of the poor and of criminals be removed from degraded surroundings and taught vocations. Others, however, took Dugdale's data and drew rather different conclusions: they argued that the transmission of depravity observed in the Jukes was due to nature, not nurture, and went on to recommend that various eugenic measures be undertaken to spare the public the harm caused by dysgenic unions.

Another important early study was conducted by Henry H. Goddard and Elizabeth S. Kite. Whereas Dugdale was interested in the transfer of depravity through the generations, Goddard and Kite were interested in the transfer of feeblemindedness. They traced another family, the "Kallikaks," back to Martin Kallikak who, at the time of the American Revolution, had an illegitimate son by a feebleminded girl. This son in turn had 480 descendants, 143 of whom were feebleminded; and of the remaining 337, only 46 were known to be normal.

But there was another side to the Kallikak family story. Martin Kallikak, after his youthful indiscretion, went on to marry a Quaker girl of good family, and from this marriage came a line of respectable citizens.

Although the Jukes and Kallikaks studies drew much popular

attention, they were not without flaws. In both studies there were serious questions about the reliability of the historical records used. Records of criminal proceedings, for example, would tend to over-represent those Jukes who were criminals and underrepresent those who had climbed from depravity. Along similar lines, how could you know for certain, as Goddard and Kite claimed to, that someone several generations back was feebleminded? And even if you knew who was feebleminded, how could you know that the transgenerational feeblemindedness was due to heredity and not environment? Many eugenicists, unfortunately, did not bother to ask these questions.

Some generational studies attempted to avoid the subjective element of the Goddard and Kite study by using objective measures, like the newly developed tests of intelligence, to measure the mentality of individuals. Unfortunately, these tests were themselves of dubious accuracy. When, for example, early intelligence tests were used by the army to weed out mental incompetents, it was found that 47 percent of whites and 89 percent of Negroes had a mental age of twelve or under. Such results proved either that you had to be dull to join the army or, more plausibly, that the tests were defective.

Flawed though they were, generational studies fostered eugenic thinking. During the golden age of eugenics—which in America lasted roughly from 1905 to 1930—the list of individuals who publicly advocated eugenic measures included Winston Churchill, Havelock Ellis, George Bernard Shaw, H. G. Wells, Sidney Webb, Oliver Wendell Holmes; economists Irving Fisher and J. M. Keynes; and presidents Theodore Roosevelt, Woodrow Wilson, and Calvin Coolidge.

To group these individuals together under the label "advocates of eugenics" is a bit misleading, though, since eugenicists differed in their reasons for advocating eugenics. A first group of eugenicists had as its primary concern the well-being of the offspring of genetically defective parents. Why should we prohibit feebleminded parents from having children? Because no one would want to be born feebleminded. A second group of eugenicists had as its primary concern the well-being, not of potential children, but of the fellow citizens of potential children. If, they argued, criminal behavior is hereditary, then we should block criminals from reproducing, not for the good of *their* children, but for the good of *our* children, who would at some future date be preyed upon by their children. A third group of eugenicists had as its primary concern the well-being not of any particular person or group of people—at least not any existing person or group of people—but rather the well-being of the "gene pool." Their fear: unless we "manage" human reproduction, our species will, as the generations pass, become woefully debased. Charles Darwin, quoted above, was apparently motivated by this concern.

Some of the eugenicists who worried about the well-being of the gene pool pointed to a particularly vicious process by which mankind can be brought down, genetically speaking. In nature, animals with defective genes are culled before they can reproduce. Evolutionary pressures keep animal species fit. In human society, however, this doesn't happen. Because evolutionary pressures are suppressed, people with undesirable genetic traits not only aren't culled, but in many cases have bigger families than those with desirable genetic traits. In time, the bad genes swamp the good, and the human gene pool is polluted.

Along these lines, eugenicist Karl Pearson lamented that the poorest quarter of married couples were producing half the children. He feared that "civilization was menaced by the fecundity of the poor." Likewise, studies at the beginning of the twentieth century suggested that college graduates were neglecting their reproductive responsibilities and thereby endangering the gene pool: every four graduates of Harvard and Yale were producing only three sons as replacements, and almost half of the graduates of women's colleges weren't even getting married.

Eugenicists also argued that the above-described process has in the past led to the fall of empires. Rome, it was suggested, fell partly because the best citizens went off to war, leaving the inferior citizens behind to reproduce. Similarly, Spain fell partly because it sent its best citizens abroad, where their superior genes were diluted by mixture with inferior races.

Let us refer to the above line of argument as the Differential Birth-Rate Argument. Its logic is impeccable: if those with trait *A* are reproducing at a faster rate than those with trait *B*, if the traits in question are heritable to the same degree, and if the offspring of these groups also reproduce at the same rate as their parents did (as will their offspring, and so forth), then in time those having trait A will far outnumber those having trait B. If trait A is less desirable, genetically speaking, than trait B, this change will be a change for the worse. We will encounter variants of this argument below.

Some Eugenic Measures

We can place possible eugenic measures on a continuum according to how coercive they are. At one end of the eugenic continuum—the end involving the least amount of coercion—the government engages in purely educational activities. It might, for instance, publicize data showing that certain medical conditions are hereditary, so couples contemplating having children can take this information into account. One step up from this on our continuum, the government provides eugenic subsidies to encourage "aristogenic" couples—those with desirable genetic traits—to have children and/or discourages dysgenic couples—those with undesirable genetic traits—from having children. (Thus, the government might offer a cash award to any carrier of Huntington's disease who agreed to undergo sterilization.) One step further up the continuum, the government requires genetic screening but leaves it open to people what they do with the data obtained; and one step up from this the government levies fines on dysgenic couples that have children and/or on aristogenic couples that don't. Beyond this we find the government handing out jail sentences and mandating involuntary sterilizations or forced matings to achieve its eugenic goals. Finally we arrive at the other end of the continuum, in which the government imposes the ultimate eugenic sanction—death to the dysgenic.

In America today the government is at the end of the continuum calling for the least interference in people's reproductive choices. It is, in other words, almost noneugenic.[2] The government funds study of hereditary diseases and distributes information about them, but in a low-key fashion. Aside from this, the government takes a laissez-faire stance with respect to reproduction: those possessing the biological ability to make a baby have the right to do so, regardless of the genetic consequences to their offspring, their fellow citizens, or the future of the gene pool.

If we look back to the golden age of American eugenics, though, we find that our forebears—more precisely, the grandfathers and grandmothers of those in my generation—thought it perfectly reasonable for the government to engage in a number of "midcontinuum" eugenic activities, including forced sterilization, custodial care, and marriage restrictions.

The first experiments with sterilization took place in the 1880s, when doctors, in an attempt to cure certain forms of insanity among women, removed their ovaries. It is unclear whether these first experiments should be termed eugenic, though, since the inability to reproduce was a side effect of the operation rather than one of its aims. These experiments were followed in the 1890s by Dr. F. Hoyt Pilcher's sterilization of fourteen girls and (by castration) forty-four boys, all feebleminded. Pilcher's experiments were motivated in part by medical considerations—it was thought that sterilization would prove medically beneficial to the feebleminded—but also by eugenic considerations. Thus, historian Mark H. Haller has labeled Dr. Pilcher's experiments "the first effort at systematic asexualization in the United States for eugenic purposes." His experiments were not, however, governmentally sanctioned; indeed, protests that his operations were illegal forced him to stop.

With the turn of the century came two new surgical procedures: vasectomy for men and salpingectomy—the cutting and tying of the fallopian tubes—for women. These operations destroy reproductive potential without altering hormone balance. Eugenicists quickly realized that these operations therefore allowed a whole range of eugenic measures that otherwise would have been impractical.

In 1907, Indiana became the first state to pass a mandatory sterilization law: it called for sterilization of criminals, idiots, imbeciles, and rapists in state institutions if a board of experts recommended it. By World War I, fifteen other states had sterilization laws. By 1931, thirty states had passed sterilization laws at one time or another, and laws were still on the books in twenty-seven states. California became the sterilization capital of America: it required sterilization of the insane and feebleminded upon their release from institutions. Virginia was still sterilizing the mentally handicapped in the 1970s.

There were court challenges to the above-described sterilization laws, but these challenges generally didn't prevail. In 1927 the Supreme Court—with Oliver Wendell Holmes writing for the majority—ruled that "sterilization fell within the police power of the state." Expanding on this thought, Holmes wrote, "We have seen more than once that the public welfare may call upon the best citizens for their lives. It would be strange if it could not call upon those who already sap the strength of the State of these lesser sacrifices, often not felt to be such by those concerned, in order to prevent our being swamped with incompetence. It is better for all the world, if instead of waiting for their imbecility, society can prevent those who are manifestly unfit from continuing their kind. The principle that sustains compulsory vaccination is broad enough to cover cutting the Fallopian tubes.... Three generations of imbeciles are enough." (There is, by the way, evidence that Carrie Buck, whose sterilization was ordered by this decision, was not an imbecile.) That such thinking, now taboo, was once considered mainstream in our country is itself a commentary on how dramatically public opinion can change.

The United States was not alone in granting a eugenic role to government. Sweden, Canada, Norway, Finland, Estonia, and Iceland all implemented laws calling for involuntary sterilization. Germany implemented its own sterilization law in 1934, years after many American states had done so.

It is interesting to note that when people *did* oppose sterilization laws in the 1920s and 1930s, they sometimes failed to offer what to us today would be the obvious argument—namely, that involuntary sterilization violates certain basic human rights. Instead, they might have advanced a "morals" argument against sterilization: there is a danger that by sterilizing people we encourage them to be sexually promiscuous, and their promiscuity can do more harm to society than their procreating. One proponent of this argument supported it by describing a feebleminded girl who had an ovariectomy. Males lined up outside her house to have intercourse with her while her mother was at work.

Americans also used to advocate custodial care of "unfortunates." The founder of the custodial care movement in America was arguably Josephine Shaw Lowell who, after making numerous inspections of New York medical facilities, observed that women who lived on the street gave birth repeatedly to illegitimate children who inherited the dissolute dispositions of their parents. "What right," she asked, "had we to permit [children] to be born of parents who were depraved in body and mind?" In 1877 she began a crusade for the state to build reformatories for delinquent and vagrant girls who had been arrested or had given birth to a second illegitimate child. Her crusade was successful, and the reformatories were built. Lowell's efforts also resulted in New York opening an asylum for the custodial care of feebleminded women of childbearing age. In the 1880s custodial care of the feebleminded became commonplace.

Advocates of custodial care had mixed motives. On the one hand, they wanted to protect unfortunate and feebleminded women from what could be a predatory environment—a noble goal. On the other hand, they realized that by keeping such women under custodial care, their reproductive activities could be blocked or at least slowed, a blessing both to their potential offspring and to society, which in many cases would have to care for their offspring.

Besides involuntary sterilization and custodial care, Americans favored eugenically motivated restrictions on who could marry (or have sexual relations with) whom. In 1896, Connecticut passed a law forbidding women under age forty-five who were epileptic, imbecile, or feebleminded from marrying or having sex; and prevented normal women under age forty-five from marrying or having sex with men who were epileptic, imbecile, or feebleminded. The minimum penalty for violating this law was three years' imprisonment. By the mid-1930s most states had eugenically motivated restrictions on marriage. Some of these restrictions were aimed at insane or feebleminded individuals, others were aimed at epileptics, and yet others were aimed at confirmed drunkards. In defense of such laws, some argued that if it is appropriate for the state to prevent people with venereal diseases from marrying in order to protect their children, then surely it is appropriate for the state to prevent people with hereditary illnesses from marrying; congenital insanity is, after all, a considerably worse affliction than syphilis.

Laws restricting marriage were also aimed at mixed-race couples: more than half the states have at one time or another had laws forbidding interracial marriage. One justification for these laws was eugenic. Some argued that racial crossings—even between two "superior" races—tend to produce physical deterioration. Others argued that some races had genetic defects in abundance and that if they married people in a different race, these defects would "overcome" the genes of the superior race.

Besides involuntary eugenic measures like those described above, the American government has been involved in voluntary eugenic programs. Consider, most interestingly, the effort by the Pioneer Fund in 1940 to encourage genetically superior Americans to have more children. Researchers at the Fund identified Air Corps (precursor to the Air Force) officers as genetically prime breeding stock. With the assistance of the Air Corps, it located officers who already had children and wanted to have more but were reluctant to do so because of the costs associated with parenting. It gave these officers $4,000—worth about $46,000 in today's dollars—if they would have another child. By the end of 1940 a dozen children had been brought into existence as a result of this program. Interestingly, these children did not grow up to be the high achievers that their fathers had been.

Besides eugenic measures aimed at its citizens, the American government has undertaken measures aimed at those who *wished to become* American citizens. The efforts of the American eugenicists culminated in what was arguably their greatest single triumph, passage of the Immigration Restriction Act of 1924 (also known as the Johnson Act). This act limited annual immigration from each European nation to 2 percent of those American residents who were of that nationality in 1890. It effectively put a lid on the number of immigrants from southern and eastern Europe. The rationale behind the Johnson Act: if "bad" genes are kept out of the country, they cannot mingle with the "good" genes already here. It was only with the passage of the Celler Act in 1965 that the eugenically motivated discrimination of the Johnson Act was significantly—but not entirely—reversed.

The Decline of the American Eugenics Movement

In the early 1900s, Americans were willing to undertake a number of eugenic measures that today's Americans would not countenance, but after 1930 eugenics declined in popularity. The deathblow to eugenics—the thing that did the most to make the subject taboo in America—was Hitler's implementation of a eugenics program that at first was content with sterilization of the mentally ill, then called for the death of the mentally ill in gas chambers, and ended by calling for the destruction of what Hitler took to be genetically inferior races.

The eugenic programs that seemed commonsensical to our grandparents have been largely dismantled. We no longer sterilize people against their will. We have emptied mental institutions and let their former inmates eke out an existence on the streets. We allow anyone at all to get married—not only those with hereditary diseases, but those with syphilis or AIDS.

This is not to say, however, that Americans oppose *all* coercive eugenic measures. They are almost unanimously in favor, for example, of laws forbidding incestuous relationships between brothers and sisters; and when asked to defend this viewpoint, they generally argue that children born to an incestuous couple are likely to be genetically defective.[3]

The battle against eugenics was arguably won in the hearts of people rather than in their minds, and because of this we have arguably gone overboard in our rejection of eugenics, much as our grandparents went overboard in their acceptance of it. For this reason, it is worth our while to take another look at the arguments by which eugenics was "refuted." As we shall see in the following chapter, these arguments are not nearly as compelling as modern Americans might expect.

CHAPTER 2

THE CASE AGAINST EUGENICS

In this chapter I will consider the three arguments commonly given against government involvement in eugenics. According to the Argument from Ignorance, the government doesn't know enough to undertake a program of eugenics; according to the Rights Argument, even if the government were smart enough to manage the gene pool successfully, any attempt to do so would violate the rights of the citizens; and according to the Slippery Slope Argument, even if the government could successfully undertake moderate eugenic measures without violating the rights of its citizens, these measures, once taken, would likely lead to extreme eugenic measures that *would* violate the rights of citizens. As we shall see, these arguments are not as compelling as many opponents of eugenics might have us believe.

My goal in reexamining eugenics is quite modest. I am not arguing that the government should undertake extensive eugenic measures like those described by Plato. I am not even arguing that the government should undertake moderate eugenic measures like those undertaken in America in the early twentieth century. I will be happy if I can convince readers that we have gone overboard in our rejection of eugenics and that there are *some* cases in which the government is justified in interfering with the procreative activities of people because of the genetic consequences these activities would have.

The Argument from Ignorance

Some oppose government involvement in eugenics by arguing that the government simply doesn't know enough to do the job. Indeed, they argue that *no one* knows enough about genetics to manage the gene pool successfully. According to this Argument from Ignorance, anyone wishing to improve mankind through genetic manipulation must overcome two significant obstacles: first, we don't know what human traits are desirable and what traits are not; and second, even if we could come to an agreement about the desirability of traits, we don't know enough about genetics to be able to improve the gene pool by means of genetic manipulation.

What Human Traits Are Desirable?

Let us first focus our attention on the claim that we don't know what traits are good and what traits are bad. Consider a trait like feeble-mindedness. A bad trait, right? Maybe not. There are those, after all, who argue that the feebleminded are not "lesser" people. It is true they cannot play chess, program computers, or do their own taxes, but there are nevertheless many things they can do. And who is to say the feebleminded do not have a better life, all things considered, than those of us who spend our days playing chess, programming computers, and doing taxes?

The eugenicists typically valued intelligence above all else—as one might expect them to, given that many of them were intelligent individuals. But is intelligence really more valuable than, say, physical strength or tallness? Indeed, perhaps great intelligence is an *un*desirable trait, since thinking too much can lead to unhappiness. Judged by the standards of the intelligent, the feebleminded may be wanting, but are these standards the right ones? And if so, why?

Besides ranking human traits, eugenicists have ranked races. Thus, Sir Francis Galton, the founder and namer of the eugenics movement, argued for the following genetic ranking of the races: the ancient Greeks were at the top, with Anglo-Saxons below them, the Negroes of Africa below that, and the Australian aborigines at the very bottom of the genetic heap. Of course, unless one judges the Australian aborigines by white, Western standards, it is hard to see why they deserve such a low ranking. The fact that they survived such harsh conditions for so long with so little itself speaks for a certain genetic robustness.

Most people today will dismiss as hopelessly subjective any attempt to rank traits or races genetically. In defense of this dismissal, they might point to the tendency of eugenicists to devise ranking systems in which they themselves rank highly. Genetic ranking systems, they will argue, tell us more about the prejudices of rankers than about the genetic fitness of those ranked. If you ask the average American whether whites are genetically superior to blacks, or blonds are genetically superior to brunets, he is likely to look at you in askance and might even accuse you of bigotry.

This is not to say, however, that Americans are incapable of ranking genetic traits and promoting the spread of good traits while limiting the spread of bad. They do it all the time—with lovers and animals. The typical American, although against eugenics in theory, is for eugenics in practice—and is in fact a practicing eugenicist. Allow me to defend this somewhat outlandish claim, after which I will return to the question of what traits are genetically desirable and what traits are not.

Closet Eugenics: Choosing a Mate

When a typical American male chooses a mate from among the earth's 3 billion women, he doesn't do so in a random fashion. Rather, he carefully seeks out women with certain traits. At first he might be concerned with physical traits like height, hair color, and race. He might then turn his attention to nonphysical traits like intelligence. (You know a relationship is getting serious when a man and woman who are dating reveal their SAT scores to each other.) Having narrowed the range of possible mates, he will probe the person's family tree. Any crazy aunts? Anyone with Huntington's disease? What he will do, in other words, is put potential mates through a genetic screening process. Would he want this woman to be the mother of his children? Would he want children, half of whose genetic makeup derives from her? And of course, women do the same thing when sizing up potential mates.

Sociobiologists argue not only that we are very good at genetic screening, but that we are often oblivious to the fact that we *are* screening. If you ask a man why he crossed the room to talk to a particular woman, he will tell you he did so because she is beautiful. Sociobiologists will point out, however, that a growing body of evidence indicates that our notion of beauty is hardwired into us. For one thing, cultures tend to share notions of beauty. Thus, if you ask someone from another culture to rank the beauty of women in our culture, he will tend to rank them in the same order as we rank them. In particular, people everywhere are attracted to symmetrical faces, and genetically speaking this is no accident: facial symmetry is a sign that all is well at the genetic level. Experiments show that it takes people only 0.15 of a second to assess the beauty of a face, meaning that we can "detect" a beautiful face before we are consciously aware of its beauty. Thus, beauty seems to be not so much in the eye of the beholder as in the hardwiring of the brain of the beholder, and when a man "selects" a beautiful woman, he is arguably engaged in an unconscious form of genetic screening.

For similar reasons, a man will probably find young women to be more sexually attractive than old women: the chance of successful reproduction is greater with young women. Likewise, he will probably find females more sexually attractive than males and find females of his own species more sexually attractive than females of other species—or than inanimate objects, for that matter. In each of these cases, the man thinks that *he* is in control—that *he* is choosing the beautiful, young woman. And no doubt he is choosing, but it is a choice billions of years of evolution have strongly predisposed him toward.

It is interesting, then, that although the average American will reject various rankings of human traits, he almost certainly possesses a personal ranking of these traits and relies on this ranking when choosing a mate. He wants his children to possess not just any traits, but certain traits he finds genetically desirable. The same is true of women choosing a mate.

Suppose someone responded to these comments by claiming that he was utterly indifferent to the genetic makeup of his mate—that he found all human traits equally desirable and chose a particular mate not as the result of genetic calculations, but because he loved her. To any such individual, I would offer the following challenge. I can see why—loving your mate the way you do—you would feel passionately about living with this particular mate or having sex with her. But since you claim to be indifferent to the genetic makeup of your mate, you should not feel nearly as passionately about whether she is the (genetic) mother of your children. A man who is truly indifferent to his wife's genetic makeup will not care whether it is her eggs or those of some randomly chosen egg donor that he impregnates— were it not so much easier to use her eggs than to implant those of a donor into her. Likewise, a woman who is truly indifferent to her husband's genetic makeup will not care whose sperm impregnates her. She might care about whom she had sex with, but—keeping in mind the possibility of artificial insemination—she will be relatively indifferent to whether it was her husband's sperm that impregnated her or the sperm of some unknown (and randomly chosen) stranger. Of course, in the real world we find that people care passionately not only about living with and having sex with one chosen person, but about making babies that incorporate *that person's* genetic makeup.

Consider the plight of a marginally fertile couple. Usually such a couple will go to great lengths to produce a baby "together"—that is, to produce a baby that incorporates both their genetic makeups. The timing of their couplings might be dictated not by lust, but by basal-thermometer readings. If that fails, they will in many cases try expensive and cumbersome in vitro fertilization techniques involving her eggs and his sperm. Only then will many couples consider abandoning the dream of making a child "together."

And when people cannot make a child "together," they often try to make a baby that is "half theirs." If the man is sterile, they might seek a sperm donor, and if the woman is infertile, they might seek an egg donor for in vitro fertilization or a "contract mother" who will agree to be artificially inseminated by the man and then turn over the resulting baby to the couple. And if they choose this route, they will invariably be picky about the sperm donor or the egg donor or the contract mother they use. They will be quite interested in the genetic characteristics of the third party involved in their procreative act and will have no trouble ranking candidates in order of genetic desirability.

It would appear, then, that nearly everyone not only possesses a ranking of the desirability of various genetic traits, but routinely makes gene-pool-affecting decisions on the basis of these rankings. In this sense, most people are practicing eugenicists. Their eugenics is, of course, wholly personal.

Why do all these closet eugenicists oppose an "official" ranking of genetic traits? In part because they fear that such a ranking will be at odds with their own private ranking. They fear that the government, on the basis of such a ranking, might force them to mate with someone they find eugenically undesirable or prevent them from mating with someone they find genetically desirable. Thus, one reason many people are opposed to *public* eugenics is that they fear it will come into conflict with their own *private* eugenics.

Closet Eugenics: Nonhuman Animals

It isn't only in our choice of a mate that we reveal our ability to rank genetic traits. Most of us do the same thing in our choice of a dog or in our choice of a dinner entrée. Those who claim to be anti-eugenics when it comes to people tend to be adamantly pro-eugenics when it comes to (nonhuman) animals.

It is agricultural heresy to suggest that farmers should take a laissez-faire approach to barnyard breeding and let animals couple as they will. This, farmers everywhere tell us, would surely lead to ruination of a herd. Furthermore, farmers will not hesitate to assert that some genetic traits are more desirable than others. For example, when it comes to turkeys, a big breast is desirable, but the ability to walk is not. Because they hold these genetic values, farmers have bred turkeys whose breasts are so big that they cannot walk—and, indeed, can't even have sex—but this, according to farmers' genetic value system, is a gain, not a loss.

And even nonfarmers—at any rate, those who aren't ethical vegetarians—will likely agree with this ranking of the genetic traits of farm animals. If we give consumers a choice between the turkeys of fifty years ago and the big-breasted but lame turkeys of today, they will choose the latter: these turkeys offer, after all, more meat for the money.

When it comes to pets, people can be quite passionate about

which genetic traits are desirable and which are not. People who buy dachshunds want them long. The length might cause the animal back problems, but a short dachshund wouldn't be a very good dachshund, would it?

A look at the breeding of pets shows how curious our ranking of genetic traits can be. There are breeders, for example, who have gone out of their way to produce pet goats that faint at the least provocation. To them, a genetic propensity to faint is a desirable trait in a goat, and they are not alone in thinking this: fainting goats can be worth thousands of dollars. Other breeders have gone out of their way to produce pet cats whose front legs are so short that to move about, the cats must hop on their back legs. Some might regard abnormally short legs as a genetic defect, but when it comes to animal breeding, one person's idea of a genetic defect is another person's idea of a genetic prize.

Not only are people capable of ranking genetic traits *within a species*, but they are capable of genetically ranking *species themselves*. One way to demonstrate the existence of this ranking is to consider the diet of the average American. He is perfectly willing to kill a cow—or, more likely, cause it to be killed—in order to have a pleasant lunch. He would be quite reluctant to do this with a chimpanzee, though; and would probably never do it with a member of his own species. (Indeed, he would probably be unwilling to dine on even a member of his species who had died a perfectly natural death.) Likewise, although he might see nothing wrong with squashing a cockroach that happened to be in the wrong place at the wrong time, he would likely be critical of a neighbor who bludgeoned a chimpanzee for escaping from its cage. The average American can draw these distinctions only because he possesses a ranking of species. He "knows" chimps are a higher form of life than cows, cows are a higher form of life than rats, and so forth. It is curious that individuals who find it so easy to rank genetic traits within species and to rank various species genetically suddenly lose this ability when we ask them to rank human genetic traits. It is curious that those same individuals who are morally disgusted by Galton's attempt to rank races are quite willing to talk about which species are "better" than which other species.

Here is one last thought on animal breeding. Consider the different breeds of dogs. They come in many different colors and shapes. In size they range from Chihuahuas—which might weigh four pounds and stand six inches tall fully grown—to mastiffs, which can weigh over three hundred pounds and be more than eight feet long, measured nose to tail. The personalities of the different breeds also vary considerably: poodles and Chihuahuas have a reputation for being highly strung, golden retrievers and English sheepdogs for being docile, Border collies for being workaholics (with an instinct for herding sheep—or cats or toddlers, if sheep aren't available), and rottweilers and Dobermans for being ferocious. Different breeds also differ in intelligence. Owners of Jack Russell terriers, for example, discover not only that they can't say "walk" without sending their dog into a frenzy, but can't even spell out W-A-L-K without their dog realizing that something is up. Other breeds—not to draw any invidious comparisons—cannot accomplish similar mental feats.

What accounts for the differences in breeds? Differences in breeding—differences, that is, in the eugenic measures our human ancestors took with respect to them. This is the astonishing thing about the breeds of dog. They all apparently trace their lineage back to the same ancestor (probably the wolf), and it took only perhaps ten or twenty thousand years to morph this ancestral dog into all the different breeds. Furthermore, our ancestors were able to pull off this impressive feat of genetic manipulation despite having only a primitive understanding of genetics. Finally, our ancestors were able to "select" not only the size, shape, and color of breeds, but the personality and intelligence of those breeds as well. It is truly a testament to the power of eugenics.

What Human Traits Will Be Desirable?

The above discussion suggests that it would be a mistake to base our Argument from Ignorance (against eugenics) on the premise that there is no way to rank the desirability of human traits. I have given reasons for thinking not just that such rankings are possible, but that most people covertly rank the desirability of human traits.

Does this mean we should give up the Argument from Ignorance? Clearly not, for notice that someone can admit that certain human traits are more desirable than others but go on to argue that in order to be successful, a program of eugenics would concern itself not with what human traits are *now* desirable, but with what traits *will be* desirable. The benefits of any eugenic program, after all, will be enjoyed not today, but in the future—indeed, several generations into the future. This means that a thoughtful eugenicist, when laying his plans, should focus his attention not on what human traits are desirable today, but on what human traits will be desirable in, say, the year 2100.

If we have trouble deciding exactly which human traits are desirable today, we will have even more trouble deciding which will be desirable a century hence. After all, the environment can change in unpredictable ways, and when it does, the desirability of traits can be affected. To see why I say this, consider the predicament of someone undertaking a eugenics program a century ago. One of the questions that would have arisen for this eugenicist is whether he should go out of his way to propagate genes for extreme tallness. In 1900 such genes weren't particularly desirable: what they made you fit for was a job as circus freak. In the century that followed, though, the "environment" changed. In particular, basketball became a popular sport, and those who played it well—generally people who were uncommonly tall—could make millions of dollars doing so. What was an undesirable trait in 1900 had become a desirable one in 2000, thanks to environmental changes that were largely unforeseeable in 1900.

It is instructive to consider the extent to which one's success in this world is due not to the traits one possesses, but to the environment in which one possesses those traits. Without basketball, Michael Jordan might have gone down in history as a second-rate minor league baseball player. Without the advent of the computer, the current crop of highly paid programmers might have spent their lives doing day labor and working crossword puzzles in their breaks. A slight change in ideals of beauty, and a number of today's movie stars might have spent their lives working as convenience store clerks. When all is said and done, it isn't who you know or even what you know that counts;

it's the interplay between the environment you were born into and the traits you were born with and developed. Stated differently, traits are not good or bad in and of themselves; they are good or bad with respect to environments, and environments routinely change in an unpredictable fashion.

In the same way as an undesirable gene can become desirable, a desirable gene can, as the result of a change in the environment, become undesirable. Consider, for example, the gene responsible for cystic fibrosis. It is a gene that even those reluctant to rank genes would be willing to label undesirable. It has been argued, however, that the gene has a "silver lining": those who possess one copy of the gene are almost immune to typhoid. Were typhoid common—as was the case in many parts of the world in the past—the advantage of having such a gene in the gene pool (namely, resistance to typhoid) outweighed the disadvantage (namely, the chance of inheriting two copies of the gene and thus falling victim to cystic fibrosis). A gene desirable when typhoid was common became undesirable when typhoid was conquered.

To carry this line of thought one step further, suppose Germany had won World War II and, acting on the conviction that "Aryan" genes were desirable, had continued and even extended its eugenic programs. Suppose that as a result, the world came to be populated by blond-haired, blue-eyed, fair-skinned people. Suppose, finally, that fears about depletion of the earth's ozone layer prove well founded and by the year 2100, those with blond hair, blue eyes, and fair skin are at a distinct disadvantage, inasmuch as they are, in a world with a depleted ozone layer, highly susceptible to skin cancer. A change in the environment would have turned "good" genes into "bad" genes.

For one last example of a desirable trait with a dark side, consider intelligence, which I will, for the sake of argument, assume is to some degree heritable. We saw above that eugenicists find intelligence to be a supremely desirable trait. Indeed, some eugenicists might even argue that as traits go, intelligence is *absolutely* desirable—that is, desirable no matter how the environment changes. They might defend this claim by pointing out that intelligence, more than any other trait, can help people cope with sudden and unpredictable changes in the environment.

This line of reasoning sounds plausible until we consider the changes that can take place in the political environment. These changes can be fatal to anyone blessed with intelligence. Consider, by way of illustration, the fate of intellectuals in Cambodia in the 1970s. During the Pol Pot regime, it was inadvisable to wear glasses even if you needed them. Glasses-wearing was taken to be evidence of literacy, literacy was taken to be a sign of intelligence, and intelligence was, in many cases, punishable by death. In Cambodia, then, political changes turned intelligence into a trait with negative survival value. And Cambodia is not the only instance in which the rulers of a country, feeling threatened by intellectuals, had them jailed or killed. In Russia under Stalin, it paid to be rather dull and unimaginative.

Consider, then, the challenge confronting anyone who undertakes a eugenics program. He should focus his attention not on what genes are *now* desirable but on what genes *will be* desirable in 2100 and beyond, when his eugenics program comes to fruition. Will he want to propagate genes for tallness? It depends on what sports he thinks will be popular in the future. For intelligence? It depends on whether he thinks future rulers will or won't feel threatened by intelligent individuals. For cystic fibrosis? It depends on whether he thinks typhoid epidemics will be commonplace in 2100. Needless to say, these sorts of questions won't be easy to answer. Indeed, some of the most important environmental changes in the future will be utterly unpredictable, even to the smartest eugenicists on the planet.

Technical Difficulties

Let us now set aside the issue of the desirability and undesirability of traits. Let us assume we are in agreement that certain traits are and forever will be desirable and certain other traits are and forever will be undesirable. Should we attempt to breed out the latter traits and propagate the former? When we try to answer this question, we confront a whole new area of ignorance: even if we can agree on where we want to go, genetically speaking, in many cases we simply don't know enough to get there.

In the first place, before a eugenic program can either propagate or breed out a trait, it must establish that the trait is heritable, and this can be difficult to do.

Consider, for example, the tendency to engage in criminal behavior. Is this trait heritable? Many early eugenicists thought so, and not without reason. There is, after all, a correlation between criminal behavior on the part of parents and criminal behavior on the part of their children. The question is whether the criminal behavior of the offspring is due to their genetic makeup or to the environment in which they are raised—whether, in other words, it is due to nature or nurture.

One way to answer this question is by examining the characteristics of identical twins. If twins differ in some respect, the difference cannot be due to their genetic makeup, since they share the same genetic makeup. The difference must instead be due to differences in their environments. (Environmental differences include not only differences after the twins are born, but differences while they are still in the womb.) If, on the other hand, twins share a characteristic, its cause might be genetic and might be environmental.

Thus, identical twins have the same color eyes because eye color is determined almost exclusively by a person's genetic makeup. Even if you separate twins at birth and raise them in radically different environments, they will still almost certainly have the same eye color. This is not true, however, of their heights. Most identical twins are of approximately the same height. Height has, after all, a strong genetic component. Nevertheless, significant height differences can result from environmental factors, like one twin experiencing malnutrition. Consider, finally, the linguistic abilities of identical twins. Suppose twins are separated at birth, with one being raised in America by English-speaking parents and the other being raised in Brazil by Portuguese-speaking parents. Although we would expect these twins to have the same eye color and be approximately the same height, we would be startled if they spoke the same language. What language a person speaks, after all, is determined almost entirely by his environment. (The *ability to speak* a language, on the other hand, is determined by both genetic and environmental factors.)

This suggests a way to establish the heritability of criminal behavior. We could locate a significant number of identical twins who had been separated at birth, with one twin being raised by criminal parents and the other being raised by law-abiding parents. If there were no differences in the criminal tendencies of the twins, we could conclude that criminal behavior, like eye color, is primarily the result of genetic factors and is therefore heritable. If, on the other hand, we found major differences between the criminal tendencies of the twins—most strikingly, if we found that all of the twins raised by criminals engaged in criminal behavior and that none of the twins raised by law-abiding parents did—we could conclude that a tendency to engage in criminal behavior, like the ability to speak English, has a large environmental component. We would therefore reject the claim that criminal behavior is heritable.

Obviously such studies are difficult to undertake, and their results are open to interpretation. Richard J. Herrnstein and Charles Murray argued, primarily on the basis of twin studies, that IQ is 60 percent genetic. They went on to show that criminal behavior is linked to low IQ, thus raising the possibility that criminal behavior is (at least indirectly) heritable. In arguing that IQ has a significant genetic component, they found themselves the object of vehement attacks, not only by shallow individuals who simply didn't want to hear that IQ (or, for that matter, criminal behavior) was heritable, but by thoughtful people who examined the evidence set forth by Herrnstein and Murray and drew the opposite conclusion.

Herrnstein and Murray frame the debate over the heritability of criminal behavior as a debate between *psychological* and *sociological* theories of crime. According to psychological theories of crime, the cause of criminal behavior is to be found within the criminal himself. Criminals might lack a sense of shame, crave excitement, or simply be bestial. Psychological theories of crime used to dominate public thinking, but in the 1950s they yielded ground to sociological theories of crime. According to these theories, it is a person's environment, not his personality or genetic makeup, that drives him to commit crimes. Since the 1970s, psychological theories of crime have made a comeback. Nevertheless, it is still possible to find people, particularly in sociology, who reject out of hand the notion that criminal behavior and other negative characteristics are heritable.

Notice that theories of crime have political implications. If psychological theories are correct, then we are (perhaps) justified in holding criminals personally responsible for their crimes and jailing them. If, on the other hand, sociological theories are correct, then it is not the criminal himself but the criminal's environment that is ultimately to blame for his criminal behavior. Therefore, our desire to punish the criminal is (perhaps) misguided; we should instead reform society. Because theories of crime have political implications, the science behind these theories tends to get subverted: people cling to a scientific theory because they don't like the apparent political consequences of abandoning it. In other scientific disciplines (for example, in astronomy), scientific theories have no political consequences, so the science done is much less likely to be corrupted by politics.

Perhaps the sensible approach—and the approach advocated by Herrnstein and Murray—is to admit that criminal behavior and various other behaviors have both genetic and environmental components. This means that it would be a mistake to think that these behaviors are as heritable as eye color is, but it would also be a mistake to think—as some opponents of eugenics do—that it is nonsense to speak of them being to any degree heritable.

In recent years eugenicists have acquired a new tool by which they can establish the heritability of traits: breakthroughs in biotechnology allow them to determine whether a trait is "in the genes" *by examining the genes themselves.*

To better understand the nature of this breakthrough, consider Huntington's disease. The gene responsible for this disease is located on Chromosome 4. Scientists are unsure of the "purpose" of the gene (that is, what function it plays in healthy individuals), but they do know that if the gene is slightly mutated (if it has extra repetitions of the genetic "word" CAG), the individual possessing it will succumb to Huntington's. If you have thirty-nine repetitions of this "word"— as opposed to the ten to fifteen repetitions in normal people—you will almost certainly get Huntington's and will probably experience your first symptoms of the disease at age sixty-six. Additional repetitions of CAG will reduce the age of onset. Someone unlucky enough to have fifty repetitions will probably "contract" the disease at age twenty-seven. It is entirely within the power of geneticists, by examining the DNA of a human fetus, to observe the gene described above and, on the basis of their observations, predict with great accuracy whether and when that fetus will succumb to Huntington's.

On the heels of this discovery came a series of "gene for" announcements: newspapers reported that scientists had found the gene for homosexuality, for asthma, for shyness, for high intelligence, and so forth. These reports were misleading, though. For one thing, traits like high intelligence have a significant environmental component that can nullify any genetic component. (Regardless of your genetic makeup, a gunshot wound in the head can have a profound impact on your intelligence.) For another thing, to the extent that these traits are "in the genes," they probably aren't in a single gene but are instead the result of multiple genes expressing themselves.

But to return to our original question, Is criminal behavior heritable? The early eugenicists felt confident it was. Subsequent generations have felt equally confident it was not. The truth seems to lie somewhere in the middle, but even this modest claim is likely to generate controversy. Of course, until we can ascertain with some degree of confidence the heritability of criminal behavior, we would be foolish to establish eugenic programs as part of our effort to fight crime.

Taking our argument one step further, suppose we could overcome our ignorance about heritability—suppose, more precisely, we could convince ourselves that a certain trait was not only desirable, but heritable as well. Would it then be safe to undertake eugenic measures to spread the trait? Not necessarily, for our ignorance of genetics makes us susceptible to another sort of mistake: attempts to improve the genetic pool can have unintended adverse consequences.

To better understand this phenomenon, consider what happens in the world of animal breeding. A hereditary retinal disease that afflicts collies seems to have been spread inadvertently by attempts to propagate a pair of traits taken to be desirable in collies: long noses and closely set eyes. It is thought that the gene responsible for the eye disease is close to the genes for these two traits, so by spreading the desirable genes, collie breeders also spread the undesirable gene. This is an example of the so-called "popular-sire effect." Because a certain male looks perfect, he is used to sire a large number of litters. Only later do breeders discover that his good looks were deceptive—that the popular sire had a genetic disease, which has now been widely propagated.

The same kind of thing can happen in humans. In our attempts to propagate a desirable gene, we might unwittingly propagate a second, undesirable gene as well. Thus, consider Nobel Prize-winning geneticist Hermann Muller's proposal that we engage in voluntary programs of positive eugenics. Muller's plan was to preserve the semen of outstanding men—the examples he gives are Einstein, Pasteur, Descartes, Leonardo, and Lincoln—for future use in artificial insemination. What is significant, for our present purposes, is his choice of Lincoln as a prime candidate for sperm donor. It turns out that Lincoln, despite all his wonderful attributes, was probably also a victim of a genetic condition called Marfan's syndrome. (Indeed, this disease was arguably responsible for Lincoln's Lincolnesque looks.) Attempts to "make more Lincolns" would have had the unintended consequence of spreading Marfan's syndrome.

The opposite of the popular-sire effect is also possible: in taking eugenic steps to eradicate a bad gene, we may accidentally eradicate one or more good genes. Once again, the best of eugenic intentions can have unfortunate consequences.

And even when we know that someone has "bad" genes, our knowledge of the genetic outcome of a certain mating is at best probabilistic in nature. If, for example, both parents have the (recessive) gene for albinism, there is a one-in-four chance that a given child will be an albino; the same is true of microcephaly, gargoylism, and some types of deafness. And if one parent has the (dominant) gene for glaucoma, cataracts, piebaldness, lobster claw, or Huntington's disease, roughly one-half of that parent's children will have the disease in question. In other cases, the probabilities are more complex: if parents have one child with pyloric stenosis, there is a one-in-ten chance that a subsequent boy will have the defect and a one-in-fifty chance that a subsequent girl will have it. So if, as part of a eugenic program, we forbid parents who have a child with pyloric stenosis from having any more children, for every hundred children we stop from being born, only six, on average, would have been afflicted by the disease—only one of the fifty girls we prevented from being born, and five of the fifty boys we prevented from being born. But is it worth preventing the birth of ninety-four "healthy" children to prevent the birth of six children with pyloric stenosis? A difficult question, but one that anyone who wants to "clean up" the gene pool must answer.

Relying on the "Invisible Hand"

The Argument from Ignorance (against eugenics) can be summarized as follows: we should not engage in eugenic programs because we don't know enough to do so successfully. It is hard enough to establish what traits are desirable today, and harder still to establish what traits will be desirable in the future; even if we can establish the future desirability of a trait, we might have a hard time establishing its heritability; and, finally, even if we can establish both the desirability and heritability of a trait, we may make a number of genetic mistakes in trying to spread the trait or in trying to eliminate it.

So what do you do if you are too ignorant to manage the gene pool? You rely on an "invisible hand" to do the job for you.

To understand the reasoning behind this suggestion, consider the following analogy: eugenics is to reproduction as socialism is to economics. If we knew enough to run an economy, socialism with its attendant governmental control of the economy would make perfect sense; but no single person—indeed, no group of people—knows enough to run an economy, and for this reason we're better off keeping the government in the background and instead relying on the private sector to determine the course of the economy. We should let millions of people start businesses. Those businesses that serve a valuable function—namely, those whose products or services people are willing to pay for—will flourish; those that do not will close their doors. A process of "natural selection" will be at work to ensure that the economy thrives and the needs of people are met.

If government bureaucrats were smart enough to tell ahead of time what sort of businesses would succeed, what sort of goods would sell, and what sort of services would be in demand, they could perhaps plan the economy. But they aren't this smart (if they were, they would be successful businessmen, not government bureaucrats), so we are better off relying on the economic law of the jungle to get the job done: profitable businesses will grow, and unprofitable businesses will perish.

What we are appealing to in this argument is what economist Adam Smith referred to as an "invisible hand." According to Smith, in a freely operating economy no one dictates how the economy will be run; instead, millions of people independently come to their own conclusions about how they can most profitably invest their money and spend their days. Curiously enough, the result of all this activity is a smoothly functioning economy—something no single individual set out to achieve. It is as if an invisible hand were leading each individual to act so as to benefit the group as a whole.

There are those who reject talk of invisible hands as bordering on mysticism. Chances are, though, that they are quite comfortable with the notion of invisible hands in areas other than economics. Consider, for example, evolution. Lots of people find evolutionary explanations perfectly satisfactory, yet according to such explanations no one "designed" the various living things that are so well suited to their environments. In particular, no one "designed" human beings. We came about despite the fact that no one intended for us to come about. We came about because of the purely self-interested decisions of our evolutionary ancestors, whose goal was not to better the species, but merely to get through the day alive and enjoy some sex at night. But these are exactly the sorts of actions that, over the course of generations, will produce a species uniquely suited to its environment. It is as if an invisible hand were at work, guiding us in our development. But of course, there is (as far as science is concerned, at any rate) no such hand.

Or consider the English language. No one designed it. And yet, here it is, one of the most stunning human accomplishments. How did it come to be? It is the end result of trillions of attempts to communicate. Those attempts that were successful were remembered and repeated; those that weren't were forgotten. The end result of these repeated—and purely self-interested—attempts to communicate is a smoothly functioning language, something no one consciously set out to create and probably something no one *could* create. Again, it is as if an invisible hand were at work.

Along these same lines, if we knew enough about genetics, a government-run program of eugenics might make sense; but we don't know enough, so the sensible alternative is to allow the future genetic makeup of mankind to be determined by billions of people, each making personal decisions about whom to marry and how many children to have. We should, in short, rely on an invisible hand to guide the destiny of our gene pool.

The Argument from Ignorance, Concluded

This, then, is the Argument from Ignorance. Some will be content to make it the core of their case against eugenics, but such a move would be ill advised.

Notice, to begin with, that the argument overstates our ignorance of genetics. It is true that we don't know everything there is to know about genetics, but we do know a lot. As a result, although the argument may rule out *extensive* eugenic measures, it doesn't rule out *all* eugenic measures. It would seem to allow a modest eugenic role for government.

Furthermore, realize that any argument that relies on our ignorance of genetics will have a limited shelf life. The completion of the Human Genome Project and other developments in biotechnology suggest that our knowledge of genetics, which took significant strides forward in the last half of the twentieth century, is about to take gigantic strides forward. In another few decades it is entirely conceivable that we will know enough to micromanage the gene pool.

Finally, opponents of eugenics should be troubled by the amoral nature of the Argument from Ignorance. The argument does not attempt to show that eugenic measures are morally condemnable, only that they are—at the present time—imprudent. Most opponents of eugenic measures, however, oppose them on moral grounds. In particular, they think almost all the eugenic measures a government might undertake would involve violation of the rights of citizens and should therefore not be undertaken. They also seek an argument that, unlike the Argument from Ignorance, doesn't risk obsolescence as a result of advances in genetics.

Let us, therefore, turn our attention to an argument against eugenics based on moral rather than scientific principles.

The Rights Argument

According to the Rights Argument, even if the government knew enough to conduct a eugenic program successfully, it should refrain from doing so, since any such program would violate a basic human right—the right to reproduce. Before trying to develop this argument, let us take a moment to get clear on the nature of this right.

Rights can be divided into two categories. On the one hand, there are the so-called *positive rights*, which are rights that someone do something *for* you. Some (alleged) positive rights are the right to employment and the right to medical treatment. If we possess such rights and are denied a job or medical treatment—if, that is, the government fails to provide us with a job or medical treatment—our positive rights will have been violated. On the other hand, there are the so-called *negative rights*, which are rights that someone *not* do something *to* you. Some (alleged) negative rights are the right of free speech and the right peaceably to assemble. The right of free speech is negative since, although the government won't force people to listen to you, it will prevent others from silencing you, say, by pelting you with eggs when you are trying to speak. Likewise, the right peaceably to assemble is a negative right since, although the government will not force people to assemble with you, it will prevent others from disrupting a peaceable assembly you attend.

The right to reproduce is a negative right. The government will not take steps to see that you procreate successfully, but it will prevent others from interfering with your reproductive activities—as long, of course, as these activities involve consenting adults and take place in private.

Among our negative rights we can distinguish between those that are *cooperative* and those that are not. To exercise a cooperative right requires the cooperation of others—more precisely, it requires that others choose to exercise this right and exercise it *with you.* Consider the (negative) right peaceably to assemble. It is a cooperative right since to exercise it, you must find someone else who wishes to exercise their right peaceably to assemble and wishes to exercise it with you. By way of contrast, the (negative) right of free speech is not cooperative. You can exercise this right regardless of whether other individuals wish to exercise their right of free speech.

The right to reproduce, besides being a negative right, is a cooperative right: it is a right you can exercise only if some member of the opposite sex also chooses to exercise the right to reproduce and exercise it with you. It is important to realize that the right to reproduce is not simply the right to make babies, but the right to make them with someone agreeable to you (as long as you are agreeable to them). A government that forces a woman to reproduce with someone of the government's choosing would presumably be infringing on the woman's reproductive rights, even though it would not, strictly speaking, be preventing her from reproducing.

Is there a right to reproduce? According to the United Nations there is: Article 16 of the International Bill of Human Rights says, "men and women of full age…have the right to marry and found a family." Although the United States Constitution makes no mention of a right to reproduce, the Supreme Court assures us—in, for example, *Griswold v. Connecticut*—that citizens have "zones of privacy" that encompass their reproductive choices.

It would be surprising indeed if, among our cherished rights as citizens, we did not find a right to reproduce. Humans have a profound attachment to their reproductive activities and will fight tooth and nail against anyone who seeks to interfere with them. Any species that lacked this commitment to reproduction would soon become extinct. As Richard Dawkins reminds us, on the genetic level we humans are nothing more than very complex gene-replication machines. (We like to think otherwise, of course, but this only shows that we are gene-replication machines that have gotten uppity.) As such, we have had programmed into us, through billions of years of evolution, a desire to reproduce.[1] All of our direct ancestors not only had this desire, but fulfilled it.

Here, then, is the Rights Argument (against eugenics) in a nutshell: if the government undertakes involuntary eugenic measures, it infringes upon the citizens' right to reproduce; therefore, it is wrong for the government to undertake involuntary eugenic measures.

Replies to the Rights Argument

Some would attack the Rights Argument by denying that there is a right to reproduce. I am going to explore, however, a more moderate line of attack: I will admit, for the sake of argument, that there is a right to reproduce, but suggest first, that it is not an *absolute* right—that is, a right without "exceptions"—and second, that some of the exceptions to the right to reproduce seem to allow for governmental programs of eugenics.

That the right to reproduce is not absolute should not be surprising: it is doubtful whether *any* right is. Consider the right of free speech. You might think it is an absolute right. Indeed, the First Amendment to the United States Constitution encourages such thinking when it says, "Congress shall make *no* law...abridging the freedom of speech."(Italics mine.) Nevertheless, government has acted to abridge freedom of speech in a number of respects. Most famously, it will fine or jail you for (falsely) shouting "Fire!" in a crowded theater. It will also jail you for relating state secrets to foreign governments, and it will allow others to seize your assets if you slander them. Likewise, the right to bear arms is not an absolute right: there are individuals—most notably, convicted felons—who are not allowed to bear arms, and those citizens who are allowed to bear them are restricted with respect to how and where they bear them. Even the right to life is not absolute. If you are trying to murder someone else and he kills you in self-defense, he will have deprived you of your right to life, but the government will not punish him for having done so; and if you succeed in murdering him, there is an interesting chance that the government itself will take your life.

Consider, then, the right to reproduce. There are certainly cases in which the American government prevents people from exercising this right. Suppose, for example, a thirty-five-year-old woman who has never reproduced commits a crime and receives a fifteen-year sentence with no chance of parole in an all-woman prison. Suppose the prison in question does not allow conjugal visits or artificial insemination of inmates. By sending this woman to prison, the government is effectively preventing her from ever reproducing.

The right to reproduce, then, is a right with which the government may sometimes interfere. The question, as we shall soon see, is whether this interference should include various eugenic measures.

Why aren't rights absolute? Because other people also have rights, and because in exercising my rights I can interfere with their rights. The only way for people to have equal rights is if everyone agrees to limitations on his rights. A good government will limit rights in a manner that yields the most desirable mix of freedom and security for its citizens.

Consider, by way of illustration, the right of free speech. We saw above that this is not an absolute right: there are circumstances under which the government can prevent you from speaking or punish you if you do speak. For the most part, government limits your freedom of speech in those circumstances in which your speaking would violate the rights of others. This is what would happen if you shout "Fire!" in a crowded theater: innocent people would be trampled to death.

When my rights and your rights come into conflict, we must make a decision about which rights are more important. My right to shout "Fire!" in a crowded theater is clearly less important than your right to life—or at any rate, than your right not to be needlessly trampled. Notice, in particular, that in forbidding me to shout "Fire!" in a crowded theater, the government is not forbidding me to shout "Fire!" at all: I can shout it to my heart's content in my living room, a cow pasture, or an empty theater. This limitation on my freedom of speech, then, will not call for much of a sacrifice on my part, but will make a major difference to the well-being of my fellow citizens. It is therefore a limitation the government should enforce.

Let us now turn our attention back to reproductive rights. Are the rights of others affected when a man and woman exercise their right to reproduce? Indeed, they are. The others in question fall into three categories: future generations, the couple's fellow citizens, and the couple's offspring. Let us consider these groups one at a time and ask whether the government can legitimately limit a couple's reproductive rights with the interests of the group in question in mind. In each case, we will do a balancing act, placing on one side of the scale the interests of a man and woman who wish to reproduce and on the other side the interests of the "others" who are affected by their procreative act.

The Plight of Future Generations

One group that can be affected by a couple's reproductive activities are the members of future generations. (In saying this, I don't mean to include the *next* generation—that is, the offspring of people who currently exist; I will deal with their plight below. Instead, I have in mind distant and unknowable generations.) If the couple in question is dysgenic and the government allows them to reproduce, their undesirable genes will be propagated and will afflict future generations. For the sake of these future generations—for the sake of the "gene pool"—it is best if the government does not allow dysgenic couples to reproduce.

How might someone defend a genetic concern for future generations? In much the same way as one might defend an ecological concern for future generations. Consider the government's role in preventing pollution. In the absence of government regulations, people will tend to dispose of their toxic wastes cheaply—say by dumping them in their backyard. The problem is that if enough people do this, the environment will be harmed. In particular, if people routinely bury toxic wastes, there will be contamination of underground aquifers.

The negative effects of the dumping just described will take decades or even centuries to be felt: it won't be our generation but some distant generation that pays the price for our environmental shortcuts. To prevent this, the government forbids our dumping toxic wastes. It makes this generation pay a considerably higher-than-necessary bill for waste disposal so future generations won't have to foot the bill for us.

Someone might now suggest that in much the same way as the government is justified in preventing pollution of underground aquifers, it is justified in preventing pollution of another sort of pool—namely, the gene pool. When a dysgenic couple reproduces, it is doing the genetic equivalent of dumping used motor oil in its backyard.

What we have just seen, and what we will see again in our discussion of population control in Chapter 4, is a fairly straightforward example of something economists are quite familiar and comfortable with: an argument that cites the "negative externalities" of an activity as justification for governmental regulation of that activity. Whereas most economists use such arguments to justify pollution control or zoning laws, they can also be used to justify a governmental role in eugenics: our reproductive activities can impose negative externalities on future generations; therefore, the government is justified in regulating our reproductive activities.

Since negative-externality arguments are a bit complex and since we will repeatedly invoke these arguments in our justification of a greater role for government in regulating parent/child relations, some clarification is in order.

Sometimes the negative externalities created by an activity are obvious. If, for example, I start raising pigs in my yard, my neighbors will be negatively affected by the resulting noise and odor. Even though the pigs never stray from my yard, their presence will cause a substantial decline in the value of my neighbors' homes. This is a negative externality most local governments would not hesitate to deal with: zoning laws generally prohibit suburban homeowners from raising pigs.

Other activities, however, are less conspicuous in the negative externalities they create. Suppose I start storing dynamite in the garage of my suburban home—and not just a stick or two, but boxes and boxes of the stuff. I could do this for years without my neighbors being any the wiser, unlike when I started raising pigs. Even though my neighbors are oblivious to my activities, most people would agree that the local government would be acting properly if it forced me to remove the dynamite from my garage. It is true that the dynamite has caused no actual harm to my neighbors (as my raising pigs did), but it does cause them "potential harm." Once word gets out about the dynamite, my neighbors will worry about the possibility of an explosion and might take precautions against one, building underground bunkers or—more sensibly—moving away. In any case, the value of their property will plummet. The costs imposed on my neighbors by the risk of an accident are less than the costs imposed by an actual accident, but these former costs are nevertheless real. Thus, the *possibility* that an activity will produce negative externalities is itself a negative externality, and one that the government can properly deal with by restricting or banning the activity in question.

For another example of an activity that creates inconspicuous negative externalities, suppose I go out in the night, dig a hole in my backyard, and dump used motor oil into it. My doing so will cause no "actual" harm to my neighbors. They will be oblivious to my dumping, so this case is unlike the case of the pigs. Furthermore, my dumping will not cause my neighbors "potential harm." It is true (as was mentioned above) that the oil I dumped will ultimately make it into underground aquifers, but these aquifers are large, so that if the amount of oil I dump is relatively small, it will be diluted and for all practical purposes be undetectable. Therefore, this case is also unlike the case in which I stored dynamite in my garage.

It might at this point seem like my dumping the oil creates no externalities at all: my dumping, in and of itself, harms no one. From this does it follow that I should be allowed to dump the oil? No, since oil dumping is an activity that raises "universalizability" concerns. I have, after all, many fellow citizens, and the question arises, What if they all followed my example? What if they all disposed of used motor oil by dumping it in their backyard? It is true that my act of dumping may be harmless, but my act of dumping, imitated by thousands of my fellow citizens, can have a serious impact on underground aquifers. Given that I am no more and no less justified in dumping the oil than my fellow citizens, the government is faced with the following choice: it can allow us all to dump oil, or prohibit all of us from dumping oil. A government that cares about the environment will make the latter choice.

Universalizability is a complex concept. There are lots of activities that, if undertaken by a single person or even by a handful of people, are harmless, but that, if undertaken by everyone (or nearly everyone), would be disastrous. Consider the activity of living in Dayton, Ohio. No problems arise if a few hundred thousand people—myself included—do it, but what if *everyone* tried to do it? Think of the chaos! Presumably, when we raise concerns of universalizability we must consider the likelihood that vast numbers of people would choose to undertake an activity if allowed. Since it is more likely that lots of people will dump oil if the law allows it than it is that lots of people will move to Dayton if the law allows it, the former activity should be subject to governmental regulation, but the latter activity should not.

It is precisely because the harm done by individual oil dumpings is *not* obvious that the government should pay attention to them; if the government doesn't, who will? If I start to raise pigs in my yard, my neighbors will quickly raise a fuss and might bring my activities to an end even without governmental intervention; likewise if I am discovered storing dynamite in my garage. On the other hand, if I and my neighbors dump oil in our backyards, none of us might think we are doing anything wrong—and treated "as individuals" we may in fact be doing nothing wrong—until with the passage of time the collective harm we have done becomes manifest. The government is wonderfully well suited to keep its eye on "the big picture" and regulate activities that are individually harmless but collectively harmful.

Above I argued that if the government allows dysgenic individuals to reproduce, future generations will be harmed. Some will respond to this argument by suggesting that I have overstated the extent of the harm. Notice, after all, that *we* are here as the result of our ancestors' unregulated couplings, and we are, genetically speaking, doing okay. We manage, despite our various genetic imperfections. Won't the same be true of future generations?

The problem with this suggestion is that things have changed since our ancestors' unregulated couplings took place. When our great-grandparents reproduced, the forces of natural selection were allowed to operate. (Our ancestors had little choice in the matter.) If you were born with a significant genetic defect, you probably would have died in childhood; and if you did not die, your existence was probably marginal.

Medical advances have changed this. I am a person who, were it not for the medical advances of the twentieth century, would not have lived to reproduce. As a baby I had pneumonia; were it not for antibiotics, I would likely have perished. And I am not alone in this respect. Suppose the medical advances that took place in the twentieth century hadn't taken place. More precisely, suppose mortality rates remained at their 1900 level. According to one study, *half of the Americans now living* would either be dead or would never have been born in the first place (since their parents would have died before having them, or their grandparents would have died before having their parents, and so on). But in saving lives, medicine undermines the forces of natural selection. Thanks to medical advances, genetically defective individuals who would never have reached puberty a hundred years ago nowadays can reproduce to their heart's content.

Consider, by way of illustration, individuals suffering from cystic fibrosis. In 1960 the average CF sufferer died at age two—before being able to reproduce. And when the parents of these CF sufferers reproduced, they usually had no knowledge of the one-in-four chance that their offspring would have CF. Thanks to medical breakthroughs, the average CF sufferer now lives to age twenty-nine. It is therefore possible for CF sufferers to reproduce—indeed, to reproduce together, in the knowledge that their child *will* have CF.[2]

As far as individuals are concerned, it is truly wonderful that people with birth defects can live long lives and experience the joys of bringing children into the world. But if we shift our focus away from individuals and toward the gene pool, we quickly realize that modern medical breakthroughs are setting the stage for what could be a future genetic catastrophe. Defective genes that would, in days gone by, have vanished from the gene pool in a few generations can now propagate. This is a central irony of modern medicine: the more medicine the current generation takes, the more medicine future generations are going to need.

Biologist and eugenics advocate Garrett Hardin has argued along these lines. He distinguishes between personal medicine and community medicine. Personal medicine is concerned with the well-being of individuals, while community medicine is concerned with the well-being of communities and society as a whole. It is possible for personal medicine to come into conflict with community medicine. In particular, when people undergo medical treatments that maximize *their* well-being, the interests of the society as a whole can be harmed. This, unfortunately, is what Hardin thinks will happen in the absence of governmentally enforced programs of eugenics: "The gravest danger arises when the use of prosthetics [that is, correction of genetic defects] in personal medicine increases the number of children produced by the bearers of hereditary defects over what it would be if prosthetics were not used…. The increase in genetic load is slow, but it is inexorable if personal medicine is not coupled with some control of breeding."

Coupled with these changes in medicine are changes in government policies with respect to the genetically disadvantaged. Consider a woman who, as the result of a genetic defect, is mentally retarded. In the past, as we have seen, the government probably would have confined her to a mental hospital and thereby severely restricted her reproductive possibilities. Today the government not only doesn't confine her, but quite possibly assists her financially. Indeed, in the recent past, the level of financial assistance the government offered her might have been proportional to the number of children she had. In short, the government (unintentionally) gave her an incentive to reproduce. More generally, the government's attempts to help those with genetic defects can have and often do have the unintended side effect of propagating "bad" genes.

All this sets the stage for what is probably the eugenicist's worst nightmare. Imagine mankind ten or twenty generations from now. Healthy individuals are rare. Most people cannot survive without medication or medical intervention. Most people suffer from physical or mental limitations that are today relatively rare. It is a world few would want to inhabit.

When eugenicists speculate about the future in this fashion, they are often dismissed as alarmists. This seems unfair. What future-looking eugenicists are engaged in, after all, is the generally admirable activity of taking a long-term view of things and suggesting small steps that, if taken today, can make a major difference in the shape of things to come. They are the genetic equivalent of those environmentalists who, in order to get us to take antipollution efforts seriously, ask us to conjure up the image of earth in the year 2100, its air unbreathable, its water undrinkable, its sunlight no longer filtered by an ozone layer, and its farmlands arid thanks to global warming. We use terms like "visionary" to refer to these environmentalists; we are not nearly so complimentary in the terms we use to describe those individuals who are concerned with the future of the gene pool.

Someone can take the argument just given and turn it on its head. It is true that technology creates problems for us—and in particular that medical technology creates genetic problems for us—but we can usually rely on technology to solve the problems it creates. Thus, technological breakthroughs allowed car ownership to become commonplace, which resulted in significant air pollution; further technological breakthroughs resulted in more fuel-efficient engines, catalytic converters, and cleaner-burning gasolines—and the pollution problem was solved. In like manner, someone might admit that recent medical advances have resulted in a greater propagation of "bad" genes than was possible in decades gone by, but argue that future medical advances will allow us to undo any harm done to the gene pool by our unregulated reproductive activities. Indeed, the time is probably coming when parents can tinker with their offspring's genetic makeup to correct any genetic defects it may possess and thereby give birth to a perfectly healthy child. Notice that these corrections will not only spare their children much suffering, but that these children, being free of defects themselves, will be able to reproduce without propagating genetic defects. Thanks to medicine, one can imagine a gene pool, twenty generations hence, that in no way resembles the nightmare scenario described above. Indeed, one can imagine a genetic paradise, in which nearly all genetic defects are a thing of the past.

In reply to this line of argument, I have three comments.

First, it is unwise to assume that technology will always bail us out of the trouble we get ourselves into. Certainly with regard to the environment, few will advocate sitting back and letting aquifers be polluted in the hope we can fix the damage done in the future. We should likewise be reluctant to sit back and let the gene pool be polluted in the hope that we can undo the damage in the future. And even if we can find a way to fix genetic defects in the future, what about the harm caused by them in the meantime?

Second, in suggesting that we fix genetic defects at some future time, the above "trust technology" argument isn't really anti-eugenic; it just wants to delay eugenic measures until some unspecified future date. Instead of keeping the gene pool healthy by regulating reproductive activities, it advocates keeping the gene pool healthy by directly tampering with people's genetic makeups.

Realize, too, that by waiting several generations before we deal with the eugenic problem created by our unregulated couplings, we transform what could have been minimal eugenic interventions into extensive ones. By way of illustration, researchers have traced back more than a thousand cases of Huntington's disease to two carriers of the disease who came to America in 1630. If these individuals had been prevented from reproducing, think of the human suffering that would, over the centuries, have been prevented. In genetics, as in the rest of life, a stitch in time saves nine. (Of course, in 1630 such measures would have been impossible: Huntington's disease hadn't been "discovered," and people's understanding of genetics was primitive.)

My third reply to the "trust technology" argument is this: if technology does indeed find a way to "fix" our genes, it raises the specter of parents not merely fixing the defective genes in their offspring, but going on to "improve" other defectless genes. Thus, besides requesting that the gene for Tay-Sachs disease be removed from their planned baby, parents might request that geneticists give him the gene for blue eyes as well. This raises a whole new set of problems for the gene pool, problems we will explore in the next chapter.

The Plight of the Citizenry

Now let us turn our attention to the second group that might be affected by a couple's reproductive activities—their fellow citizens. Suppose a man and woman make a baby knowing it will likely have a serious birth defect that will require extensive—and exorbitantly expensive—medical treatment. Suppose they are too poor to pay for this treatment; their plan is to go on public assistance after the baby is born and have the government—more precisely, their fellow citizens—foot the bill. Above we worried about the impact the reproductive activities of such a couple could have on future generations; in this case, we are concerned with the impact this couple's reproductive activities will have on the *present* generation—more precisely, on the tax bills of members of the present generation. Shouldn't taxpayers have some control over the activities of others if they will ultimately be asked to foot the bill for the consequences of these activities?

The perceptive reader will recognize this as yet another negative-externalities argument for a eugenic role for government. The couple's reproductive activities impose costs on outsiders, much as my raising pigs in my yard imposes costs on my neighbors. In the same way as zoning regulations are an appropriate way to deal with these latter costs, eugenic regulations—it is argued—are an appropriate way to deal with the former costs.

Even if we take a taxpayers-be-damned approach to this issue—even if we think that an impoverished couple's right to reproduce dysgenically must be guaranteed, regardless of the expense to taxpayers—we should be concerned about the effect dysgenic coupling has on the health-care system. Health-care resources are not infinite. When a baby with, say, Tay-Sachs disease consumes hundreds of thousands of dollars in health-care resources in its inevitably losing battle with the disease, it takes a significant slice out of the health-care-resources pie. Is this sensible—or fair?

If a couple were able to pay for the medical care their child required, their reproductive act would not affect their fellow citizens in the manner described. We would then be confronted with a new question: is it fair *to their offspring* when a man and woman reproduce in the knowledge that any offspring could have a serious genetic defect? It is to this question that we now turn.

The Plight of the Offspring

To keep this discussion concrete, let us focus our attention on the reproductive activities of a particular couple—call them the Smiths. Suppose, for the sake of argument, this couple knows there is a good chance that if they procreate, their child will be born monstrously deformed—so deformed that he will suffer terribly through his childhood and will spend the bulk of his childhood years not playing, but in hospitals undergoing various operations. Suppose, too, that the child's deformity will cause him to die at a relatively early age—say, three.[3]

It is important to realize that the case I have described is much more serious than, say, a case in which a child is born with Down's syndrome or missing limbs. In these latter cases, it would still be possible for a child to have a good life—good from his perspective, at least, and that is presumably what counts. In the case I have in mind, the deformity is so horrible that the child will be nothing but a bundle of frustration and pain, especially when viewed from his own perspective—which, again, is the one that counts. The case I am describing is one about which almost any thoughtful person would say the following: "It would be better not to be born at all than to be born into that life." Readers who think the case described is unworthy of such a comment are free to imagine the plight of the child being even worse than the one I have described.

Consider, then, the plight of the Smiths' potential offspring. It may be true that the Smiths have always longed for a child and that a reproductive act would be the fulfillment of their dream. But is it acceptable for a couple to fulfill their dream if doing so means a shortened life of horrible suffering for an innocent child? It may be true that the couple will suffer if their procreative dream remains unfulfilled, but surely this suffering pales compared to that of the child they would create.

Turning our attention back to free speech, it is true that some people will be frustrated if we forbid them to yell "Fire!" in crowded theaters. They may enjoy the attention it gets them or enjoy watching the ensuing panic, but this enjoyment pales in comparison to the suffering others will experience if we allow them freedom in this respect. For this reason we must not allow it.

Suppose, then, that the government were to forbid the Smiths to procreate. In doing so the government is not forbidding them to live together, get married, or have sex. The Smiths can, after all, do these things without procreating, as long as certain precautions are taken. Nor is the government asking them to give up parenting: they can always adopt. (We can imagine that the government, to make up for the sacrifice the Smiths endure in not procreating, attempts to compensate them by moving them to the head of the line for adoptions.) Nor, in fact, is the government forbidding them to procreate "individually." Suppose, for example, that even though any baby Mr. and Ms. Smith made *together* would likely be defective, we determine that if Mr. Smith acts as sperm donor for someone other than Ms. Smith or Ms. Smith is artificially inseminated by the sperm of someone other than Mr. Smith, the resulting babies would be perfectly healthy—and the Smiths would have fulfilled their wish to procreate. Thus, in forbidding the Smiths to procreate, the government isn't even saying that they can't make babies; it is saying only that they can't make babies *together*. It is a small sacrifice to ask for, especially when weighed against the likely suffering of any baby they did make together.

Some opponents of eugenics will be unimpressed by the above line of reasoning. They might argue that I am underestimating the joy that comes from making a baby *with the person you love*. It is far more significant than the joy that comes from living with, marrying, or having sex with that person. It is also far more significant than the joy that comes from making a baby with someone other than that person. Indeed—according to this line of reasoning—the joy is so great that it more than counterbalances the suffering the baby they made would probably experience.

There are problems with this reply. For one thing, I doubt whether the joy of making a baby with the person you love outweighs the suffering described above. Indeed, I doubt whether *any* human joy outweighs that suffering. For another thing, if someone really thinks the joy of reproducing with the person you love is so great, I ask him or her to consider a slight variation on the above story. Suppose the child the Smiths wish to have is not their first. Suppose, to the contrary, that the thrill of making a baby with the person you love is a thrill they have already experienced—three times, to be exact, with three monstrously defective children to show for it. Even if we think the Smiths should be able to experience "reproduction with the one you love," we might think it appropriate for the government to step in and say, to paraphrase Oliver Wendell Holmes, that three defective children are enough.

A hard-core opponent of eugenics might dig in his heels at this point and assert that the logic of the above argument is mistaken. I said our rights must be limited by the government inasmuch as our exercise of these rights can negatively impact other individuals. The opponent of eugenics might argue that a couple's children do not count as "other individuals." To the contrary, their children belong to the couple, and as such are theirs to do with as they please. If they want to make a defective baby, it's their business and no one else's.

Few, I think, will accept the claim that a couple's children "belong to the couple, and as such, are theirs to do with as they please." In particular, most people will be opposed to child abuse and will see nothing wrong with governmental interference with families to prevent its occurrence. This last point is significant inasmuch as there is a connection between child abuse and dysgenic acts like the one being contemplated by the Smiths. Notice that there are lots of "nongenetic" ways to make a baby who will suffer like the Smiths' child would. You can give birth to a healthy baby and then beat it until it resembles the Smiths' child; you can give birth to a healthy baby but just after it is born inject it with a substance that ruins its health and makes it resemble the Smiths' child; or you can inject a perfectly healthy fetus, while it is still in the womb, with a teratogen, and thereby produce a baby whose birth defects make it resemble the Smiths' child. In each of these cases we would accuse the parents of child abuse. The first case described involves straightforward physical abuse. The other two cases involve poisoning. Virtually everyone would agree that the government has a role to play in preventing these forms of abuse and in punishing parents who engage in them. But if the government is justified in preventing these forms of abuse, is it not likewise justified in preventing the abuse the Smiths would inflict upon their child by bringing it into existence?

At this point someone might suggest that the Smiths are not *inflicting* abuse on their child; indeed, they aren't *doing* anything to their child. They are doing something to each other—namely, having sex. Their child's suffering is a side effect of this interaction.

I have two replies to this suggestion. First, I would argue that while the case of the Smiths is indeed importantly different from the case in which parents beat their baby, it is rather like the other two cases in many important respects. There is a sense, I think, in which the Smiths *are* guilty of poisoning their child. They are poisoning it not with a chemical in a syringe, but with a chemical (defective DNA) in the father's sperm and the mother's egg. It is a high-tech form of poisoning. And second, even if we accept that the Smiths are not "doing something" to their child, it does not follow from this that the government should not step in and act on their child's behalf. Suppose, for example, that a couple, rather than abusing their child, simply neglect him. Suppose, more precisely, that they routinely leave their baby without any adult supervision for extended periods of time and that, as a result, their child experiences malnutrition and is injured in various accidents. Suppose their child is damaged until it comes to resemble the Smiths' child in its life prospects. In this case the parents "did nothing to" their child, and that's just the problem. Their failure to look out for the best interests of their child had tragic consequences for their child, and this is something the government should not tolerate. But can't we say the same thing of the Smiths?

Isn't it true that by having unprotected sex they are failing to look out for the best interests of their (potential) child?

Opponents of eugenics might, at this point, seize on an ambiguity in the forgoing argument. I have repeatedly said that if the Smiths make a baby together, the baby will "probably" inherit the defect. But this simply isn't true in the case of most serious genetic defects. In particular, in the case of the Smiths, one would assume that each parent carries only one copy of the defective gene. (If they carried a double complement of the gene, they would have died in childhood.) But if this is so, then there is only a one-in-four chance their child will inherit both copies of the defective gene and thus be afflicted by the disease. Some would argue that these are pretty good odds—that there is nothing wrong with taking an action that might produce a baby whose life would be hell on earth as long as there is a three times greater chance it will produce a healthy baby.

This attempt to "hide behind probabilities" is arguably misguided. To see why, consider the following analogy. Suppose you do some research and find that if you drop bricks from a certain highway overpass, there is a one-in-four chance that you will cause significant injury to someone driving under the bridge. Suppose you drop one brick and cause significant injury to a driver. If, when arrested, you point out that there had been only a one-in-four chance your act would hurt someone, the legal system is unlikely to be sympathetic. Yours was an act, after all, that exposed others to a significant risk (a one-in-four chance, to be exact) of significant harm and an act you could easily have avoided doing. Much the same, of course, can be said of the Smiths.

Suppose the opponent of eugenics, at this point, is willing to concede that it would be wrong for the Smiths, in the circumstances described, to make a baby, and is even willing to concede that the government is justified in preventing them from making one. As far as a governmental role in eugenics is concerned, this isn't much of a concession. Notice, after all, that the case I have described is an extreme one and is therefore an easy one to argue. If we turn our attention to less extreme cases—cases in which, for example, the genetic defect won't mean suffering and an early death for a child, but will mean a somewhat less-than-ideal existence—it would be much more difficult to argue that parents should be forbidden to reproduce.

I intentionally chose an extreme case as the focus for my defense of eugenics. Eugenics is, after all, a taboo subject. Most people, if you ask them what role the government should play in eugenics, will answer, without hesitating, "None at all." Those who are more thoughtful—but still taboo-ridden—will answer that the government should perhaps fund genetic research and publicize the results, but nothing beyond that. For present purposes, I am delighted if I do nothing more than make the reader see that our ancestors were not simply speaking ignorantly when they said, "Three generations of imbeciles are enough." If we are interested in the well-being of children, there almost certainly will be cases in which we will want to say to people, "It would be morally reprehensible for you to reproduce." And if these individuals ignore our rebukes, we should turn to government to enforce morality, the way we turn to it in the case of parents who physically abuse or poison their children.

The Limitations of the Rights Argument

Before we leave the Rights Argument, here is one last thing to consider: there is less to this argument than meets the eye. To see why I say this, suppose we grant—in keeping with the Rights Argument—that people have an absolute right to reproduce. It does not follow from this that the government cannot engage in eugenic programs; for as long as the government restricts its eugenic endeavors to *voluntary* measures, it will not be interfering with anyone's right to reproduce. Thus, if the government were to offer me ten thousand dollars if I would undergo a sterilization operation and I took them up on the offer, they would not be violating my right to reproduce; instead, I would be waiving my right in return for a cash payment.

We do this sort of thing all the time. When we sell a car, we waive our ownership rights in exchange for cash. When we go to work for a corporation and sign an agreement not to divulge corporate secrets, we waive part of our freedom of speech in exchange for a job. Indeed, a case can be made—and I have made it elsewhere—that what makes our rights valuable is our ability to waive them for a consideration. Remember that a right you cannot waive is more properly called a duty.

Likewise, suppose the government announced that it would cut off government aid—including medical aid and welfare payments—to dysgenic individuals who chose to reproduce. It is not immediately obvious that the government would be violating anyone's reproductive rights in imposing such a condition, particularly if the prime reason for imposing it was to keep down the long-term costs of the aid programs in question. In such a scenario, dysgenic individuals would still possess the right to reproduce. What they would be deprived of is the option of having their reproductive activities subsidized by the government.

Some would respond to this suggestion by claiming that government aid is an *entitlement*, so to take away someone's aid is to violate his rights. This claim, however, is debatable. Generations of Americans—namely, those who lived before the New Deal—considered the issue and concluded, without any hesitation, that people did not have a right to government aid. And even if we come to the conclusion that government aid is an entitlement, it certainly isn't an "absolute" entitlement—that is, something to which people are entitled, *no matter what.* To qualify for welfare, you must meet certain conditions: you must be impoverished, unemployed, and actively seeking a job. The above eugenic suggestion simply expands this list of conditions.

It is only when we consider *involuntary* eugenic measures, like involuntary sterilization, that the Rights Argument comes fully into play. But this means that a government can be quite active in the realm of eugenics, offering dysgenic couples incentives not to reproduce and placing eugenically motivated conditions on its welfare or medical-care programs, and not raise any serious issues about reproductive rights; and this in turn means that individuals who contend—as many Americans apparently do—that the government should *never* undertake eugenic measures will have to rely on something other than the Rights Argument to buttress their position. Let us now consider what will, for many hard-core opponents of eugenics, be the argument of last resort.

The Slippery Slope Argument

According to the Slippery Slope Argument, even if (contrary to the Argument from Ignorance) we are smart enough to manipulate the gene pool successfully and even if (contrary to the Rights Argument) we can do so without violating people's rights, we must not allow the government to engage in eugenic measures, even voluntary ones. Why the prohibition? Because—the argument goes—once government gets started in the eugenics business, even in a minor way, it will start sliding down the slippery slope to ever-more-objectionable forms of eugenics. What lies at the bottom of this slope? Eugenic programs whose goal it is to eliminate undesirable races and traits— if not by sterilization, then by death. Some will point to history in defense of the Slippery Slope Argument: Hitler, they will remind us, started out with a few innocuous eugenic measures, but soon found himself sliding down the slippery slope, much to the dismay of his fellow human beings.

Before I respond to the Slippery Slope Argument, a word of clarification is in order. Some might interpret the Slippery Slope Argument to say that if a government takes moderate eugenic measures, it is *inevitable* that it will subsequently engage in extreme eugenic measures. This form of the argument, I think, we can dismiss out of hand. For notice that even though the United States undertook moderate eugenic measures years ahead of Hitler, we not only avoided a slide down the eugenic slope, but went on to renounce eugenics. Thus, if it is to be taken seriously, the Slippery Slope Argument should be understood to say that if a government takes moderate eugenic measures it is *probable* that it will subsequently engage in extreme eugenic measures. The idea is that the probability of a slide is high enough and the consequences of a slide are odious enough that the gamble is not one worth taking.

I have mixed feelings about the Slippery Slope Argument against eugenics. For one thing, arguments of this sort generally fail. We could, for example, develop a slippery slope argument to show that the government should not tax us (since if it taxes us at all, it will ultimately take all we've got) or place any limits on free speech, not even the prohibition on yelling "Fire!" in a crowded theater (since if it starts placing restrictions, it is just a matter of time before we have no free speech left). It is clear in both of these cases that we have not slid down the slippery slopes described. Indeed, in both cases we have successfully resisted numerous attempts by politicians—many of whom would be delighted if we citizens were taxed more and talked less—to pull us down the slippery slope. But if we can draw lines in these cases, why not in the case of eugenics? Why not allow the government to undertake some modest eugenic measures and say, "That's it; that's where we draw the line"?

Thus, an advocate of the Slippery Slope Argument would have to show that there is something special about eugenics that makes the pull of the slippery slope almost irresistible. And it won't do to tell us what the Nazis did when they were atop the slippery slope. We aren't Nazis.[4]

Many of those who advocate the Slippery Slope Argument against eugenics do so partly because they fear governmental abuse of power. I am sympathetic to this fear. In fact, because I appreciate the danger of such abuse, I go much farther than most of my fellow citizens in advocating strict limits on the role of government. The fundamental principle is this: if a goal can be accomplished without resorting to government, then don't resort to government to accomplish it. What you are left with, if you accept this principle, is a starkly minimal government. It is one that provides national defense, since if not provided by government, effective national defense would be impossible. On the other hand, this minimal government wouldn't be in the mail delivery business. The private sector can not only accomplish this goal, but probably would accomplish it better than the government does.

What about the goals of eugenics? Can they be accomplished without resorting to government? Probably not. Although some dysgenic individuals will behave responsibly and refrain from reproducing, others will not. (Think of the dysgenic Smiths.) Unless the government intervenes, these last individuals will reproduce with tragic consequences. More generally, consider the gene pool. Remember that in the same way as it is not in the immediate interest of any one person to avoid polluting underground aquifers, it is not in the immediate interest of any one person to avoid polluting the gene pool. If the government doesn't protect the gene pool—or underground aquifers, for that matter—then who will?

Conclusions

There was a time, as I've said, when the average American took it for granted that government had a eugenic role to play. Since then, the case for eugenic measures has, if anything, grown stronger. For one thing, our knowledge of genetics has leaped forward. People in the 1920s had a pretty good idea of which conditions were hereditary and which weren't; we today have an excellent idea. People of the 1920s possessed only crude tests for a handful of genetic conditions; we possess reliable tests for a wide variety of genetic conditions. For another thing, the "cost" of eugenic measures has declined dramatically. In the 1920s, the only way to keep dysgenic people from reproducing was either to keep them locked up or to sterilize them. Thanks to breakthroughs in contraception, it is now fairly easy for people to avoid reproduction without losing their freedom (and in particular, without losing their freedom to engage in sexual relations) and without rendering them permanently infertile. If eugenics was a defensible idea in the 1920s, it is arguably even more defensible today.

So what happened? Hitler happened. People lost their stomach for most things eugenic. What was commonsense to our grandparents—the view that the reproductive activities of dysgenic individuals must be curbed—became for us an abomination.

Is there a role for government with respect to eugenics? If we think people have an absolute right to reproduce, regardless of the consequences their reproduction will have for their children and for others, we will answer this question in the negative; but if we value the well-being of children, we will answer it in the affirmative.

Certainly the government has a role to play in disseminating the results of genetic research and possibly in funding such research as well. Caring parents, if they know there is a significant chance their offspring will be defective, will choose not to reproduce. Indeed, in some populations, people routinely take the results of genetic tests into account when deciding whom to marry and whether to reproduce. Thanks to this sort of genetic thoughtfulness, cystic fibrosis has been all-but-eliminated from the American Jewish population.

The problem, of course, is that not all would-be parents are this thoughtful. Some pregnant women don't even bother to get prenatal care; it would be unrealistic to expect such women to submit to genetic testing before they reproduce. Other individuals are more thoughtful than this but nevertheless decline genetic testing because they fear bad news. (What if they are told that there is a chance any baby they make will have terrible birth defects? Then they would, in their decision whether to reproduce, be faced with a real moral dilemma. Decline the testing, and you can circumvent the dilemma.) For such individuals, ignorance is bliss, at least until their child is born. Finally, there are those individuals whose defective genes render them indifferent to the results of genetic testing. Included in this group are those who are mentally retarded as the result of genetic defects.

Most states used to and many states still do require people to get blood tests before being married. Part of the rationale for these tests is to prevent an "innocent spouse" from contracting a sexually transmitted disease. Equally important, though, is the medical well-being of any children the couple conceive: a fetus can be harmed not just by the venereal disease that might afflict its mother, but also by diseases like rubella. If these measures are within the proper scope of government, won't the same be true of tests for common genetic disorders? If the government has a legitimate interest in preventing children from experiencing rubella, doesn't it have a legitimate interest in preventing children from experiencing the far worse horrors of, say, Tay-Sachs disease?

Mandatory genetic testing is not such a radical idea. Indeed, in every state but one, genetic testing is required by law; and when the government tests people, they are usually unaware that they are being tested. The tests in question involve newborn babies. Hospitals test them (usually with a "heel stick," shortly after the delivery) for genetic illnesses like phenylketonuria (PKU). Parents are not asked if they want their baby tested; indeed, they are probably in such a daze that they don't realize that their baby is being tested. If the tests come back positive, the parents are informed of the results—but are not forced to get medical attention for their child.

If we can accept mandatory genetic testing after children have been born (when the harm has already been done), why not test the genetic makeup of potential parents before the child is conceived (so the harm can be prevented)? It is true that some parents will find such tests worrisome or annoying, but is that too high a price to pay to avoid the creation of children with serious birth defects? If individuals wish to avoid worry and annoyance, they are probably making a mistake having children; and in any case, the worry and annoyance of preconception genetic testing is a pale shadow of the worry and annoyance they will experience if their reproductive activities result in a child who has serious birth defects.

Presumably, requiring genetic testing before marriage would force dysgenic couples to acknowledge the risks they run in reproducing. Hopefully, many of these couples, after confronting the risks they—and, more important, their offspring—face if they reproduce, will rethink their reproductive plans. This eugenic measure, however, will have absolutely no effect on those dysgenic couples that do not think of marriage as a prerequisite to reproduction. (In America today, nearly one-third of babies are born out of wedlock.) Nor will it have any effect on those parents who are perfectly content to expose their offspring to enormous risks in order to fulfill their desire to "make a baby."

What about more extreme forms of eugenics? In particular, is the government ever justified in forcing individuals to undergo sterilization operations? How we answer such questions will depend in large part on how seriously we take the interests of children. Thus, consider again the imaginary couple described above. The Smiths put satisfaction of their desire to make babies ahead of the interests of the babies they made, who were born with monstrous birth defects. It seems to me that the only way we can support the Smiths' right to reproduce—as a hard-core opponent of eugenics might—is if we are utterly indifferent to the interests of their offspring. Perhaps this is the key difference between us and our eugenics-espousing grandparents: they were more concerned with the interests of children than we are. If I am right in thinking this, then our grandparents' advocacy of eugenics—rather than being a sign of moral depravity, as many modern opponents of eugenics will claim—was a sign of moral enlightenment.

What lies in the future for eugenics in America? Let me take this opportunity to predict a revival of eugenics—the dawning of a second golden age of eugenics, as it were. The New Eugenics will be unlike the old, though. In the 1920s it was *the government* that forced citizens to behave in a eugenically responsible manner. In the New Eugenics, it will be *the citizens* who are pushing for eugenic measures. The role for government, if it has one, will be in blocking citizens from undertaking the eugenic measures they seek. In the following chapter we will take a closer look at the New Eugenics.

CHAPTER 3

DESIGNING CHILDREN

So far we have considered the government's role in *promoting* eugenic measures, both voluntary and involuntary. We can also imagine a role for government in *preventing* people from taking eugenic measures.

When a man and woman decide to create a child, the genetic makeup of their offspring is a probabilistic function of the genetic makeup of the father and mother. Usually they have no control over this function, but there are some exceptions. Instead of passing on the mother's genes to the child, the couple can find an egg donor whose genetic makeup they prefer; or instead of passing on the father's genes, they can find a sperm donor whose genetic makeup they prefer. They can even use the sperm of a Nobel Prize winner. (Some winners have been so kind as to donate their sperm for the betterment of mankind.) In this way, the couple can affect the genetic destiny of "their" child and perhaps get a smarter child, a taller child, or a more attractive child than if they simply let nature take its course.

If a man and woman insist on using their own genetic material, there are some fairly low-tech ways to affect the genetic makeup of their offspring. They can, for instance, create fetuses and abort those with genetic characteristics they find undesirable. Thus, they might sample the pregnant woman's amniotic fluid to learn whether the fetus they have conceived has Down's syndrome; if it does, they can abort it. Or they might get a sonogram to learn the sex of the fetus they have conceived; if it is not the sex they desire, they can abort it. This last technique has been quite popular in India, and its use there has skewed the male/female birth ratio.

Recent medical advances allow couples to do even more than this to "filter" the genes of their offspring. One couple, for example, wanted to have a child but found themselves confronted with a pair of obstacles. The first was that the man carried a defective gene that causes both cystic fibrosis and congenital infertility: men born with the gene usually lack vasa deferentia, the tubes that carry sperm out of the testicles. The second obstacle was that the woman also carried the gene that causes cystic fibrosis, which meant that if the man's infertility could be overcome and they had a child, there would be a one-in-four chance the child would have both copies of the defective gene and therefore be born with cystic fibrosis.

Doctors used a microsurgical technique to extract sperm directly from the man's testicles. They removed a dozen eggs from the woman, injected the sperm into these eggs, and succeeded in fertilizing five of them. When these five eggs had begun to divide, researchers removed a cell or two from each embryo. They tested the removed cells and found that although none of them was free of the defective gene, three of them carried only one copy of it and would therefore produce a child who would carry the gene for cystic fibrosis but wouldn't have the disease. The three "good" embryos were implanted in the womb of the woman. The end result: a baby boy who was healthy and who, unlike his father, had vasa deferentia. This tale, as incredible as it seems, is old news: the case in question dates from 1994.

As long as we understand the genetic basis of a human trait and can test for the presence of those genes in an embryo or a fetus, parents can "filter out" that trait in their offspring, either by not implanting genetically undesirable embryos—this process is called *preimplantation genetic diagnosis,* or PGD—or by aborting genetically undesirable fetuses. As we gain knowledge of genetics, these filtering techniques will become increasingly powerful. It is not difficult to imagine a time when parents can filter out not only genetically defective embryos and fetuses, but also those that are genetically suboptimal. In this eugenically brave new world, parents could select hair color, eye color, and even to some extent the height and intelligence of their offspring.

The filtering technique has some obvious drawbacks. First, it is cumbersome and inefficient. It is one thing to filter out one in four embryos to find the three that don't have a double complement of the gene for cystic fibrosis; it is quite another to filter out, say, the 999 out of 1,000 embryos lacking the exact combination of eye color, hair color, and so forth that the parents desire. Second, discarding embryos or aborting fetuses, as the filtering technique requires us to do, raises a number of ethical issues (some of which will be examined in Chapter 10). And third, parents might be supremely choosy, meaning that none of the billions of genetically distinct children that can be made from their genetic material is to their liking. Suppose, for example, both parents have blue eyes and therefore have a double complement of the gene for blue eyes. These parents are incapable (barring mutation) of producing a child with brown eyes; the laws of genetics will not allow it. Consequently, for these parents, filtering out non-brown-eyed embryos and fetuses is tantamount to filtering out *all* embryos and fetuses.

Blue-eyed parents who want a brown-eyed child have two options. They can, on the one hand, "import" genetic material. They can, for example, find a brown-eyed sperm-donor—more precisely, a brown-eyed sperm-donor with a double complement of the gene for brown eyes. The problem with this option is that even though the resulting offspring will have brown eyes, it will be only half "theirs," genetically speaking. It won't look like one of them. The other option is to tamper with the parents' genes before the fetus is conceived. This might be done by taking the father's sperm and altering its chromosomes so as to produce a child that is genetically "theirs" except for the addition of the gene (or, more likely genes) for brown eyes. (Scientists have not yet altered human genes in this manner but someday surely will.)

Or suppose a man and a woman are each carriers of (one copy of) the gene for cystic fibrosis. There is a one-in-four chance that if they mate, their offspring will have the disease. They could eliminate this risk if, rather than relying on the usual sexual act to determine (in random fashion) the genetic makeup of their offspring, they created a child who was, say, a clone of the mother. A variety of mammals have been successfully cloned and one supposes that it is a matter of time before human beings are cloned. Indeed, it may turn out that cloning is technically less difficult than gene manipulations like the one described in the preceding paragraph.

When we tamper with another person's genetic identity, we are engaged in gene therapy. In *somatic* gene therapies we alter the genes in the nonsex cells of an already existing individual. We might, for example, direct a somatic gene therapy only at the lung cells of someone suffering from cystic fibrosis; this, after all, is where his defective genes are expressing themselves and thereby making him ill. Since only his lung cells are affected by the therapy, the genetic changes we make will not be passed on to his offspring.

Someone who has been a successful recipient of somatic gene therapy will come to embody two different genetic identities. The chromosomes in (some of) his lung cells, for example, will be different from the chromosomes in his liver cells. He will have two different genetic fingerprints, depending on which of his cells we sample.

Other gene therapies involve *germline intervention*: we alter a person's genetic makeup in a way that will be transmitted to his offspring. Thus, if we genetically alter the sperm of the blue-eyed father or the egg of the blue-eyed mother in the manner described above, we will be affecting the genetic identity of their offspring. Every cell of that offspring will have different chromosomes than if we hadn't intervened. This in turn means that we will affect the genetic identity of the offspring's offspring, and so forth.

Somatic gene therapies are currently a reality. Such therapies have been used, for example, to treat some forms of severe combined immune deficiency (SCID). Somatic therapies are also being attempted on those suffering from cystic fibrosis. Doctors have been reluctant, however, to attempt germline therapies, in part because of medical concerns—we aren't yet confident enough of our genetic skills to try them on people—and in part because of ethical concerns.

One can imagine, though, that growing use of somatic gene therapies to treat genetic illnesses will lead to the use of germline therapies. These latter therapies, after all, get to the root of the problem. Why allow someone to be born with a defect you have to treat, when you can, by a bit of germline intervention, create a person who won't need treatment and whose offspring won't need treatment?

One can also imagine that although gene therapies, both somatic and germline, will initially be directed toward the treatment of genetic illnesses, they will ultimately be used to "improve upon" individuals who are essentially healthy. This, after all, is how things happen in medicine.

Consider, by way of example, drugs like somatrem and somatotropin. They were initially developed to help children who, because they were deficient in human growth hormone, would be abnormally—indeed, distressingly—short as adults. It was a matter of time before parents sought these drugs to turn their ordinarily tall offspring into extraordinarily tall individuals, perhaps to improve their chances of success on the basketball court. Likewise, the drug epoitin was developed to help those suffering from anemia. Before long, athletes—who already enjoyed exceptionally good health—sought the drug: they hoped taking it would enable their blood to carry more oxygen and thus improve their athletic ability. Along similar lines, cosmetic surgery was originally developed to help those whose faces had been disfigured by accidents regain a normal appearance and thus a normal existence. Cosmetic surgical procedures were subsequently adapted to fulfill the desires of parents who wanted to beautify, say, the nose of their offspring. The old nose was perfectly functional, but the new nose was nevertheless seen as an improvement. And from cosmetic surgery, the American health establishment has moved on to "cosmetic psychopharmacology." The drug Prozac was originally developed to treat depression, a serious mental illness that can result in the death (through suicide) of its victims. It wasn't long before people who were mentally healthy but wanted to feel "better than well" started using it.

One imagines that this sort of transition will happen with germline therapies. At first these therapies will be used to prevent parents from transmitting serious genetic defects, like the gene for Huntington's disease, to their children. Enterprising doctors will adapt these therapies to enable parents to improve on what would otherwise have been perfectly healthy offspring. The day might come when parents can in effect design, by means of genetic manipulations, the child they want to have. They can specify eye color, hair color, IQ, and so forth. It does not strain credulity to suggest that such a day is coming, particularly when we look at the breathtaking advances in genetics that have taken place in the last fifty years. It also does not strain credulity to suggest that when this day does come, America will experience a eugenic revival.

The New Eugenics will differ from the Old in two important respects. In the Old Eugenics—which reached its zenith in America in the first decades of the twentieth century—the *government* was the driving force, and the thrust of the eugenic measures taken was *negative:* the point of the Old Eugenics was to prevent dysgenic individuals from reproducing. In the New Eugenics it will be the *citizens* who are the driving force, and the thrust of the eugenic measures taken will be *positive:* citizens whose genetic health is satisfactory will tamper with the genetic makeup of their offspring in an attempt to improve on nature.

When the New Eugenics finally arrives, what should the government do? Should it take a laissez-faire attitude and let the citizens do what they will, genetically speaking? Or should government play an anti-eugenic role and regulate the genetic choices of its citizens, allowing some choices and prohibiting others? It is to this question that we now turn.

The Role of the Government

Let us focus our attention on "designer babies." Let us imagine, in other words, that we live in a world in which it is medically possible for parents, by making use of germline therapies, to determine the genetic makeup of their offspring. They can make a daughter who is the spitting image of her mother, a son who is a carefully chosen amalgam of his parents' features, or a child who looks like neither parent, but instead resembles a certain movie star.

Some would argue that in the world just described, the government should ban *all* use of germline therapies. Let us now consider and dispose of three ways this argument can be developed.

To begin with, someone might point to an important difference between somatic and germline therapies. In somatic gene therapies we are dealing with an already existing person and can therefore ask his permission before we change (part of) his genetic identity. In germline therapies, on the other hand, we are affecting the genetic identity of someone who does not yet exist and therefore cannot obtain his permission to make the changes. Having drawn this distinction, the opponent of germline therapies might go on to argue that it is morally wrong for us to tamper with someone's genetic identity without his permission and that the government ought to prohibit such tampering.

Then again, *whenever* parents mate, they are affecting the genetic identity of their offspring and are doing so without his permission. No child asks to be born, and no child asks to be born with the precise genetic makeup his parents are capable of endowing him with. Permission of the future offspring is not a concern when parents reproduce in the natural way. Why should it be a concern when they "improve on" nature by means of germline therapies?

A second argument given against germline therapies is that they are irreversible: once we change the germline, we change it for all time, and all subsequent generations will feel the effects of our tampering. In reply to this concern we might point out that what genetic technology does, it can presumably undo. Geneticists can as easily tamper with the genetic makeup of a child's children as it did with the genetic makeup of the child himself. There is, in short, every reason to believe that if we don't like the effects of a germline intervention, we can undo that intervention in the next generation.

A third argument against germline interventions is that they can have unforeseen and undesirable consequences. Since it is wrong to expose our offspring to genetic risks, it is wrong for us to engage in germline interventions. The problem with this line of argument is that even if we *don't* engage in germline interventions—if, that is, we make our children in the natural way and let chance decide their genetic makeup—we are exposing them to genetic risks. Indeed, as our knowledge of genetics increases, we will probably be exposing our children to a higher level of risk if we make them in the natural way than if we thoughtfully tamper with their genetic makeup.

Let us now consider three cases in which parents design a child—in which, more precisely, they engage in a germline intervention that alters the genetic identity of their offspring. In the cases in question, parents have different motives in designing their child and are faced with different genetic tradeoffs in their chosen designs. What soon becomes clear is that if we value the well-being of children, we will advocate a governmental role in regulating the genetic choices of parents.

Case #1: Parents have geneticists perform a procedure that will result in their child being born with an IQ fifteen points lower than would otherwise have been the case. The motives of these parents are selfish and negative: they don't want their child to be smarter than they are.[1]

It is clear these parents are doing something wrong: they are engaged in a high-tech form of child abuse. It would be wrong, after all, for parents to inject a two-year-old child with a substance that reduces his IQ. In such a case we would say they had poisoned their child. It would likewise be wrong for parents to inject something into the mother's womb—e.g. alcohol—that would reduce their child's IQ. Isn't it equally wrong for parents to inject something—namely, altered genetic material—into (say) the mother's egg and thereby reduce their child's IQ? If we answer this question in the affirmative, we will conclude that the government has a role in preventing parents from engaging in genetic measures that will harm their offspring as well as a role in punishing those parents who engage in such measures.

Case #2: In this case, as in Case #1, parents make a genetic choice that causes their offspring to lose fifteen points of IQ, but unlike the parents in Case #1, the parents in Case #2 have positive motives in making this choice: they are reducing their child's IQ because it is the genetic price they must pay in order to confer a certain genetic benefit on him. For the sake of concreteness, let us suppose that the parents "buy" their child five extra inches of height by giving up fifteen points of IQ, that they do this so he will be better at basketball, and that there is no way for him to gain the height without giving up the points of IQ. This genetic tradeoff is admittedly far-fetched, but the idea of genetic tradeoffs is not. In many cases parents who are designing a child will learn that in order to obtain a desirable trait they must give up something, genetically speaking. Designing a child will, in other words, be somewhat like designing a home: the architect says, "Yes, you can have a bigger kitchen, but it means a smaller family room."

In Case #1 we invoked the "child abuse" argument to justify governmental intervention. In the present case this argument won't work. Most people think it is permissible to "inflict harm" on a child as long as some more-than-counterbalancing good comes of it. Is it wrong to make your child cry by sticking a needle in his arm? Not if you are doing it to vaccinate him against some deadly disease. The question raised by Case #2, then, is this: does the benefit a child would receive from five extra inches of height more than counterbalance the genetic cost to him to obtain this benefit—namely, the loss of fifteen points of IQ?

One way for us to determine what *genetic* tradeoffs should be allowed by the state is to consider the *nongenetic* tradeoffs parents are allowed to make when raising their children. Suppose, then, that a pair of parents—call them the Browns—have a son who came into existence without benefit of genetic engineering. Suppose the Browns want their son to be a better basketball player, and to accomplish this goal, they enroll him in basketball leagues, send him off to basketball camps, install a basketball court in the backyard, and buy him season tickets for the local NBA team. Suppose, finally, that because of the time and money spent on basketball, there will be no time or money left for, say, cello lessons. The Browns have made a tradeoff: they have swapped musical ability in their son for basketball ability. The state will find nothing objectionable about this tradeoff.

Now suppose that because they are so busy developing their child's basketball ability, the Browns spend little time reading to and conversing with him. Psychologists tell us that parents can, by raising their child in a stimulating environment—for example, by reading books to him and engaging him in conversation—add points to their child's IQ. In failing to provide such an environment, the Browns are arguably depriving their offspring of IQ points. Once again, though, it is a tradeoff to which the state will not object: the state does not fine or jail parents for failing to read to their children.

But if it is permissible to trade, in a *nongenetic* fashion, musical ability or even intelligence for basketball ability, shouldn't it also be permissible for parents to engage in the tradeoff described in Case #2? Shouldn't they be allowed to swap points of IQ for inches of height? This line of reasoning is quite tempting, but before we give in to temptation, we should consider a pair of points.

First, it is worth noting that although the state will allow parents to make *many* tradeoffs with respect to developing their children's talents, it won't allow them to make *just any* tradeoff. Parents, for example, would be in very big trouble with the state if the child started skipping school in order to get more time for basketball. When it comes to genetic tradeoffs like the one between height and IQ, the same will presumably hold true. The state might allow parents to swap *fifteen* points of IQ for five inches of height, but not *fifty* points of IQ.

Second, there is an important difference between the genetic steps parents might take to enhance a child's abilities and the nongenetic steps. The Browns can easily reverse the nongenetic steps they might take to enhance their child's basketball abilities: they can, for example, stop sending him to basketball camp. The same cannot be said of the genetic steps they might take. Suppose parents, when designing a child with basketball in mind, give up fifteen points of IQ in their child to gain him five extra inches of height. What if it turns out he doesn't want to play basketball? What if despite his extra height he is no good at basketball? What if he wants to be a logician, an occupation for which a few extra IQ points never hurt? There is, in these cases, no turning back.

The bottom line: if there is reason for thinking the government is sometimes justified in interfering with the *nongenetic* steps parents take on behalf of their children, there is probably even better reason for thinking the government will sometimes be justified in interfering with the *genetic* steps parents take. Parents should have a large degree of autonomy with respect to "developing" their children's talents, but not absolute autonomy.

Case #3: In this final case, parents make a genetic choice they believe benefits their child but involves negligible genetic costs, or genetic costs that are clearly more than counterbalanced by genetic benefits. Suppose, for example, that another basketball-loving couple want to gain their child five extra inches of height. Suppose geneticists tell them that because of a lucky genetic circumstance, their child won't have to give up any IQ points in order to get the height; indeed, the only genetic price he will have to pay is that his eyes will be a slightly less dazzling shade of blue than would otherwise have been the case—admittedly another far-fetched tradeoff, but bear with me.

In Case #3 we will not be able to argue that the parents are abusing their child, as we did in Case #1, and we will not be able to argue that the parents are engaging in a foolish genetic tradeoff, as we might have done in Case #2. Thus, someone might conclude that the government has no business interfering with this particular genetic choice. Before we accept this conclusion, though, we should remember that—as we saw in Chapter 2—the government has a role to play in regulating activities that create negative externalities. In particular, the government is justified in regulating activities (like dumping a few quarts of used motor oil in one's backyard) that are harmless if one person engages in them, but quite harmful if lots of people do. It is, in other words, important for the government to be concerned with the "big picture" implications of individual acts.

Thus, suppose a man and woman choose the sex of their offspring: they select a son. This is a harmless choice for any one couple to make, but when large numbers of people make the same choice, the ratio of males to females is upset, and the result—a world in which men far outnumber women—is one that even those who prefer sons will agree is undesirable. Similarly, if parents tend to choose alike when specifying the other traits of their offspring, the result will be diminished genetic diversity in the human gene pool. This outcome is genetically worrisome, inasmuch as a diverse gene pool has a greater chance of adapting to unforeseeable changes in the environment than a homogeneous one. When parents don't genetically design their offspring—when they rely on chance to determine their offspring's genetic makeup—these issues don't arise: nature will set the ratio of males to females at approximately one-to-one, and the gene pool will be wonderfully diverse.

Is it likely that parents who design their children will settle on similar designs? Quite possibly. One imagines that they will be almost unanimous in removing known defects from the genetic makeup of their offspring. After that they will tend to select certain physical traits that are valued in their culture. They will tend to add inches to their son's height and remove inches from their daughter's waistline. They will do what they can to give their child clear skin, beautiful hair, and a nice nose. They will tend, consciously or unconsciously, to make their child resemble the "beautiful people" of their culture: children might be designed to resemble famous actors and actresses.

Suppose the government, as the result of monitoring parents' design choices, discovers a worrisome trend. One way the government could respond to this situation is simply to announce its discovery and hope "market forces" will correct the situation. Suppose, for example, government statisticians found an unusually large number of parents designing sons instead of daughters. Parents might react to this information by changing their designs: in a world with too many men, there are advantages to being a woman, and parents will want their children to be able to enjoy these advantages. Similarly, suppose lots of parents are designing daughters to resemble a certain actress. If the government informed parents of this trend, many would rethink their designs. If lots of girls resemble the actress in question, the look will lose much of its appeal.

There is reason to think, in other words, that the government has noncoercive ways to deal with many of the "big picture" problems that will arise when parents design their children. We shouldn't, however, count on market forces *always* to work. It might sometimes happen that parents persist in making choices that, because so many people are making similar choices, will have collectively objectionable consequences. In these cases, if the consequences are sufficiently objectionable, the government arguably will be justified in playing an anti-eugenic role: it should ban certain genetic designs and punish doctors who implement them.

Perhaps the world described above will never come about. Maybe human genetics will be more complex than we thought, and we will never gain the ability to design children; or maybe we will figure out how to design children, but the technology in question will be extravagantly expensive, meaning that only a few parents can take advantage of it. And even if we can come up with an affordable technology, we might find ourselves with little desire to use it. For many parents, after all, making a baby is an act of narcissism. They want the baby to be like them and look like them, even if this means that their baby is imperfect in the eyes of others. For parents to design a daughter to look like Gwyneth Paltrow or a son to look like Brad Pitt is to admit that they themselves are not beautiful people, which is more than many parents can bring themselves to do.

Whatever happens in the future, one thing seems clear. Breakthroughs in genetics are going to give parents genetic information and choices with respect to reproduction that former generations lacked. As a consequence, parents will be forced to deal with a variety of eugenic issues that they are at present reluctant to consider.

CHAPTER 4

POPULATION CONTROL

So far our discussion of the question "Who shall be allowed to have children?" has been concerned primarily with the role the government might play in controlling the genetic characteristics of its citizens. We will now turn our attention from the role the government can play in determining *what kinds of* citizens it has, to the role it can play in determining *how many* citizens it has. In this chapter we will ask whether the government is ever justified in taking measures to restrict people from having babies so population growth can be checked, and if it is justified, what form these measures should take. In the next chapter we will ask whether governments concerned about an underpopulation problem are justified in taking measures to promote population growth.

A Brief History of the Population Problem

For the longest time, the earth was relatively underpopulated. Before the invention of agriculture in around 8000 B.C., the human population stood at perhaps 5 million; two thousand years ago it stood at 200–300 million; and by the seventeenth century it stood at 500 million. This puts the current human population of 6 billion into historical context. Not only are the current numbers huge compared to the relatively recent (in geological terms) past, but the rate of population increase has risen dramatically.[1] It used to take thousands of years for the population to double. By the 1960s the rate of population growth was high enough that, if sustained, it would result in a doubling of the population in thirty-seven years.

Thomas Malthus was probably the first person to take seriously the dangers of overpopulation. In his *Essay on Population,* written and revised around 1800, Malthus argued that overpopulation and its attendant evils were the inevitable result of some basic mathematics. As long as the average couple has more than two children, population will grow at an exponential rate, like the series 1, 2, 4, 8, 16, ... does. But while this is happening, said Malthus, the ability of people to feed themselves will grow at an arithmetic rate, like the series 1, 2, 3, 4, 5, ... does. This means population will show an irresistible tendency to grow until the means of subsistence is outstripped, at which point people will perish.

Is there a way to prevent the population bomb from exploding? Malthus pointed to various "checks" to population growth, including war, famine, and pestilence. He presented us with a distressing dilemma: either various calamities—involving war, famine, and pestilence—keep the population in check, in which case we suffer from the calamities in question, or there will be no calamities to keep the population in check, in which case we will likely suffer from the evils of overpopulation—namely, war, famine, and pestilence. It is not a pretty picture.

Malthus's logic was impeccable, but his two premises were mistaken—or rather, were made false by technological advances. The development of effective contraception enabled couples to have as much sex as their hearts desired and still have two or fewer children, thus blocking the exponential growth rate Malthus worried about; and the rise of industry and mechanized agriculture allowed us to produce food at a rate that would have astonished poor old Malthus. Indeed, in much of today's developed world, it is the production of food that has been growing at an exponential rate, while the population has been growing at an arithmetic rate—if it has been growing at all.

Despite these criticisms, Malthus still has followers who predict an impending population crisis. They argue that the technological breakthroughs of recent decades haven't saved us from disaster; to the contrary, they have only bought us time.

Malthus Redux: The Population Bomb

After World War II, governments grew increasingly concerned about the problem of overpopulation. The level of concern peaked when biologist Paul Ehrlich published *The Population Bomb* in 1968. The view Ehrlich presented was essentially an updated version of Malthus. He warned of impending disaster as population growth outstripped our resources. The turning point, he said, came sometime around 1958, when "the stork passed the plow" and food began to be transferred from developed countries to underdeveloped countries.

In defense of this prediction, Ehrlich pointed out that human beings are very good at reproducing. There is an evolutionary reason for this: creatures that are good at reproduction survive, and those that aren't don't. As a consequence, the ability to reproduce, even under adverse circumstances, has been genetically programmed into us. There can be no quarreling with this observation. Nor can anyone quarrel with Ehrlich's observation that when faced with a population crisis—that is, when the ratio of births to deaths is unacceptably high—only two solutions are available. The first is the *birth-rate solution*, in which we find ways to lower the birth rate. The second is the *death-rate solution*, "in which ways to raise the death rate—war, famine, pestilence—*find us.*" Ehrlich's conclusion: we must take measures to lower birth rates.

What measures? Some were benign. Ehrlich suggested, for example, that Americans could respond to the population crisis by becoming "hippies." Other measures were more extreme. He discussed the possibility of adding temporary sterilants to the water supply in order to control the birth rate, but concluded that such a measure was not technically possible. He also advocated formation of a federal Department of Population and Environment, one of the functions of which would be to overcome the technical difficulties presented by the just-described mass-sterilization program.

Ehrlich criticized our government for wrongheadedly being more concerned with the health of the population (and thereby causing an undesirable decline in the death rate) than it is with population control. He argued that the system of taxation, which gave taxpayers a deduction for each child they made, should be changed so that rather than having a tax incentive to reproduce, people would have a tax disincentive. He also suggested levying luxury taxes on children's furniture and toys. If these proposals were implemented, it would cost a taxpayer to have a big family, but this is only fair since big families require more governmental services than small families.

Ehrlich also proposed a government lottery in which only the childless would be given tickets, as well as government grants to couples that delayed having children and to men who agreed to have vasectomies before having two children.

Ehrlich recommended even more drastic actions for other nations. He promoted the policy set forth by William and Paul Paddock in their 1967 book titled (unfortunately) *Famine—1975!* This book, Ehrlich remarked, "may be remembered as one of the most important books of our age." The Paddocks claimed that because the world's resources were so limited, we must engage in triage with respect to countries. We should, in other words, divide countries into three groups: those that can pull through even without our help, those that probably cannot pull through even with our help, and those for which our help will be a key factor in determining whether or not they pull through. Countries in this last group should get most or all of our aid. Countries in the first two groups should get aid only if we have any left over after the needs of the last group are taken care of—an unlikely event.

The Paddocks, by the way, offered India as an example of a country in the "hopeless" group. India, they claimed, was "so far behind in the population-food game that there is no hope that our food aid will see them through to self-sufficiency." Ehrlich agreed with this pessimistic assessment of India's population situation. He supported an Indian plan to sterilize all Indian males with three or more children. That such a plan was coercive didn't bother Ehrlich, inasmuch as it was coercion "in a good cause."

When would the population bomb explode? Ehrlich begins *The Population Bomb* with this prophecy: "The battle to feed all of humanity is over. In the 1970s the world will undergo famines—hundreds of millions of people are going to starve to death in spite of any crash programs embarked upon now. At this late date nothing can prevent a substantial increase in the world death rate...." And in case anyone misinterprets him, he later declares that "massive famines will occur soon, possibly in the early 1970's, certainly by the early 1980's." Needless to say, although the 1970s and 1980s saw famines, they were nothing special, as famines go, but the run-of-the-mill sort.[2]

In retrospect Ehrlich appears to have made the same mistakes as Malthus. To begin with, Ehrlich assumed, as did Malthus, that without the application of "outside forces," population would grow at an exponential rate. He was oblivious to the possibility that large numbers of people would voluntarily choose to have small families, as in fact happened in America and much of the developed world. In his second mistake, Ehrlich appears to have outdone Malthus. Whereas Malthus thought a society's resources would grow, but only at an arithmetic rate, Ehrlich predicted that our society's resources would shrink. Thus far, this prediction has been profoundly wrong. If anything, our access to resources since 1968 has increased dramatically—but this is precisely what one would expect when one considers the technological breakthroughs that have taken place in agriculture, mining, and manufacturing.

In an attempt to demonstrate the mistake in Ehrlich's reasoning concerning the future supply of resources, Dr. Julian Simon in 1980 offered Ehrlich a bet on the future prices of various natural resources. Ehrlich got to choose the five metals he thought would be in shortest supply in the future—and whose price would rise as a consequence—and got to pick the time span of the bet. He chose chrome, copper, nickel, tin, and tungsten, and a ten-year time span. At the end of the decade, the metals Ehrlich chose had *fallen* in value by 57 percent (in real terms), and Ehrlich had to send Simon a check for $576.07.

Ehrlich was not alone in predicting a coming shortage of resources. In 1972 the Club of Rome published *The Limits to Growth*, in which they predicted that the world would run out of gold by 1981, mercury by 1985, tin by 1987, zinc by 1990, petroleum by 1992, and copper, lead, and natural gas by 1993. Both Ehrlich and the Club of Rome failed to appreciate that in a capitalist economy, shortages of a resource today almost invariably lead to an abundance—if not a glut—of the same resource in the future. When a resource is in short supply, its price goes up, and it pays people to find and develop new supplies of that resource.

The Population Bomb Defused

By the 1980s it had become apparent to most people that although population growth was a problem, it was not necessarily a catastrophe waiting to happen. The rate of world population growth started slowing in the mid-1960s. This meant that although the earth's population continued to grow in absolute terms, an Ehrlichian population explosion was unlikely. There was light at the end of the population-growth tunnel.

How was the population bomb defused? In part by population control programs undertaken by developing nations. In one Thai program, for instance, women were encouraged to space their next pregnancy "with a pig." They were given piglets in exchange for a promise not to get pregnant until the piglets had fattened, in eight or nine months. Women who kept the promise were given a share of the profits from the sale of the grown pig. This program carried with it a built-in form of advertising, since villagers could see for themselves that families with few children and lots of pigs were better off than families with lots of children and no pigs.

The program just described was voluntary, but not all the programs proposed or implemented have been. In 1976, Indira Gandhi implemented a sterilization program in India. She made public employees' salaries contingent on the number of people they could talk into sterilization operations. Couples that had three children but refused sterilization were threatened with fines and imprisonment. Sometimes police raids were used to round up men "eligible" for sterilization. In the last half of 1976, more than 6 million people were sterilized.

China likewise resorted to force to deal with its population problem. Its infamous one-child policy restricted citizens' procreative activities. Parents that had more than one child had to pay an "excess child levy" that might mean a 5 to 10 percent deduction from their income for the next ten to sixteen years. They had to pay all the medical and educational expenses for their excess child. They could not apply for additional housing space or for more land, as could parents who were having their first child. They had to forgo promotion bonuses. By way of contrast, those who signed the single-child pledge got cash subsidies, priority access to housing, supplementary retirement benefits, and (in the countryside) more land for the family's private use. Their one child got priority access to nurseries, schools, clinics, and, ultimately, employment.

One-child programs like China's typically have unintended side effects. One is a rise in female infanticide because of "son preference." In many developing countries, sons are more valuable to parents than daughters. A son will typically stay at home even after marriage and continue to work on behalf of his family; a daughter, on the other hand, will typically live with in-laws, meaning that her labor is lost to the family. But if couples that want a son are told that they can have only one child, and if their first child is a daughter, they might solve their dilemma by resorting to infanticide. Another curious side effect of one-child programs is that a society with nothing but "only-children" will be a society without brothers and sisters, without uncles and aunts, without nephews and nieces. If one imagines that society gains something important from these relationships, a society that implements a one-child policy will end up paying an interesting, although largely invisible price.

China's one-child program has been criticized for being "generationally unfair": the penalties it levies are often paid not by parents who have excess children, but by the excess children themselves. If, for example, the government forces parents who have excess children to pay for their children's education, and if the parents cannot afford to do so, it is the children who suffer, not the parents.

China's one-child policy has also been criticized for being unnecessarily harsh. There was, after all, another, less oppressive way China could have achieved its desired reduction in population growth: it could have allowed people to have two children, but required women to wait till age twenty-five to have their first child and wait four to six more years before having their second.

Some might suggest that neither the Indian nor the Chinese programs described above are truly coercive. After all, citizens have the option of nonparticipation: they *can* say no. But one must consider the cost of saying no, for if this cost is sufficiently high, nonparticipation won't truly be an option. The problem of coercion is particularly significant in socialist countries, in which the government controls many aspects of day-to-day living. In the China of the recent past, if you were denied housing space by the government, you were out of luck, for the government controlled housing space. If you were denied medical care for your children in government clinics, you were out of luck, for there were no private clinics. Thus, there is a sense in which, in many socialist countries, to have your government benefits removed is to be punished, meaning that any governmental program that threatens the removal of benefits is in fact coercive.

What is Overpopulation?

Before we get further into the topic of population control, we would do well to address a semantical question: what do we mean by "overpopulation"? As it turns out, the answer to this question is not as obvious as it first might appear.

To begin with, it would be a mistake to define "overpopulation" solely in terms of an absolute population figure. Population is a problem only when there are too many people in relation to something else. Thus, we might define "overpopulation" in relation to land. We might, in other words, declare a region to be overpopulated when its population density—the number of people per square kilometer of land—is "too high." Such a definition, however, would have some obvious counterexamples: even though Monaco's population density is nearly fifty times higher than that of India, the general consensus is that it is India, not Monaco, that has an overpopulation problem.

Here is another way to think about the issue of population density. Six billion people is a very big number, but earth is a very big planet. Indeed, it would be possible for the entire population of earth to stand (sardine-like) within the city limits of Jacksonville, Florida; and if every man, woman, and child on the planet had a house the size of the average U.S. house, they could all live in Texas, with room to spare.

Although Ehrlich did not define "overpopulation" in *The Population Bomb*, in *The Population Explosion* he agrees that it is a mistake to define "overpopulation" as simply being too many people on too little land and advocates instead a definition of "overpopulation" that is based on "carrying capacity": "When is an area overpopulated? When its population can't be maintained without rapidly depleting nonrenewable resources (or converting renewable resources into nonrenewable ones) and without degrading the capacity of the environment to support the population. In short, if the long-term carrying capacity of an area is clearly being degraded by its current human occupants, that area is overpopulated." This definition is an improvement on the population-density definition of "overpopulation," but it produces a number of strange consequences, some of which Ehrlich himself notes: "*By this standard, the entire planet and virtually every nation is already vastly overpopulated....* The United States is overpopulated because it is depleting its soil and water resources and contributing mightily to the destruction of global environmental systems...." And if this consequence doesn't seem strange, imagine an island on which, because of population increases over the centuries, a large number of people are trying to wrest a living from a limited amount of land. Suppose the islanders experience severe overcrowding, with a dozen people living in each tiny hut. Suppose, too, that these islanders are undernourished because the land is capable of only so much and impoverished because all their time and energy is spent in food production. According to Ehrlich's definition of "overpopulation," as long as these islanders respect the land—as long as they close the ecological circle, use their own wastes as fertilizer, and so on—their island will not count as overpopulated.

The problem with Ehrlich's characterization of overpopulation is that it assumes that respect for the environment is the only thing that matters. (Indeed, for Ehrlich, this *may be* the only thing that matters.) Most people would argue, however, that there is more to life than respecting the environment. In particular, it is permissible to harm the environment to accomplish various human goals.

Allow me, then, to suggest a different characterization of overpopulation: a region is overpopulated when its population density creates significant problems for the people who live there. (Thus, I am advocating an *anthropo*centric rather than an *eco*centric definition of "overpopulation.") A high population density can—as Ehrlich is eager for us to realize—cause environmental problems, but it can also cause problems like starvation, an unacceptably high crime rate, or the easy transmission of disease.

On this characterization of overpopulation, the question of whether a particular region is overpopulated is somewhat subjective. Suppose, for example, that because of high population density, people in a certain region cannot afford to live in separate houses but must instead live in apartments. Is the region overpopulated? It depends in part on whether people mind living in apartments rather than houses. If they do, there is an overpopulation problem; otherwise, there is not.

Also, from the mere fact that a region has a high crime rate, it does not, according to the above characterization of overpopulation, follow that the region is overpopulated. What, after all, is the cause of the crime? Only if it is a fairly direct consequence of overcrowding will we be able to point to it as evidence of overpopulation. Thus, America's high crime rate—which is presumably due to social factors like the breakdown of the family rather than overcrowding—should not be taken as evidence that America is overpopulated.

Notice, finally, that even a region with a low population density can, according to the above characterization, be overpopulated. Thus, an enormous island with only two human inhabitants would have a very low population density; but if there were food enough for only one person, the island is, as far as its inhabitants are concerned, overpopulated.

One consequence of the above characterization of overpopulation is that population can grow—even dramatically—without overpopulation resulting. As long as the people's needs are met, there will be no population problem. Thus, countries that suffer from overpopulation are typically countries that have allowed their population to grow at a faster rate than their ability to meet the needs of this population. This is why India has a population problem, while Monaco, with a population density fifty times higher, does not.

Overpopulation and Poverty

There is a connection between overpopulation and poverty. It is clear, on the one hand, that overpopulation can cause poverty: if a country allows its population to grow at a faster rate than its citizens' needs can be met, many citizens are likely to become impoverished. It is also possible for poverty to cause overpopulation.

When people are poor, it generally makes sense for them to have lots of children. At first this sounds illogical: why have lots of children when you can barely take care of your own needs? The reasoning of the prolific poor only makes sense when we remember that in many impoverished countries, parents operate on the ownership rather than the stewardship model of parenting. They have lots of children not because they have their children's interests in mind, but because they have their own interests in mind. They might want lots of children, for example, so they can benefit from the children's labor. (Notice that the labor of a child is more valuable in an agricultural economy than in a developed country.) Also, in many impoverished countries it is difficult to save for old age, inasmuch as any wealth produced must be consumed in the struggle to stay alive. Because of this, couples in impoverished countries might have lots of children in the hope that their children will support them when they are aged. Call it a low-tech form of social security.

These motives for having children are intensified by high infant mortality rates. In some places infant mortality is so high that couples must produce six to ten children just to have a good shot at one surviving son—sons being, as we have seen, more valuable in many impoverished countries than daughters.

And when an impoverished country starts to prosper, the result, paradoxically, is often a surge in population, a surge explained by the theory of demographic transition. Increased affluence means better nutrition and improved access to medical care for a country's citizens. It therefore typically results in a decline in the rate at which these citizens die. People's notions about the "right" number of children to have, however, are slower to change. (Lots of people take the family they grew up in as being the ideal-sized family.) But constant (or slowly declining) birth rates in the face of rapidly declining death rates means an increase in the total population.

In saying all this, I do not mean to suggest that parents in impoverished countries never take the interests of their children into account or, for that matter, that they don't love their children. I *am* suggesting, though, that in countries with overpopulation problems, many procreative acts are motivated by parental self-interest. Indeed, in many impoverished countries a parent who was primarily concerned with the well-being of his offspring—a parent who operated on the stewardship model of parenting—might choose not to have any children at all, even though doing so was contrary to his own interests. I will have more to say about this below.

Solutions to the Overpopulation Problem

How should we deal with the problem of overpopulation? In the following discussion, I will distinguish between *systemic* and *programmatic* solutions. Systemic solutions attempt to deal with overpopulation by changing the political and economic systems of a country. Advocates of systemic solutions argue that if we fix a country's "system," the overpopulation problem will, in the course of time, take care of itself. As we shall see, advocates of capitalism and socialism have proposed rival systemic solutions. Programmatic solutions, on the other hand, attempt to deal with the problem of overpopulation by dealing with its immediate causes rather than its root causes. India's "forced" sterilizations and China's one-child policy are examples of programmatic solutions to the problem of overpopulation.

Systemic Solutions to Overpopulation

Capitalists and socialists agree that poverty is a cause of overpopulation and that one excellent way to restrict people's reproductive activities is to enrich the people in question. They will no longer need to make ten sons in order that one survive; they will be able to afford medical care for their children. They will no longer need to have lots of children in order to work the farm; they will be able to acquire machinery that can do the job much better. They will no longer need to create children as part of a "social security" plan; they will be able to save for their old age. Where capitalists and socialists disagree is over the best way to end poverty.

Capitalists argue that there is no better way to fight poverty than by reforming an economy along capitalistic lines. People are poor, they tell us, because they lack property rights or because the government does not protect what property rights they have. They are poor because government obstructs the functioning of the economy, preventing productive enterprises from arising and keeping unproductive enterprises in business. Capitalists will remind us that even Marx tipped his hat to the productive powers of capitalism.

Socialists, on the other hand, argue that the best way to fight poverty is to provide people with the things they need. Give them medical care, land to work, and pensions when they are too old to work, and they will no longer need to make children just to survive.

Betsy Hartmann advocates a socialist solution to overpopulation in *Reproductive Rights and Wrongs*. According to Hartmann, "the solution to the population problem lies not in the diminution of rights, but in their expansion. This is because the population problem is not really about a surplus of human numbers, but a lack of basic rights. Too many people have too little access to resources." The socialist solution? Divide the wealth of a nation among the poor of that nation, and then, of course, they will cease to be poor. According to Hartmann, one of our basic rights is "the right of everyone on the earth today, not just in the future, to enjoy a decent standard of living through access to food, shelter, health care, education, employment, and social security."

A capitalist might respond to this analysis by pointing out that the countries with the greatest overpopulation problem—for example, India and China—tend to be socialist. To such a challenge, the socialist can reply—and rightly, I think—that many of the countries with overpopulation problems, although socialistic in theory, fall far short of the socialist ideal. Along these lines, Hartmann points out that in the late 1960s and 1970s—back when socialism reigned in China—the population growth rate in China slowed dramatically. According to her, it was only when China let capitalism poke its nose under the tent that population growth became a problem. Hartmann's China solution is to return China to its pre-economic-reform days. In particular, she thinks it was a mistake to decollectivize agriculture.

Hartmann doesn't have much patience with the capitalist solution to overpopulation. She uses the term "Cornucopian" to describe those who advocate capitalism as a cure for overpopulation. According to her, these Cornucopians "believe that free enterprise and nuclear energy can do the trick, just as long as there isn't too much government interference through environmental regulation." She doesn't trust the Cornucopians' "unbridled faith" in science, technology, and human inventiveness.

Presented with these criticisms, capitalists might point out that the decline in China's population growth rate in the 1960s and 1970s corresponded with the country's Cultural Revolution—a point Hartmann conveniently overlooks. During the Cultural Revolution, love was declared bourgeois, and many people went hungry. It was not, in short, an ideal time to start or expand a family. Capitalists might also point to the startling difference between Taiwan and China. Taiwan has the "same people" as China, the same culture, and five times the population density, and yet it avoided China's overpopulation problem. How so? A capitalist will remind us that in 1949 the Chinese capitalists moved to Taiwan while the Chinese socialists stayed behind in China.

The capitalism/socialism debate is not, of course, going to be settled in these pages. Let us, therefore, turn our attention to another way in which people have tried to deal with the problem of overpopulation.

Programmatic Solutions to Overpopulation

Unlike systemic solutions, programmatic solutions to overpopulation leave a country's political and economic systems intact. Within these systems, programs are implemented to encourage or force citizens to have fewer children. India's forced sterilizations, China's one-child policy, and Thailand's use of pigs as an incentive for would-be parents to space their children further apart are all examples of programmatic solutions to overpopulation.

When governments are confronted with an overpopulation crisis, they generally favor programmatic solutions over systemic solutions. This is in part because governments feel threatened by systemic solutions. In favoring a systemic solution, politicians must acknowledge that they and their policies were in part responsible for the overpopulation crisis—something politicians are reluctant to do. On the other hand, there is nothing a politician loves more than creation of a new program, since more programs typically mean more power for politicians.

Another advantage of programmatic solutions: they are more "direct" than systemic solutions and as a result yield their benefits more quickly. A government can sterilize a significant part of the population in under a year. Such a program will have an immediate and indisputable impact on birth rates. Transforming a country's economic system, on the other hand, might take a decade, and the transformation's impact on birth rates will be debatable. Thus, the more urgent the overpopulation problem is, the more attractive programmatic solutions will be.

Even when a government favors a systemic solution to overpopulation, it may want to supplement this solution with programmatic solutions. Thus, suppose a government implements capitalistic reforms, and as a result its citizens begin to experience relative prosperity. The infant mortality rate is likely to drop, but the citizens (in accordance with the theory of demographic transition) will be slow to curb their rate of reproduction. The result might be a baby boom. (It has been suggested that many Third World countries are now experiencing this phenomenon.) Thus, a country making a transition to capitalism in order to deal with its long-term overpopulation problem might want to implement programmatic solutions to deal with the short-term overpopulation problems caused by this transition.

Overpopulation: The Political Debate

Above I described the steps a government might take to "do something" about overpopulation. Many of these steps raise important political questions. In particular, some would argue that when governments engage in programmatic solutions involving mandatory contraception, forced sterilization, or limits on family size, they violate their citizens' right to reproduce.

Someone could respond to this argument by claiming that as long as a government lets citizens have one child, it has allowed them to reproduce and therefore hasn't violated their right to reproduce. Those offering this response take the right to reproduce to be a *limited* right—that is, a right you can "use up." A classic example of a limited right is the right to vote. In any given election, you can exercise this right only once. The right of free speech, by way of contrast, is an *unlimited* right: the fact that you have spoken once in no way diminishes your right to speak again.

Most of those who think there is a right to reproduce think it is an unlimited right, meaning that you have as much right to make a thirteenth child as you had to make a first. According to this understanding of the right to reproduce, it is as wrong for the government to stop you from having a thirteenth baby as it would have been for the government to stop you from having a first.

There is a second sense in which the right to vote is limited: the government gets to decide when (that is, how often and beginning at what age) you will have an opportunity to exercise this right. By way of contrast, the government does not decide when you may exercise your right of free speech. Those who hold the right to reproduce to be *numerically* unlimited also generally hold it to be *temporally* unlimited: the right to reproduce includes the right to determine not only *how many times* you reproduce, but *when* you reproduce. You can reproduce when you are a teenager or when you are in your fifties (if it is biologically possible for you to do so), and you can space your babies a year apart or a decade apart. If the right to reproduce is indeed temporally unlimited, a government that makes its citizens space their children three years apart is violating their right to reproduce, even if this temporal restriction does not result in citizens having fewer children, over the course of a lifetime, than they want.

In the remainder of this chapter I will assume, for the sake of argument, that there is an unlimited (in both the numerical and temporal sense) right to reproduce. I will go on, however, to argue that sometimes, in response to an overpopulation problem, a government is justified in restricting its citizens' reproductive activities. In other words I will argue, as I did back in Chapter 2, that the right to reproduce isn't an absolute right.

A couple's decision to reproduce appears, at first blush, to be a private decision, affecting only the couple in question—it is, after all, *their* family that they are planning. But of course, the man and woman aren't the only ones affected by their reproductive activities. Their children (both potential and currently existing) and fellow citizens are also affected.

Consider first the children they bring into existence. Suppose that because they live in an extremely overpopulated country, the best their children can hope for is an infancy ravaged by malnutrition and illness, an adolescence spent in unending manual labor, and (if they survive childhood) an adulthood spent in poverty, compounded by the burden of having to support their parents. Would anyone choose to be born into such a life? Given a choice between living that life and not being born at all, many would prefer nonexistence.

Suppose that when we inquire into the motives of the couple just described, we find that they wish to have children because they wish to exploit the labor of their children and because they wish to use the children as a form of old-age insurance so that they—the parents—will not starve on the streets when they are old. (In having these motives, they reveal themselves to be advocates of the ownership model of parenting rather than the stewardship model.) The man and woman in question, then, are attempting to lessen their own suffering and reduce their own chance of starving to death by creating children who will suffer and quite possibly starve to death. In fact, because the children come into existence later in the population explosion than their parents did, it is likely that the children's suffering and risk of starvation will be *greater than* that of their parents.

Many would argue that it is morally wrong for a person to avoid suffering by taking steps to increase the suffering of another person—that it is wrong to "shift" your suffering onto someone else. By way of illustration, for me to save myself from drowning by using another person as a flotation device—and thereby drowning him—would be wrong. But in having children, the man and woman described above *are* attempting to "shift" their suffering onto someone else. What they are doing is arguably wrong, and it is arguably within the proper scope of government to prevent them from doing so, much as it is within the proper scope of government to stop me from using you as a flotation device.

Here is another way to think about the ethics of reproduction in overpopulated countries. Most people agree that it is proper for governments to prevent parents from withholding food from their children and thereby starving them to death. Suppose, however, that people have children in the knowledge that, once they exist, there will be insufficient food for them and they will starve to death. In one sense these parents will not be responsible for the starvation of their children: they have no food to give them and thus prevent them from starving. In another sense, though, these parents *will* be responsible: realizing how limited their resources were, they could have chosen not to have children and thereby prevented their children from starving. In failing to make this choice, they arguably become responsible for their children's starvation.

Besides wronging any children they bring into existence, the couple described above, if they reproduce, can also wrong the children they have already brought into existence. It is likely, after all, that by continuing to reproduce, they make life harder for their currently existing children: a bigger family typically means fewer resources per child. Thus, if we think it appropriate for the government to force parents to fulfill the obligations they undertake in becoming parents, we might come to the conclusion that the state can legitimately prevent parents who are barely capable of caring for their currently existing children from having any more.[3]

Philosopher Onora O'Neill has written about the reproductive rights of parents. Although she thinks there is a right to reproduce, she does not think the right is absolute. Instead, it is "contingent upon begetters and bearers having or making some feasible plan for their child to be adequately reared by themselves or by willing others. Persons who beget or bear without making any such plans cannot claim that they are exercising a right." The idea is that when you exercise your right to reproduce, you undertake certain obligations to the children you bring into existence. If, because of an overpopulation problem, the people in a country can't meet these parental obligations, then their government can legitimately interfere with their reproductive activities.

In summary, it would appear that for people in overpopulated countries, having children is, in many cases, an intensely selfish act— an act that could only be undertaken by someone firmly entrenched in the ownership model of parenting and an act that a government that cares about the interests of children will forbid.

Besides affecting their children (both potential and currently existing) when they reproduce, a couple in an overpopulated country can also affect their fellow citizens. Life in an overpopulated country is already bad enough for these fellow citizens. The reproductive activities of the couple can only make things worse. There will be more starvation, more crowding, and a greater chance of contagion. It may be true that the couple has a right to reproduce, but the couple's fellow citizens have rights, too. In such cases, the rights of the couple must give way to the rights of the fellow citizens.

Someone might reply to this line of reasoning by pointing out that *one* couple's having a baby will have negligible effect on the well-being of the couple's fellow citizens. Suppose a country has 10 million people living in it. If a man and woman have a child, the increase in the country's population—and therefore the increase in crowding and starvation—will be negligible. The couple's fellow citizens therefore have no grounds for complaining about the couple's reproductive activities. Indeed, even if they have a dozen children, there would be no grounds for complaint.

These claims are true but irrelevant, for remember our discussion of universalizability back in Chapter 2. It may be true that *my* dumping motor oil in my backyard won't hurt anyone, but if enough of my fellow citizens imitate me, significant harm will be done. The same can be said for reproductive activities in an overpopulated country. A single act of reproduction will have a negligible impact on the country's well-being, but if the government grants everyone the right to reproduce (without limits) and if everyone exercises this right, the consequences can be disastrous. In the same way as it is appropriate for the government to restrict the activities of polluters, it is appropriate for the government to block the reproductive activities of couples in overpopulated countries.

Overpopulation and Eugenics

Let us end our discussion of the government's role in dealing with overpopulation problems by comparing the sacrifices expected of citizens in an overpopulated country with those that might be expected of dysgenic citizens under a government that undertakes eugenic measures. Although Americans are generally opposed to both population control measures and government mandated eugenic measures, they tend to find the former measures less odious than the latter. There are, in other words, Americans who are tolerant of China's one-child policy or maybe even of India's involuntary sterilization policy—who can see why China and India "had to" take these steps—but who are nevertheless intolerant of any eugenic role for government. This viewpoint is curious, since the sacrifices citizens are asked to make in population control programs are typically greater than the sacrifices they are asked to make in eugenic programs.

In forbidding a dysgenic couple to reproduce, we aren't forbidding them to have sex. We aren't even forbidding them to reproduce. We are forbidding them to reproduce *with each other*. In forbidding a couple in an overpopulated country to reproduce, we are forbidding them to reproduce, period—not with each other and not with anyone else. We are probably asking them to make other sacrifices as well. In a poor country, in which effective means of contraception are unavailable, to ask a couple not to make babies is tantamount to asking them not to have sex. It is also tantamount to asking them to spend their later years in abject poverty, since they will lack offspring who might otherwise take care of them. Notice, finally, that although the eugenic measures a country takes might affect relatively few citizens—those with defective genes—the population control measures a country takes might affect *all* its citizens. In summary, a government that undertakes population control measures is generally asking its citizens to make far greater sacrifices than a government that undertakes eugenic measures.

All this suggests that if we are opposed to governments interfering with the lives of citizens, we should be more reluctant to implement population control programs than we are to implement eugenic measures, but as I've said, many Americans find population control programs to be less objectionable than eugenic measures. This is one more indication of how muddled our thinking can be when it comes to the issue of "reproductive rights."

CHAPTER 5

THE POPULATION IMPLOSION

In the previous chapter we considered the problem of too many people on the face of the earth—a population explosion. Some fear the opposite problem—a population implosion. In many developed countries, women are reproducing at below the replacement rate. This means that in much of the world the population is declining or soon will decline. The possibility of a population implosion presents us with yet another question concerning the relationship between parents, children, and the state: under what circumstances should the government encourage or even force people to have children?

The Coming Population Implosion

A few statistics put the population implosion into perspective. In 1790 the average American woman had seven children. By 1890 that number had dropped to four, a number that remained fairly constant through the first half of the twentieth century: in 1945, 47 percent of Americans took four or more children to be the ideal family size. Then things started changing dramatically. By 1985 only 11 percent of Americans favored four-child families. During this same period, the percentage of parents favoring two-child families rose from 16 to 56. In four decades, two children were effectively lopped off the ideal American family.

In 1972 the American *total fertility rate*—the number of children had by the average woman during her lifetime—dropped below 2.1. This number is significant, inasmuch as it is the *replacement rate,* the number of children each woman must have in order for the population to remain stable. (This number is greater than two since not all children make it to adulthood.) American fertility has not risen above 2.1 since then. This means that although the population of America continues to rise, it will stop growing sometime this century and then start shrinking. America is experiencing what author Ben Wattenberg calls a Birth Dearth.

The Birth Dearth is not a uniquely American phenomenon. In almost every politically free, industrialized country, much the same thing is happening, often more dramatically than in the United States. After the breakup of the Soviet Union, Eastern Europe was hit hard by the Birth Dearth. Current reproductive rates imply that in Ukraine and the Czech Republic, the average woman will have only 1.1 children in her lifetime, and in Bulgaria and Russia only 1.2 children. In Europe as a whole, forty of forty-two countries and territories are reproducing at below replacement level. In the words of French Prime Minister Jacques Chirac, "Europe is vanishing." He cautioned that if current rates of reproduction continued, "our countries will be empty." Japan not only has a Birth Dearth, but began to experience it ahead of most Western nations. Even Third World nations show signs of susceptibility to the Birth Dearth phenomenon: the island of Java in Indonesia and the city of Addis Ababa in Ethiopia are, surprisingly, reproducing at below the replacement rate.

The world has experienced population declines in the past, but whereas those declines were due to external factors like wars, famines, and plagues, the current Birth Dearth is the result of conscious human choice. In saying this I don't mean to suggest that people are consciously choosing to shrink the population; they are, however, consciously choosing to have only two children, one child, or no children at all even though it is within their power to have three or more. This phenomenon is unprecedented in population history.

Suppose the Birth Dearth continues. What does this mean for future population figures? In the United States it means that our population will top out in a few decades and then start to decline. By the end of the century our population will be not much higher than it is today. In other nations the mathematics of the Birth Dearth is rather more cruel. West German women had an abysmally low fertility rate in the late 1980s. Had this rate continued—it was disrupted by reunification with the rather more prolific East German women—the population of West Germany would have gone from 60 million in the late 1980s to 50 million by 2000, and down to 16 million by 2100.

The Birth Dearth, besides affecting the number of people in a country, affects their age distribution. When the population is growing, the age distribution typically resembles a pyramid, with lots of people under ten years old, fewer people between ten and twenty, fewer still between twenty and thirty, and so forth. If population growth drops to the replacement rate, this pyramid will, in the course of time, transform into a column, with about the same number of people under ten years old as there are people between ten and twenty, and so on. And if population growth drops *below* the replacement rate for a prolonged period, this column will become an inverted pyramid, with few babies, more children, even more adults, and lots of senior citizens. Some students of the Birth Dearth phenomenon find the change of age distribution within a country to be even more disturbing than the associated decline in population. I will explain why in a moment.

When a nation experiences a Birth Dearth, its national identity, or even, as we shall see, its national sovereignty, might be imperiled. As a result, some nations with low rates of reproduction have established pronatalist programs to ensure adequate reproduction rates. In the mid-1960s, for example, Romania banned abortion, restricted the use of contraceptives, and discouraged divorce in an attempt to stave off a population implosion. As the years went by, the Romanian government became even more intrusive in citizens' lives. By the mid-1980s, women were required to have a monthly gynecological exam to make sure they weren't "cheating" by taking steps to avoid pregnancy. Romania also offered couples incentives to reproduce, including maternity leaves, tax benefits, and birth premiums. Whatever we may think of the legitimacy of the program, it accomplished its goal: Romanian birth rates went up.

Other Eastern European countries also implemented pronatalist programs, but theirs were not as coercive as Romania's. Western European countries have been reluctant to initiate pronatalist programs but have not rejected them out of hand. In the 1930s, sociologist Gunnar Myrdal advocated welfare state proposals to boost Swedish reproduction. Simone Veil, the former French Minister of Health and Family Affairs and President of the European Parliament, wanted France to implement pronatalist policies.

Why an Implosion?

A number of interrelated factors are responsible for the Birth Dearth. Until the second half of the twentieth century, the only sure way for families to stay small was for parents to avoid having sex. Forced to choose between less sex and more children, many parents viewed the latter as the lesser of two evils. Breakthroughs in contraceptive technology—and in particular, the invention of the birth-control pill—changed all this. It became possible for parents to have sex to their heart's content with negligible risk of pregnancy. Along with improved contraceptive technology came an increased willingness, on the part of politicians, to allow citizens to avail themselves of this technology. (Not so long ago even low-tech means of contraception like condoms were prohibited by law in many places.) And when abortion was legalized, many people who would otherwise have given birth to (unwanted) babies remained child-free. In America in the 1990s, more than a million fetuses were aborted each year.

Legalized abortion and improved access to reliable contraception didn't in and of themselves guarantee the onset of a Birth Dearth: people could have chosen not to use contraception or have abortions. For a slowdown in the birth rate to take place, parents had to modify their views concerning ideal family size, and this is apparently what happened.

A number of social changes in the 1960s and 1970s caused people to reduce their reproductive goals. One such change was the rise of the women's movement, which encouraged women to stop seeking fulfillment as housewife/mothers and instead seek it the way men did—at the workplace. A large family, which can be a blessing to a housewife/mother, is likely a curse to a woman who wants to focus her time and energy on her career. Wattenberg lists the migration of women out of the home and into the workforce as perhaps the single most important factor giving rise to the American Birth Dearth. Another change that triggered a reassessment of American views on ideal family size was the liberalization of divorce laws. The no-fault divorce revolution of the 1970s (which I will discuss in detail in Chapter 11) meant that if a woman chose to play the role of housewife/mother, her husband would no longer be required to support her in the event of a divorce. She therefore risked future destitution, and the risk was particularly high if she chose to have a large family. Finally, there were people who would have preferred a large family but felt guilty about bringing children into an already overpopulated world. In other words, by acting on their fears of global overpopulation, they contributed to a national underpopulation problem.

It is also possible that the Birth Dearth is the result of a substitution, in some countries, of materialistic values for familistic values. Perhaps people are simply less in love with family life than they used to be. Perhaps their increasing reluctance to have children is the result of their realization that children get in the way of other things—like a lavish lifestyle and maximal personal freedom—and their conviction that the rewards of parenthood are not sufficient to compensate for the sacrifices required by it. It is also possible that the Birth Dearth in much of the developed world is simply the last stage of the demographic transition triggered by the Industrial Revolution: at long last our notions about the "right" family size have caught up with—indeed, have overshot—the reduction in death rates brought about by the affluence resulting from industrialization.

Why Worry?

The natural reaction to the above comments is to ask, What's so bad about a population decline? In the previous chapter we spent a fair amount of time describing the harm done by a population explosion. If population explosions are bad, doesn't it follow that population implosions are good?

Here is another way to put this point. We have seen that if recent reproductive trends continue, the population of the United States will peak in the middle of this century and will end the century at about its present level. Can this be such a bad thing? Our current level of population isn't causing us too many problems. If 280 million is an acceptable number of Americans today, why would it be any less acceptable in a hundred years?

Because they carry us into uncharted territory, population explosions are intrinsically more scary than population implosions. Since our planet has never supported 12 billion people, we can only speculate on what conditions would be like if the population of the earth were to double. On the other hand, imagining what the world would be like with half as many people as it now has is easy to do: just picture the world as it was in 1960. Not a bad world, all things considered. So why should we fear a population implosion? For a number of reasons.

For one thing, a shrinking population is bad for the economy. To see why I say this, consider two towns—call them Growville and Shrinksberg—that have the same number of residents, the same number and types of businesses, and the same level of affluence. Indeed, suppose they differ in only one significant respect: Growville's population is growing at a rate of 10 percent per year, while Shrinksberg's population is shrinking at a rate of 10 percent per year. If a corporation were given the choice of opening a new store in either Growville or Shrinksberg, which should it choose? In Growville it could count on an increasing number of customers for its store, even if all it did was maintain its market share in coming years. In Shrinksberg, on the other hand, the only way it could increase its customer base would be to take market share from other stores. Shrinksberg would be a more competitive business environment than Growville; for this reason alone, many corporations would favor Growville over Shrinksberg. Growville would likely be the recipient of more investment capital—and would therefore probably come to possess a more vibrant economy—than Shrinksberg.

If a *shrinking* population is bad for an economy, a *shrunk* population is even worse. Decrease the population of the world and you decrease the ability of its inhabitants to specialize in their vocations. Less specialization in turn means a less productive economy, and lower productivity means that people have to work harder to maintain a given standard of living—something people are generally reluctant to do.

To better understand the benefits of specialization, consider the pencil. It is not an exaggeration to say that a great many people—probably numbering in the millions—had a hand in making any given pencil. There were the people who obtained the wood for it, the people who manufactured the tools with which the trees were felled, the people who manufactured the tools with which *these* tools were manufactured, and so on. There were the people who transported this wood, the people who built the trucks that transported it, the people who mined the ore that became the steel in these trucks, the people who made the mining equipment with which the ore was mined, and so on. The drift this argument is taking is, I hope, clear. The reason pencils are cheap and plentiful is that our planet is populated with people who are vocational specialists. Someone who set out to manufacture a single pencil without taking advantage of the specialized labor of others might spend decades in the attempt. Thus the absolute number of people inhabiting the earth makes a very real difference to how well those inhabitants will live. The more people there are, the more easily they can specialize, and the better off, materially speaking, everyone can be.

And these aren't the only ways in which a population implosion can hurt the economy. As we saw above, during a population implosion the standard "population pyramid"—with lots of babies and relatively few senior citizens—will tend to transform into a "population column" or even an "inverted population pyramid." Thus, when a population starts to shrink, the average age of its inhabitants tends to rise. But with this higher average age comes, one supposes, a personality shift. Older people may be wiser than younger people, but they tend to be less innovative and less tolerant of risk. If one assumes that innovation and risk-taking drive economies—or, at any rate, contribute significantly to gains in productivity—then a shrinking population is likely to result in a stagnant economy.

Besides harming the economy, an inverted population pyramid

can damage the retirement prospects of a country's citizens. When a young American deposits money into "her" Social Security account, it doesn't stay there, but is immediately transferred to the account of an older, retired American, who thinks—quite mistakenly—that the money she is receiving is the money she deposited into Social Security decades before. This transfer scheme will work—in the same sense as a Ponzi scheme or a chain letter can be said to work—as long as there is an ever-increasing number of young people to make deposits. When a population starts shrinking, though, the jig is up. Before long, the money taken out exceeds the money going in, and ultimately, unless drastic measures are taken, there is no money left.

What about the Third World?

Some, on hearing the above concerns, will argue that for the American economy to slow down would not be such a bad thing. We Americans are, after all, affluent beyond the wildest imaginings of our great-grandparents. For us to be forced, by declining population, to cut back on our extravagant lifestyles would be a blessing, not a curse.

It is therefore worth noting that a decline in affluence isn't the only thing a country with a declining population has to worry about. It also risks loss of national sovereignty. Fighting wars successfully takes a lot of people, both to manufacture weapons and to use them. But a country with a declining population might lack sufficiently many people for its defense. A superpower with a declining population is arguably a superpower in decline.

As I mentioned in the previous chapter, although much of the developed world is experiencing a Birth Dearth, many Third World nations are experiencing a population explosion. At first these might seem like offsetting factors, with the net result being a relatively stable population for the planet as a whole. This, unfortunately, isn't the end of the story. For if the developed world is shrinking at the same time as the Third World is growing, then the "developed population" of the world must necessarily decline as a percentage of the total world population: fewer and fewer people will live lives of affluence, while ever more will live lives of poverty. Here are some numbers to put this process into perspective. In 1950 the "free, modern world" was 22 percent of the global population. By the late 1980s that number had fallen to 15 percent. By 2025 it is projected to be 9 percent, and down to 5 percent by the end of the century.

Does it matter if the population of the "free, modern world" shrinks relative to the population of the Third World? Indeed it does. To begin with, there is a danger that as the relative size of the free, modern world declines, so will its influence on the international stage; and this would be tragic since the developed world has been (many would argue) an extraordinarily good influence on less developed countries, revealing to them, for example, the advantages of democracy. Furthermore, as the population of the developed countries declines, so will their ability to help overpopulated Third World nations, meaning increased suffering for the citizens of these nations. Finally, consider again the issue of national sovereignty. Above I pointed to the danger of a country with a declining population being overrun by a larger country. If countries in the developed world continue to shrink while Third World countries continue to grow, it is conceivable that at some future date, the Third World will come to dominate the developed world militarily. Inasmuch as the governments of many Third World countries are neither enlightened nor benevolent, this is not a pretty picture to contemplate.

What to Do?

Whether or not we think the Birth Dearth is a serious problem at present, let us suppose, for the sake of argument, that it gets sufficiently bad in the future that people implore their government to "do something" about it. Would the government be justified in acting on these requests? And if it did act, what steps would it be justified in taking?

Before attempting to answer these questions, let us consider the range of steps the government can take in response to a population implosion. Least intrusively, it can engage in informational campaigns, urging its citizens to have many children and warning them of the dangers of a population decline. It can promote voluntary measures: it can give citizens who have babies cash payments or make tax breaks available to them. It can also implement involuntary pronatalist measures and fine or jail citizens who (in the absence of a medical explanation) fail to reproduce. In extreme cases it might even force men to act as sperm donors and force women to undergo artificial insemination. Can any of these steps be justified? And if so, what sort of argument can be used to justify them?

The arguments we develop with respect to population implosions will necessarily differ from those we developed (in the previous chapter) with respect to population explosions. In those arguments, the basic issue was when, if ever, it is permissible for the government to interfere with someone's right to reproduce. In the present discussion, this right is not at issue. Notice, in particular, that if we force men to act as sperm donors or force women to become pregnant, *we are not violating their right to reproduce.* Instead, we are violating, if anything, their right *not* to reproduce.[1]

Suppose we admit—as most people unhesitatingly will—that there is a right *not* to reproduce. From this alone it does not follow that the government is never justified in interfering with this right. There are times, after all, when one person's rights come into conflict with another person's, and when this happens, someone's rights must give way. We encountered this basic ethical fact in our discussions of eugenics and population control. We saw that when dysgenic parents reproduce and when parents in an overpopulated nation reproduce, the interests of others can be harmed—arguably harmed sufficiently that the government is justified in interfering with its citizens' right to reproduce. Let us undertake a similar investigation with respect to the right not to reproduce. Let us ask, in particular, whether an individual's failure to reproduce can harm the interests of others and harm them sufficiently that the government is justified in encouraging or even forcing this person to reproduce.

Whose interests are affected when a man and woman in an "underpopulated" country refuse to reproduce? Two obvious groups would be the couple's offspring and the couple's fellow citizens.

Consider first the (currently existing) children of the nonreproductive couple. Suppose a couple, call them the Greens, live in a country whose population is declining in a worrisome fashion.

Because it is shrinking, the country's economy is languishing and its national sovereignty is threatened by the malevolent dictator of the neighboring Third World country, who has a massive army at his command. Suppose that under these circumstances the Greens, who are biologically capable of having a dozen children, quit after having only one. It could be that the Greens, in having this one child, become obligated to have more. Their child, after all, would appear to have a legitimate complaint: no thoughtful person would ask to be born into such a situation. Having chosen to create him, his parents, if they wish to do right by him, should have additional children.

This makes it look as though parents in an underpopulated country, if they reproduce, create for themselves a vicious circle of obligation: each child they create obligates them to have another child, whose creation in turn obligates them to have yet another. This appearance is misleading, though, for presumably in the case in question there is a number that, if every couple had that many children, would be sufficient to alleviate the underpopulation problem. Once parents had that many children, they could rest.

Now consider a second couple, call them the Whites. Suppose the Whites are countrymen of the Greens, but unlike the Greens, have no children at all even though they are biologically capable of doing so. The argument we used to show that the Greens had an obligation to reproduce obviously won't work on the Whites: they have no offspring who can complain about their failure to reproduce. The Whites *do* have fellow citizens, though, and *they* might not be too happy about the Whites' decision not to reproduce. Suppose, after all, that lots of couples followed the Whites' example and chose not to reproduce. The result—a rapidly declining population—would presumably be undesirable to all, including the Whites.

In such cases it might be appropriate for the government to encourage reproduction. The most obvious step would be to offer incentives for reproduction. Such a course of action would not be coercive. Furthermore, since it is the citizens who will benefit from a couple's reproduction, it seems fair that these citizens be asked to fund (through taxation) cash grants for prolific couples.

What if cash grants are insufficient to spur a public interest in reproduction? Would the government then be justified in forcing couples to reproduce? Such an action on the part of government would be odious. For one thing, it would involve a high degree of coercion. For another, whereas a cash-grant program distributes the program's costs among taxpaying citizens, a program of forced reproduction will compel certain couples to bear the major part of the program's costs.

Be this as it may, it seems clear that in times of national emergency, governments are entitled to ask for great sacrifices on the part of citizens. In the case we are considering, the sovereignty of the country in which the Whites and Greens live is threatened by the malevolent dictator of a neighboring country. Were this dictator to attempt to invade their country, the government would ask citizens to fight—indeed, fight to the death—to block the invasion. But this sacrifice is far greater than the one the government would be asking if it forced its citizens to reproduce so as to forestall an invasion. Perhaps, then, there are times when a government is justified in taking aggressive steps to ensure that its citizens reproduce.[2]

Having said this, I would add that in most cases, governments simply don't know enough about population trends to be justified in dictating family sizes to their citizens. Although a country can accurately tell how many citizens it currently has, it is much harder for it to say how many citizens it will have in, say, ten years. The population trends of countries are changeable because the reproductive plans of their citizens are changeable. Yes, the women of the Czech Republic are currently having only 1.1 child, but that could change literally overnight. All it would take is for these women to move reproduction up a few notches in their list of priorities. Because population changes are so difficult to predict, governments should be very cautious about taking steps to "fix" what they regard as an errant population trend.

PART TWO

WHO SHOULD BE ALLOWED TO RAISE CHILDREN?

CHAPTER 6

CHILDREN WITHOUT PARENTS

We normally assume that children need parents and that the state should designate a particular man and woman (in most cases the man and woman who brought the child into existence) as a child's parents. Both these assumptions are open to challenge.

Advocates of Children's Liberation argue, contrary to the first assumption, that children don't need parents; indeed, they argue that adults wrong children when they undertake the role of parent. This role, after all, requires adults to interfere with the freedom of children. It is, they tell us, as wrong to parent a child as it is to parent an adult. Advocates of Children's Liberation call for a radical reform of the parent/child relationship.

And in response to the second assumption—that the state should designate a particular man and woman as the parents of a child—some argue that children are better off raised by the state than by a traditional parent-pair. In particular, when children are born, they should be taken from their biological parents and placed in state-run nurseries, staffed by squads of government-employed nannies. After that, children should have no contact with their biological parents. The parent/child relationship is severed—for the good, it is claimed, of the citizens of the state. Let us now examine the reasoning of those who wish to discard the traditional parent/child relationship.

Children's Liberation

American parents have an impressive array of legal rights with respect to their children, including the right to determine a child's standard of living and administer a child's property; to decide where and with whom a child lives; to determine where and how a child is educated; to decide what medical care a child receives (and whether their son is circumcised); to choose a child's name, religion, and nationality; to control with whom a child associates; and to veto a child's marriage plans or passport application. Parents also possess the right to arrange the details of a child's life, including what books he reads, what he eats, when he goes to bed, what television shows he watches—and indeed whether he watches television at all. Finally, parents have the right to discipline a child should he disagree with their ideas about how he should live his life. The punishments might include being spanked, being locked in his room, or being denied food. This list of rights makes it clear that in America today, parents have considerable power over their children.

Advocates of Children's Liberation argue that parents have too much power and that as a result their children have too little freedom. One of the most outspoken advocates of Children's Liberation is Richard Farson who, in his book *Birthrights*, argues that the government should extend the same rights to children as it extends to adults. The liberated child, according to Farson, will have the right to self-determination in decisions about eating, sleeping, washing, and dressing. The parents of such a child could no more force him to eat spinach, go to bed at eight, or wash his face than they could force their (grown-up) next-door neighbor to do these things. The parents of a liberated child would have no control over what games he plays and over what he listens to or reads. Liberated children would have the right to engage in the same activities as adults, including the right to smoke, drink, and have sexual relations.

Farson wants to abolish compulsory education: it is, according to Farson, as wrong to force a six-year-old to go to first grade as it would be to force a thirty-year-old to go to college. If Farson had his way, children would have the right to decide what life goals to pursue. If a child, at a tender age, decided to become a juggler or garbageman, his parents would have to respect his career choice, even if they thought his talents would be wasted in these occupations.

Children would have the same economic rights as adults. In particular, they would have the right to enter into binding contracts and the right to a certain share of the family wealth.

The parents of an unruly liberated child could not punish him. Indeed, if the child didn't like the way his parents treated him, he would have the right to leave home. His parents would find themselves childless.

Farson would extend the right to vote to children. If we were to point out, by way of criticism, that children are not competent to vote inasmuch as they don't understand the issues, Farson would reply that the state, when it allows *adults* to vote, does not require them to be competent. If competence is not required in adult voters, why require it in children?

It may sound like Farson is willing to let children do *anything*, but this is not the case. He wants, for example, to place limits on children driving cars: adults can drive a car only if they can pass the driving test; the same should be true of children. Driving tests, according to Farson, are not objectionable because they treat adults and children alike, which is the whole point of Children's Liberation.

Farson is not alone in advocating expanded rights for children. Others who seem sympathetic to the goals of Children's Liberation include Jean Jacques Rousseau, John Dewey, Paul Goodman, Carl Rogers, A. S. Neill, and Wilhelm Reich.

Some might dismiss the Children's Liberation movement as nothing more than an excuse for parental laziness. Notice, after all, that it costs parents considerably to curb their children's freedom. Children spend vast amounts of time and energy, first in determining what the limits of their parents' tolerance are and then in attempting to push back these limits. Parents are thus faced with a choice: either draw lines (by restricting their children's freedom) or draw no lines at all. The former course of action will require parents, who typically have far less time and energy than their children, to spend what little they have justifying and enforcing the lines they have drawn.

If you tell your child that he cannot go out to play until his homework is finished, you might have to endure his tantrum. If you send your child to his room for an hour, you will have to monitor his behavior for that hour and make sure he stays put. If you tell your teenager to be home by midnight, you will have to stay up until midnight to make sure the edict is obeyed. Letting your child do whatever he wants would avoid this ongoing expenditure of energy and thus represents, for parents, the easy way out.

Before dismissing Children's Liberation, though, we should realize that it is based on a principle that most would unhesitatingly accept: that all men are created equal—that the state should extend the same rights to all persons. Children are persons. It therefore follows that the state should extend the same rights to children as it extends to adults.

The American government, to be sure, has not always extended the same rights to all persons. For much of our history, blacks and women were not granted the same rights as white males. If we asked a white male to justify this exclusion, he might have argued that blacks and women aren't "men" and therefore the principle that all men are created equal simply does not apply to them. Or more interestingly, he might have argued that blacks and women have "diminished capacity" and therefore would be harmed rather than benefited by being granted the full range of rights. If the state wanted to look out for their interests, the argument went, it had to treat them paternalistically—treat them, that is, like children.

In the case of both blacks and women, it took liberation movements to overcome the views that blacks and women weren't "men" or that they suffered from diminished capacity. Children's Liberation is an attempt to overcome the parallel view that most people now have about children: in the same way as we shouldn't treat blacks and women like children, we shouldn't treat children like children.

Double Standards

This line of argument is seductive, but we should think twice before allowing ourselves to be seduced. In what follows, I will suggest two different sorts of reply that can be given to the advocates of Children's Liberation. The first is theoretical and the second is practical.

The above argument for Children's Liberation, stated simply, is that we are guilty of a double standard in our treatment of people: we extend a full complement of rights to adults but a severely restricted set of rights to children. No one would deny that we have a *different* standard of treatment for children. Whether this difference constitutes a *double* standard depends on whether we are able to come up with reasonable grounds for the difference in treatment. If such grounds are forthcoming, the *different* standard is not a *double* standard.

Are we justified in treating children differently than we treat adults? Consider a newborn baby. It differs from a typical adult in a number of respects. It cannot reason. It cannot take care of itself. Left to its own devices, it would be dead within a week. A newborn baby is unquestionably a case of diminished capacity. Furthermore, its diminished capacity is due not to the way society has treated it—as might at one time have been true of blacks or women—but to nature itself.

Infants are also victims of diminished capacity. Their reasoning ability is still impaired and they lack an understanding of the way the world works. For this reason they have a hard time connecting acts with ultimate consequences, a potentially fatal shortcoming in this dangerous world.

By the time they are teenagers, children have better reasoning ability and a greater experience of the world than they did as infants. Unfortunately, this reasoning ability is often, thanks to hormones, overcome by their emotions. Although they know much about the world, they have not been around long enough to appreciate the fact that they will—with luck—still be inhabiting their current bodies sixty years hence and that activities that give them a few moments of pleasure today can subsequently yield decades of pain. They also fail to appreciate their own mortality.

A newborn baby resembles someone in a coma; older children resemble, in a number of respects, someone mentally ill. If we think paternalistic treatment is appropriate for comatose or mentally ill people, then it is appropriate for children, too. Thus, in treating children paternalistically, we are not guilty of a double standard.

While we are on the subject of double standards, it is worth noting that liberationist Farson himself seems to be guilty of one. He allows, as we have seen, children to walk out on parents who don't please them. But if the claim is that adults and children should have equal rights, then does it not follow that parents should also have the right to walk out on children who don't please them? If parents do indeed have this right, they would have a powerful bargaining chip in dealing with their liberated children: "Yes, my darling daughter, you have the right to get drunk, but if you exercise this right, I'll exercise my right to throw you out of the house." Life for the liberated child would not be the playground that Farson apparently envisions.

Along with this theoretical reply to Children's Liberation, many parents will offer some practical observations. Children raised with too much freedom tend to lack self-discipline and respect for the rights of others. Give a child enough freedom and he might end up ignorant (since he might choose not to go to school) or even dead (since he might choose to abuse drugs). Thus, many parents would agree, Children's Liberation would appear to provide us with a blueprint for the production of spoiled or even ruined children.

Advocates of Children's Liberation are not likely to be swept away by this appeal to parental views on the importance of child discipline. Parents, after all, are hardly impartial commentators on the relationship between themselves and their children: asking parents how freedom would affect children is like asking a slave owner how freedom would affect slaves. The slave owner would probably argue that freedom would be a bad thing for slaves. Freed slaves would tend—we can imagine the owner arguing—to use their freedom to drink themselves to death. In the same way as we should be skeptical of the comments made by a slave owner, we should be skeptical of similar comments made by parents.

How are children affected by freedom? We know how children turn out when raised with conventional limitations placed on their freedom. It is instructive to contrast these children with those who have experienced considerably greater freedom. Along these lines, let us consider the plight of so-called feral children who were raised by animals or by no one at all and thus were not subject to adult-imposed limitations on their freedom. Then let us consider the plight of children who, because their parents fell under the spell of unorthodox theories of child psychology, were raised with what by any standards would count as extensive childhood freedom.

Feral Children

From time to time children are lost in the wilderness. Sometimes these children are neither found nor perish but instead survive a parentless childhood. They live a life of perfect freedom, with no one around to tell them what to do.

One of the most famous of these feral children was Victor of Aveyron. He lived in France and was first seen in 1798, running naked in the woods. He was captured but escaped. Fifteen months later he was captured again but after eight days escaped again. Finally, he was recaptured and slowly came to trust people. At the time of his capture, he was perhaps eleven or twelve years old and was quite short. He had apparently been without human companionship since age four.

Victor was found with a shirt draped around him but refused to wear clothes when they were offered. He preferred nakedness—even in winter—and was utterly lacking in shame. His hearing was excellent but curiously selective: he could easily hear the sound of a chestnut cracking but did not react to a gun fired near his ear. He appeared to be immune to physical discomfort and could withstand great cold. His activities consisted of sleeping, eating, doing nothing, and running about. He would spend hours staring at the moon, his body motionless. He appeared to be without emotion, except when he thought a display of emotion could get him food. He was described as being "essentially selfish."

It was Victor's fortune to come to the attention of Dr. Jean-Marc-Gaspard Itard. When he first met Victor, Dr. Itard described him as "a disgustingly dirty child affected with spasmodic movements, and often convulsions, who swayed back and forth ceaselessly like certain animals in a zoo, who bit and scratched those who opposed him, and who showed no affection for those who took care of him." Dr. Itard treated Victor with great kindness. He tried to teach Victor both written and spoken language. (It was thought that if Victor could learn language, he could account for his early years and thus solve the mystery of his existence.) In the end, though, there was not much Dr. Itard could do to bring back the humanity that Victor's existence had cost him.

In the twentieth century the most famous feral children were probably the wolf-children of Midnapore, India. In 1920, Reverend J. A. L. Singh, a missionary, found two girls living with wolves. Several other people were present when the wolves were dislodged from their cave, and the children were found inside the cave with two wolf cubs. The children were taken to an orphanage, where Reverend Singh tried to keep their existence a secret.

One girl was thought to be eight years old and the other a year and a half. They had sores all over their bodies, so much so that they looked like lepers. They could not stand erect, but got around by crawling and spent much of their time crouching quietly in a corner of their room. Their eyes had a "peculiar blue glare," and they had excellent night vision. They ate as dogs do, by lapping their food. Their perception of heat and cold was essentially absent, as was the case with Victor of Aveyron. They were incapable of making sound except for cries and howling.

The younger wolf-child died within a year of her discovery. Reverend Singh continued to work with the older wolf-child and made some progress. Three years after her discovery, the girl could stand; she later learned to walk. Five years after her discovery, her vocabulary consisted of thirty "words," which were in fact approximations of actual words. She died nine years after being rescued.

Some have studied feral children in an attempt to gain insight concerning the nature vs. nurture debate. Feral children, after all, grow up in a "culture-free" environment, so their behavior is presumably a good approximation of "natural" behavior—or at any rate is more natural than that of regular children. For our purposes, though, feral children are of interest because they provide us with an illustration of what becomes of children who are given perfect freedom. There were no oppressive parents around to tell Victor of Aveyron what to do—no one to tell him to bathe, eat his spinach, or learn to read. How did Victor use this freedom? To grub for food in the woods. To the extent that the existence of feral children demonstrates anything, it demonstrates that too much childhood freedom can be a very bad thing.

It is, by the way, a mistake to think that in America feral children are a thing of the past. Modern feral children spend their lives not in caves or in the woods, but running free in urban and suburban environments in which parents are either absent or grotesquely dysfunctional. We see pictures of these children being rescued from homes in which the adults are more interested in obtaining and abusing drugs than in raising their children. What modern feral children have in common with Victor of Aveyron and the wolf-children of Midnapore is that they have to raise themselves. No one teaches them manners, how to shake hands, wash their clothes, brush their teeth, keep themselves clean, or control their emotions. Because their parents are unwilling or unable to shape the lives of these children, they enjoy considerably more freedom than "raised" children do. They often use this freedom to take drugs and hang out on the streets; and because they lack self-control, they often end up in jail.

There are several ways advocates of Children's Liberation might respond to stories about feral children.

In the first place, they might argue that such stories are not to be trusted. Some are utterly fictitious, and most probably contain significant factual errors. Thus, even though the story of the wolf-children of Midnapore is relatively well documented, it gives rise to some important questions. For instance, Reverend Singh describes the eyes of the wolf-children as glowing blue at night. Living with wolves can certainly affect a child's personality, but it cannot, one would suppose, affect the anatomy or physiology of her eyes. One might wonder whether human eyes are capable of glowing blue, and if they are not, suspect that Reverend Singh was guilty of making the children more wolflike than they in fact were. But if Reverend Singh was guilty of embellishing the children's story in this respect, perhaps he has embellished the story in other respects as well.[1]

The wolf-children's ages when they were discovered is also problematic. The girls were thought to be eight and one-and-a-half years old, respectively, an age difference that is, in the current context, extremely curious. If the girls were sisters who had gotten lost together, the age difference means they could not have been with the wolves for more than one and a half years, and the older girl would have been six and a half when the wolves adopted them. Wouldn't a six-and-a-half-year-old girl have known better than to let wolves adopt her? Would a year and a half have been sufficient time to make the older child go wild? In particular, could a six-and-a-half-year-old child unlearn walking in a year and a half?

There are ways around this difficulty. Perhaps the girls were sisters who were abandoned years apart by their parents and adopted by wolves; or perhaps the girls weren't sisters at all, but were unrelated girls who just happened to be adopted at different times by child-loving wolves. This is probably the best explanation for the age difference, but even it isn't particularly plausible.

An advocate of Children's Liberation could accept the authenticity of feral-child stories but reject the conclusions we drew from them. We suggested above that it was the excessive freedom of their feral childhoods that ruined the abandoned children. It might be, however, that the children had been "ruined" *before* their feral childhoods—indeed, that their parents had abandoned them because they were "ruined." The wolf-children of Midnapore, for example, might have been abandoned by their parents *because* they were mentally retarded. If this were the case, it would be a mistake for us to blame their lack of speech and social skills on their period of feral freedom.

It might also be suggested that it is wrong to think that a feral existence invariably ruins a child. In reply to this criticism, I must confess that it is possible to "undo" a feral childhood: the "cure" is to put the child under the control of loving adults—that is, to take away its feral freedom.

Finally, an advocate of Children's Liberation might argue that even if we could produce a believable case in which a "normal" child went wild as a result of a parentless existence, it is unclear what consequences such a case has for Children's Liberation. In particular, an advocate of Children's Liberation might remind us that liberated children will not be feral children: they will not be left to nature or left to the wolves, but will have parents to care for them. Thus, the argument goes, the wildness of feral children is irrelevant as a criticism of Children's Liberation.

This last line of reply might work for moderate advocates of Children's Liberation, but not for radicals like Farson. Under Farson's principles children will have a breathtaking amount of freedom. Their parents can't force them to bathe, eat their spinach, or come inside when night falls. It would therefore be inconsistent for someone like Farson to tell us that under his scheme, children would be utterly free but well cared for. To "care for" a child necessarily means depriving him of a considerable amount of freedom.

Experiments in Freedom

Let us turn our attention from feral children to cases in which children, although raised by people, were given extensive freedom. In the cases in question, parents took an experimental approach to child rearing and "freed" their children in the conviction that doing so would benefit their children.

In his *Emile*, published in 1762, Jean Jacques Rousseau argues for liberated childhoods, although less liberated than Farson would recommend. According to Rousseau, parents should let experience teach their children: "Give your scholar no verbal lessons; he should be taught by experience alone." Rousseau's goal is to produce a child who is free of the pernicious influences of society—who will, as an adult, become a Natural Man. The book was one of the first "bestseller" books on parenting.

While most of the parents who read *Emile* accepted some of Rousseau's advice and rejected the rest, there were parents who attempted to raise their children in complete conformity with his theories. According to social historian Christina Hardyment, these experiments in freedom were less than successful: "Richard Lovell Edgeworth's boy became so unmanageable that he was sent away to boarding school. David Williams described one little child of nature who, aged thirteen, slept on the floor, spoke 'a jargon he had formed out of the several dialects of the family', could neither read nor write, and was 'a little emaciated figure, his countenance betraying marks of premature decay, or depraved passions; his teeth discoloured, his hearing almost gone.'" Rousseau, by the way, was not interested in testing his child-rearing theories to see whether they would indeed produce the Natural Man he claimed they would. Indeed, Rousseau secretly ridiculed those parents who took his child-rearing advice to heart. He appears to have intended his *Emile* more as a literary work than a handbook on how to raise children.

In another experiment, children were raised in extreme freedom because their parents were in the grip of Freud's views on child psychology. The theory was that if children weren't forced to repress various instinctual urges, they would grow up free from the neuroses that plague most adults. In the experiment in question, parents did not curb their children's thumb sucking, exhibitionism, or masturbation, and did not stop their children from expressing jealousy, hate, or discontent. Indeed, parents tried, to the extent possible, to avoid prohibiting *any* of their children's behavior.

Unfortunately, the children in this experiment did not outgrow their infantile behavior the way theory said they would. By the time researchers were done with them, they showed little interest in the world around them. They were egoists who had trouble working in groups. They were not toilet trained, lacked table manners, and failed to see the point of personal hygiene. They were irritable, emotionally volatile, and displayed a tendency to obsessive behavior and depression.

An advocate of Children's Liberation might respond to the above-described experiments by denying that they were the failures I make them out to be. In saying that the children turned out badly, I am obviously relying on my culture's value system, according to which children who are clean, polite, and well educated count as better people than illiterate children with missing teeth or children who fail to outgrow infantile behavior. But is this value system correct? Alternatively, a liberationist might admit that the children described above did not turn out well, but point out that this hardly proves that liberated children *always* fare poorly. The sample of children described is minuscule, and it is dangerous to generalize from a small sample.

A more promising way for advocates of Children's Liberation to respond to the above experiments is to produce examples of children raised in freedom who nevertheless turned out well. Indeed there *have* been instances in which children were given considerable freedom without disastrous consequences. Consider the children of A. S. Neill's experimental Summerhill School. We might argue about whether these children turned out better or worse than children raised at conventional schools, but clearly they turned out better than the children described above. Then again, the children at Summerhill School, although they had more freedom than conventional children, had less freedom than the ones Farson has in mind. What radical Children's Liberationists need are cases in which children were raised in extreme freedom but turned out fine—or at least moderately well. I wish them luck in finding such cases.

Some people are drawn to Children's Liberation because they value freedom: children are people, and people should be free. Although it sounds paradoxical to say so, most parents who restrict their children's freedom do so because they, like advocates of Children's Liberation, value freedom—because they want their child to be free. Where they differ from advocates of Children's Liberation is in their views on how childhood freedom affects adult freedom. According to the antiliberationist, experiencing excessive freedom as a child will drastically diminish the amount of freedom a person will experience as an adult. Thus, if the goal of parents is for their offspring to experience not just the maximum possible freedom *as a child*, but the maximum possible freedom *over the course of a lifetime*, they must restrict the childhood freedom of their offspring. They will be willing to restrict their child's current freedom in order to "buy" him a more-than-compensating amount of future freedom.

In defense of the claim that less freedom now means more freedom later and more total lifetime freedom, notice that a child who is allowed to behave foolishly now and thereby kill himself will not be able to enjoy his freedom in the future: he will have no future. Likewise, a child who is allowed to skip school may not find himself feeling particularly free when, later in life, time comes to choose a career. Furthermore, a child who does not learn some degree of self-discipline will not, at a later date, be able to choose the life he leads. Instead he will find himself and his fate bandied about by external forces. He will not end up doing the things that he chooses to do, simply because choice-making requires a degree of self-discipline that he lacks.

Children's Liberation: Some Afterthoughts

Even though the arguments of the Children's Liberationists are flawed, they deserve our attention. Notice, to begin with, that liberationists are right in thinking that the considerable power parents have over their children can be abused. Besides restricting a child's present freedom in order to enhance his future freedom, parents might have other motivations—either conscious or unconscious—for restricting their child's freedom. They might, for example, restrict it to keep him in a state of prolonged dependence. It is nice to be needed, and one of the joys of being a parent is the realization that someone truly needs you. Indeed, the dilemma faced by every parent is this: if you teach your child how to stand on his own two feet, he someday probably will, and you will become obsolete. There is, in other words, a temptation for parents to keep their children in a state of "diminished capacity," for then they will always be needed as parents.

Alternately, parents might restrict their child's freedom in a vicarious attempt to live out their own fantasies. Thus, the sports-oriented father might force his child to join Little League rather than take ballet lessons, or the classical musician mother might force her child to play the cello rather than the electric guitar. Parents are in constant danger of being corrupted by the power they wield, and good parents will be ever cognizant of this fact.

The arguments offered by advocates of Children's Liberation can also inspire us to reconsider the nature of adulthood. The thinking that leads us to act paternalistically toward children—namely, that by restricting their freedom today, we can maximize their total lifetime freedom—can also be applied to certain adults. We choose not to apply it to adults, however; instead, we draw a line at, say, age eighteen and make the following declaration: "If you are under this age and behave childishly, we will treat you paternalistically to protect you from your behavior, but if you are over this age and behave childishly, we will allow you to self-destruct." Can such a division by age be justified?

Thus, consider two individuals: a sixteen-year-old who gives ample evidence of being physically, mentally, and emotionally mature, and a thirty-year-old who, despite his age, still lacks the basic ability to think through the consequences of his actions. As things now stand, we will behave paternalistically toward the sixteen-year-old even though he probably doesn't need and won't benefit from our paternalism, and we will refuse to act paternalistically toward the thirty-year-old, even though he would benefit greatly from our paternalism. If our goal in acting paternalistically is to protect childish people from their behavior, then our treatment of the above-described sixteen- and thirty-year-olds seems inconsistent.

Why did Americans, until the 1970s, think that children became adults at age twenty-one? This age was chosen not because of a biological transformation that occurs on one's twenty-first birthday and brings with it instant wisdom and emotional maturity. Nor was it chosen because researchers, after years of study, determined that the average twenty-one-year-old had advanced sufficiently far physically, mentally, and emotionally that he no longer needed our protection. Rather, twenty-one was chosen because it is the age our ancestors chose. It was good enough for them, so it was good enough for us.

Why did our ancestors choose twenty-one as the age of adulthood? One theory is that twenty-one used to be the age of eligibility for knighthood. A second is that in England, children of the aristocracy could inherit property at nineteen, but the transfer of property took two years, thus making twenty-one the age at which a young aristocrat came into his own. We can, of course, ask why people were required to wait until they were twenty-one before they became knights, or why people were required to wait until they were nineteen before they could inherit property, but the answers to these questions are lost in the mists of time.

Even if our ancestors had good reasons for choosing twenty-one, it is not at all clear that these reasons, if applied to today's Americans, would yield twenty-one as the age of adulthood. For one thing, life spans used to be far shorter than they are at present. By making someone wait until he was twenty-one before becoming an adult, our ancestors were in many cases making him spend half his life as a "child." Perhaps our ancestors felt that an even later entry into adulthood would have been appropriate, but chose twenty-one because they wanted a significant number of people to reach adulthood before dying. (You need some adults around to run the show.) If this were the case, then today's Americans, relying on the reasoning of our ancestors, might want to make a human half-life—at present, about forty years—the age of adulthood.

On the other hand, someone might argue that our ancestors picked twenty-one years because that is how long it took people to achieve a working knowledge of the world. Thanks to mandatory schooling, though, people now achieve that knowledge at an earlier age than in days gone by: the average sixteen-year-old of today—if he has taken his education seriously—knows far more about the world than the average thirty-year-old medieval Englishman did. Thus, today's Americans, relying on the reasoning of our ancestors, might want to set an age of adulthood considerably lower than twenty-one. (Conversely, someone might argue that children, although more knowledgeable at age twenty-one than their ancestors were, are less mature—that the modern tendency to shelter children retards their maturation.)

The preceding discussions, of course, are highly speculative. As I've said, we don't really know why our ancestors picked twenty-one as the age of adulthood. My point in the above comments is to show that their reasoning—whatever it was—might, if applied today, lead us to pick some other age as the threshold of adulthood. Furthermore, in the same way as we have learned to ignore our medieval ancestors' reasoning about, say, medicine, we might do well to ignore their reasoning about how to set the age of adulthood. We have a much better understanding of human development than they did, as well as a better understanding of the benefits and dangers of paternalistic behavior.

We are therefore probably in a much better position than they were to make an informed judgment on what qualifies a person for adulthood. It is, in short, high time we reconsidered the age of adulthood.

It is misleading to talk about *the* age of adulthood, since there is no one age at which adulthood happens; to the contrary, the "rights of adulthood" are phased in. People in America generally gain the right to drive a car—if they pass the test—at age sixteen, the right to vote and sign contracts at age eighteen, and the right to drink at age twenty-one.

There seems to be precious little logic in our choice of these particular age limits. We allow someone to drive a car two years before allowing him to sign contracts. What can go wrong when we allow an immature person to drive? He can maim or kill himself, his passengers, and innocent bystanders. What can go wrong when we allow an immature person to sign a contract? He can be forced into bankruptcy—an unpleasant experience, to be sure, but not nearly so unpleasant as a car crash. One suspects that we allow people to drive at a relatively early age not because we feel that they are ready for the responsibility involved in driving a car, but because we, the adults of the world, are tired of acting as their chauffeurs.

Let us now consider a radical proposal: instead of setting arbitrary ages at which people gain the various rights connected with adulthood, why not dispense with age limits altogether and "test for adulthood"? Those who pass the appropriate test will be granted the right in question, regardless of their age.

What would be involved in testing for adulthood? To answer this question, let us focus our attention on one particular right of adulthood—the right to vote. It used to be that in some places, Americans had to pass a literacy test before being allowed to vote. These tests were abandoned when it became clear that they were being used not to weed out illiterate voters, but to discriminate against blacks. There is, however, much to be said for restricting the right to vote to those who are not only literate, but also reasonably well informed about their political environment and the tradeoffs involved in certain political decisions.

Suppose we were able to develop a test that effectively measured a person's competence as a voter. The test in question might test his knowledge of the positions of the candidates and of the economic and political consequences of these positions. One use of such a test would be to weed out the electorally incompetent. We might, for example, say that citizens could vote only if they had reached a certain age *and* passed the voter's test. This would mean that some people—those too lazy to take the test or too ignorant to pass it—would *never* be allowed to vote. A second, presumably less controversial use of the test would be to allow electorally precocious children to vote at an earlier age than is now the case. Under this plan, you could vote at age eighteen or when you passed the voter's test, *whichever came first.* A sixteen-year-old who passed our test would arguably have a better grasp of the political landscape than many sixty-year-olds do. Why not let him vote?

Some will respond to this question by arguing that no matter how politically well informed a sixteen-year-old is, he would necessarily lack the maturity and the life experience that would allow him effectively to judge the personalities of candidates. He would therefore be unfit to vote. In reply to this suggestion, we might point out that while it is doubtless important for voters to be mature and to possess extensive life experience, it is also important for them to be politically well informed. Indeed, some would even argue that a callow but well-informed person would be a fitter voter than a mature individual who has no idea at all what the issues are in an election. If we are willing to let this latter individual vote, why not the former?

Alternatively, someone could argue that it would not be cost-effective to construct and administer tests of voting competence that would enable children under eighteen to vote. It is clear that sixteen-year-olds want to be able to drive cars: indeed, they are willing to take driving lessons and practice for months to pass a driving test. How many teenagers, though, would be similarly motivated to study for a voter's test so they could vote before age eighteen? Not many, one assumes, in which case we will be wasting our time and money if we attempt to create voter's tests.

In the final analysis, when we set age limits for the various rights connected with adulthood, we do so with political considerations in mind. We are not so much concerned with the question of whether sixteen-year-olds are more or less competent to vote than sixty-year-olds, but with the political ramifications of extending the vote to them. If sixteen-year-olds were clamoring for the right to vote—the way eighteen-year-olds were in the late 1960s—they might gain this right; their current silence on the topic, however, insures that they will not.

The State as Parent

Suppose, contrary to the advocates of Children's Liberation, we think children should be raised. We are then faced with a new question: who, exactly, should raise them? The obvious answer is that children's biological or adoptive parents should raise them, but this is not the only answer possible. In particular, some will argue that *the state* should raise whatever children its citizens bring into existence.

I first came across the idea of the state acting as parent when, as a college freshman, I read Plato's *Republic*. I remember feeling shocked that anyone would make such a suggestion—that anyone would break up the traditional family or seriously argue that the government should have a significant role in raising children. In the decades since then, we have come a long way in America. Many of my fellow citizens are petitioning the government to take their children—during the day, at least. They are, more precisely, petitioning the government to get into the day-care business. They argue that privately-provided day care is unsatisfactory and that the government would do a better job at a lower cost. But if the government is competent to act as parent for eight hours a day, why not for ten, twelve…or even twenty-four hours a day?

Let us, then, take a moment and consider the view that children should be raised by the government. Let us first consider Plato's plan for state-as-parent.

As we saw in our discussion of eugenics, Plato did not cherish people's right to choose a mate and start a family. He argued, for instance, that the government should implement programs to promote aristogenic couplings and deter dysgenic couplings, and it should keep the citizenry in the dark about these eugenic activities—thus, his plan for a fixed "lottery" to determine who should marry whom. He also advocated the abolition of marriage, in the common sense of the word. Men and women would stay together long enough for the woman to get pregnant. The next marriage lottery might or might not match them up again.

You could do all this and still allow biological parents to raise the children they had created. Plato rejects this idea, though. In his plan, when state-sanctioned unions yield offspring, "officials appointed for the purpose...will take them." The genetically fit children of genetically fit parents are turned over to nurses living apart; unfit children are taken to a "secret and unknown place," where they are set out to die. By taking children at birth, the city breaks the parent/child bond: "The nurses will...see to it that the mothers are brought to the rearing pen when their breasts have milk, but take every precaution that no mother shall know her own child...."

Plato wants to break the parent/child bond because he wants to eliminate our tendency to favor our relatives. Family ties, he argues, get in the way of the ties that should bind citizens to their state. Plato's ideal city would be populated by people who, for all they knew, were the father or mother, brother or sister, or son or daughter of the other citizens they encountered. As a consequence the city would—in theory, at any rate—be one big happy family. Thus, Plato tells us that allowing the state to act as parent would be "the cause of the greatest good" for his ideal city.[2]

Plato's views on family structure appear to be based on—but were more extreme than—the policies of nearby Sparta. The Spartans pressured men to marry (a pronatalist measure), but did not allow them to live with their wives until after the birth of a child; instead, the husband spent the night at his barracks. Even after a child was born, the father was expected to have his evening meal not at home, but in a common dining hall. Some eugenic measures were taken, including encouraging old men to allow vigorous young men to impregnate their wives and mandatory infanticide of children born unfit. Healthy children were not snatched from their mothers at birth, as Plato wanted to do, but were allowed to stay with their mothers until age seven, at which time their training (for soldiering) began.

Would abolishing the traditional family in favor of state-parenthood increase the harmony in his ideal city, as Plato thought? Arguably not. Plato worried, as we have seen, that (inferior) men would dissent if assigned inferior wives by rulers. (It was to avoid this dissent that the assignment of wives was disguised as a lottery.) It does not seem to occur to Plato that people would likewise dissent if romantic attachments were forbidden—if, after mating, one had to return one's mate to the "common pool"—or if officials came to take a couple's newborn baby. One suspects, though, that most parents would not happily hand over their child; instead, they would take extreme measures to avoid this coerced parting.

Plato's plan to make the city one big happy family by keeping people in the dark about the identity of their relatives could also backfire. Instead of treating everyone in the city as (possibly) a relative, the citizens of Plato's ideal city might treat everyone as a nonrelative—indeed, as a complete stranger. Instead of thinking of themselves as the parent, sibling, or offspring of the other citizens they encounter, they might think of themselves as state-created orphans, without parents, siblings, or offspring. If this happened, Plato's plan, rather than promoting harmony in the city, might promote uncaring selfishness in its citizens. Why should they make sacrifices for strangers?

Most people will reject out of hand the idea of the state acting as parent. For one thing, the state is incapable of giving children the love and attention they need. For another, state-parenthood gives a government enormous power over the lives and destinies of its citizens. No one can be trusted with this much power.

Interestingly, governments also reject the idea of state-parenthood. Even totalitarian governments—which one might think would want to take control of their citizens' lives at the earliest possible moment and begin the indoctrination process—rarely want to play the role of nanny. It isn't that totalitarian governments care about the emotional needs of children or are reluctant to gain additional power over the citizenry. What stops them is the realization that it simply isn't cost-effective for the state to act as parent. State-run nurseries and boarding schools would be expensive. Why pay to raise children when the citizens will do it for free? Furthermore, totalitarian governments realize that by letting parents raise their children but forcing the children to attend state-run schools, they can indoctrinate the children *and simultaneously use them to monitor the lives of the children's parents.* In many totalitarian countries, children act as unpaid spies. They can be induced to report what goes on in the privacy of the citizens' own homes. From the point of view of a totalitarian dictator, what could be better?

It seems unlikely, therefore, that governments—even totalitarian governments—are going to assume the role of parent. Let us, therefore, bring our discussion of state-as-parent to an end and instead assume that governments will allow citizens to act as parents. The question we must now address is, *Which* citizens should the government let play the role of parent?

CHAPTER 7

LICENSING PARENTS

In America today we license any number of professions and activities. We license doctors, dentists, nurses, pharmacists, plumbers, electricians, teachers, and lawyers; we license drivers and pilots; we even license barbers. We do not, however, license parents, and this seems inconsistent. If the harm done by incompetent barbers is sufficient that we license the profession, shouldn't we also license parents? Doesn't bad parenting cause far more harm in our society than bad barbering?

Before launching into the argument for licensing parents, let me clarify what is involved in licensing a profession or activity.

It is important, to begin with, to distinguish between *licensing* and *certification*. To obtain a license or certification, people must demonstrate competence in a certain field, usually by taking classes or passing exams. Where the procedures differ is in what happens to people who don't take the classes or don't pass the exams. In the case of licensing, such people are prohibited from engaging in the activity in question. If they ignore this prohibition—if, for example, they get caught practicing medicine or driving a car without a license—they will be fined or jailed. In the case of certification, the person who doesn't take the classes or pass the exams can still engage in the activity in question. Consider, by way of example, state-certified tree experts. The state will not penalize someone for doing tree surgery without having been certified. Then why bother with certification? Because some people will go out of their way to hire tree surgeons that the state, through its certification program, has declared competent.

It is also important to distinguish between *licensing* and *registration*. If the state requires those engaged in a certain activity to register with the government, and if an individual engages in the activity without registering, the state—as is the case in licensing—can fine or jail him. The difference between registration and licensing is that to be licensed, a person must take classes and/or pass exams, whereas registration has no such requirement. To register, one simply signs one's name in a book or fills out a form. Thus, the state does not make you take classes or pass exams before you buy certain poisons, but it does require that you "register" as a user of a poison.

The terms I have just defined are often used interchangeably and therefore confusingly. A fishing "license," for example, is really what I would call a fishing registration: you don't need to pass a test or demonstrate your competence to get a fishing license, but the state will punish you if you fish without one. Similarly, teaching "certificates" are really teaching licenses: if you lack a teaching certificate, the state typically will not let you teach in public grade schools. And "registered" pharmacists are really licensed pharmacists.

Rationales for Licensing

Why do we license professions and activities? Three rationales are commonly offered. To better understand these rationales, let us focus our attention on the sorts of arguments that might be given in favor of licensing airplane pilots.

A first rationale for licensing pilots is *economic:* by restricting entry into a profession, we increase the wages of those who practice the profession. If anyone at all is allowed to fly a plane (or fill cavities or repair plumbing), the supply of pilots (or dentists or plumbers) will swell, and the wages of these people will presumably plummet.

I happen to be a practitioner of an unlicensed profession: you may need a "license" to teach in a public grade school, but you don't need one to teach at a state university. I would benefit financially if the government started licensing those wishing to enter my profession—if it made people pass difficult tests and meet stringent requirements before they could teach at a state university but allowed people like me who were already teaching to be "grandfathered" in (that is, be licensed without having to meet the requirements or pass the tests). Licensing shrinks the supply of practitioners of a profession and thereby boosts the income of those in the profession.

A second rationale for licensing pilots is *paternalistic.* The assumption here is that a significant number of people are incapable or only marginally capable of looking out for their best interests. If flying were an unlicensed activity, people would (foolishly) try to pilot airplanes without proper training and would periodically crash, thereby injuring or killing themselves. And when these pilots crashed, they would take their passengers down with them.

These first two rationales for licensing airplane pilots are questionable. To begin with, it is far from clear that the government should take steps to inflate the earnings of those in certain professions. Why help pilots—or dentists or plumbers—earn more money? And if you help *them,* why not help every other profession? (In particular, why not help college professors like myself earn more?) Why not simply let every profession's earnings depend solely on how much people are willing to pay its practitioners, which in turn presumably depends upon how much the public values the service they provide? Furthermore, anyone opposed to governmental paternalism will be opposed to many forms of licensing. Being free in part means being free to behave foolishly. We cannot undertake paternalistic measures to prevent individuals from harming themselves without reducing their freedom. Opponents of governmental paternalism will also point out that such paternalism has an undesirable side effect: when the government gets into the business of looking out for the interests of its citizens, those same citizens lose some of the incentive to look out for their own interests and consequently become more likely to do foolish things.

This brings us to the third and most compelling rationale for licensing. Consider again the risks posed by an airplane pilot. His incompetence, as we have seen, poses risks to himself and to his passengers. These risks, however, are voluntarily assumed: the pilot could have gotten better training but chose not to, and his passengers could have ascertained the qualifications of the pilot before boarding but chose not to. The risks posed by the pilot, however, do not end there, for his flying also puts at risk those who live below his intended flight path; and these people, unlike himself or his passengers, have not voluntarily undertaken the risks to which they are exposed. The people on the ground are therefore "innocent bystanders" with respect to his flying.

The most compelling rationale for licensing an activity is *to protect innocent bystanders from the risks posed by that activity*. Piloting an airplane, therefore, is a perfect example of an activity that government ought to license. So is driving a car on public roads. (If you drive on your own property, you place only yourself and those who are voluntarily on your property at risk; for this reason the government allows people to drive on their own property without a license.) At the same time, the innocent-bystander rationale for licensing does not appear to apply to dentistry: incompetent dentistry can harm the dentist—he might accidentally drill his finger—or his patients, but in either case the person harmed is someone who was a knowing risk-taker. In the case of dentistry, there do not appear to be any innocent bystanders who can be harmed.

Does the innocent-bystander rationale for licensing apply to doctors? It depends on what branch of medicine they practice. Doctors who treat communicable diseases should be licensed, since if they misdiagnose an illness, innocent bystanders—namely, the people their patients come into contact with—can be harmed. On the other hand, doctors who treat sprained ankles or perform cosmetic surgery need not be licensed since they are unlikely to harm anyone other than their patients.

It should by now be clear that if we licensed only in accordance with the innocent-bystander rationale, we would license far fewer professions and activities than we presently do.

Let us turn our attention back to parenting. If we think it appropriate for the government to license activities that impose serious risks on innocent bystanders, then there is every reason to license parents. When two people decide to become parents, they expose themselves to certain risks—most notably, the risk that they will not enjoy parenting. They are, however, voluntarily undertaking this risk. (Even if they become parents "by accident," they have the option of giving up their child for adoption and thus avoiding the risks of parenthood.) Much more serious are the risks parenting creates for that most innocent of bystanders—namely, the child they bring into existence. This child did not ask to be born, did not ask to be born to these parents, and certainly did not ask to be raised by them. And yet, if they have him and do a bad job of raising him, they can make his life miserable.

Incompetent parents can harm their children in a number of respects. Most obviously, they can physically or emotionally abuse them. And even in the absence of outright abuse, parents can harm their children if they do not understand their children's physical and emotional needs or if they understand these needs but are unable, because of shortcomings of their own, to fulfill them.

A child, in other words, is like a person who lives under the intended flight path of an unlicensed pilot, but in many respects the child's plight is worse. The person who lives under the flight path could, after all, take steps to lessen the risks posed by the pilot. This person might build a bunker to hide in, move elsewhere, or shoot down approaching planes. The child cannot take similar steps to protect himself from bad parenting. He is stuck with his parents, unless they are unusually brutal.

Notice, too, that far fewer innocent bystanders will be harmed by incompetent piloting than will be harmed by incompetent parenting. Incompetent piloting is, after all, a self-limiting activity: not many people are tempted to go up in a plane without having had proper instruction. On the other hand, the world is full of people who want to have a go at parenting despite never having spent time dealing with babies. Similarly, while it is presumably no fun to be up in an airplane when you don't know how to fly, some incompetent parents seem to enjoy their incompetence: they enjoy abusing their children. Finally, when incompetent pilots crash, the odds are that they *won't* hit an innocent bystander on the ground: most of the ground, after all, is unoccupied. On the other hand, when incompetent parents "crash," the innocent bystander that is their child will almost certainly be harmed.

We should also bear in mind that the harm done by incompetent parents can extend beyond their child. A child may, as a result of bad parenting, become a sociopath, in which case people the parents have never even met will be harmed by their bad parenting. Also, when an abused child grows up and has children, they are likely to be abused. Thus, the harm done by incompetent parents can be transmitted through many generations.

A Parent's License Described

What would a prospective parent have to do to obtain a parent's license? Before attempting to answer this question, it is useful to take a look at the requirements that must be met in order to obtain a pilot's license and to consider the reasoning behind these requirements.

To obtain a pilot's license you must, first and foremost, be in good health. You cannot have epilepsy, a serious heart condition, or other diseases that could cause you to lose control of an airplane. You must have good eyesight: in particular, if you are blind, you will not be allowed to fly, since you would almost certainly crash a plane during or shortly after takeoff. But even if you are in perfect health, you cannot get a pilot's license unless you possess the skills and knowledge necessary to keep a plane safely aloft. You have to know airspeak, the restricted form of English used in air traffic control. You must have logged a certain number of hours of hands-on experience, flying alongside an instructor, and you must pass a written exam. Finally, even though you meet all the above conditions, you will not be able to obtain a pilot's license until you are seventeen, the reasoning being that someone under seventeen would lack the good judgment necessary for safe piloting.

The above requirements have one thing in common: they are designed to weed out those individuals most likely to crash an airplane. In much the same way, a parent's license would be designed to weed out those individuals most likely to "crash" as parents. To begin with, there will be health requirements for a parent's license—although the requirements won't be quite as stringent as those for a pilot's license.

We would probably tolerate poor eyesight, occasional seizures, or a heart condition in parents, but we wouldn't grant a parent's license to a person whose physical condition clearly would interfere with the activities involved in parenting. Consider an extreme case—a quadriplegic. It is inconceivable that such a person, by himself, would be able to take care of a newborn baby. We might be willing to issue such a person a "restricted" parent's license: we would allow him to become a parent only if a second parent—one who possessed a "full" parent's license—was present in the household. Similarly, we would be reluctant to issue a parent's license to someone with an addiction or to someone who had a terminal illness that in all likelihood would result in his death in a half-dozen years.

When it comes to parenting, mental health is as important as physical health. Thus, someone with schizophrenia would not be granted a parent's license, nor would someone who is mentally retarded. To get a parent's license a person must be rational and emotionally stable.

What about the *genetic* health of parents? Should we allow, say, two carriers of the Tay-Sachs gene to get a parent's license? Absolutely, as long as they meet all the qualifications. Whether we should allow them to reproduce is an entirely separate issue, one we examined back in Chapter 2. In other words, although their genetic health may disqualify them from creating children, it need not disqualify them from adopting.

Besides the health of prospective parents, we will be concerned with their knowledge of children and parenting techniques. We will want to make sure that they understand the physical, emotional, and intellectual needs of children. We might require them to take classes in child-rearing—classes that will provide them with information about infant and child nutrition, about nonviolent techniques for dealing with unruly children, about what sorts of things children like and dislike, and about common childhood diseases and how they can be prevented or dealt with. We also might require them to take a course in infant first aid. And it would not be enough for them simply to sit through a class. They would also have to pass an exam demonstrating that they had mastered its content.

In the same way as we require prospective pilots to log hours in the air, we could require prospective parents to have a certain amount of "hands on" experience with children of various ages before granting them a license. It would be highly instructive for a young couple to change a few diapers, spend the night attempting to calm a baby, rearrange their job schedules and lifestyle around a child's needs, or attempt to reason with a teenager. (Indeed, exposure to flesh-and-blood children might convince a number of people who had romantic notions about parenting that they weren't really ready to undertake the huge commitment that parenting involves.) Prospective parents who, in the course of their practice parenting, constantly made mistakes—like hitting babies that refused to stop crying—and showed themselves to be unable or unwilling to change this behavior would be denied a parent's license.

In the same way as we regard some people as being too young to fly a plane even though they can pass all our tests, we will regard some people as being too young to parent. This will presumably include thirteen-year-olds. We might also put an upper limit on the age at which someone can become a parent. In particular, someone who becomes a parent at age eighty-four (as novelist Saul Bellow did) is unlikely to live long enough to complete the task of parenting he has taken on—which is arguably unfair to the child in his care.

We should also be reluctant to license someone who has committed crimes against children in the past—not only crimes of violence like child abuse, but "financial crimes" like failure to make court-mandated child support payments. A father's inability or unwillingness to support his current children should make us doubt that he would support additional children.

And this isn't all we will expect of potential parents. We will, for one thing, want them to possess a certain financial wherewithal. Parenting is expensive. There is, at the very minimum, the cost of medical care for a child and the cost of food, clothing, and shelter. We will also want to take into account the cost of providing a child with educational and recreational opportunities, and maybe even the cost of providing him with postsecondary job training or a college education. Finally, and quite significantly, there is the cost of providing "day care" for children. If parents put their child in a day-care center, this cost will be obvious; but even if they avoid the expense of a day-care center by having a parent stay at home with the child, they will experience a "day-care cost"—namely, the opportunity cost equal to the income the stay-at-home parent forgoes by staying at home rather than working.

Since parenting is an activity best undertaken by two people, we might want to issue parent's licenses in pairs; and since good parenting requires that the *same* two people act as parents throughout a child's upbringing, we might insist that a pair be married before being licensed.[1] Along these same lines, we might be reluctant to grant parent's licenses to individuals who, though married, had been divorced many times in the past. We might infer from their past divorces that they would be unlikely to stay together through the two decades of parenting required to raise a child.

A parent's license would place limits on the number of children a couple can parent. It is reasonable to think that a young, affluent couple would be better able to fulfill the demands of parenting than an old, impoverished couple. It is also reasonable to think that no one—not even a young, affluent couple—could fulfill the needs of, say, thirteen children. The family-size limits imposed by parent's licenses would take this into account. Those wishing to have unusually large families would have to meet additional requirements. (In much the same way, a pilot's license does not permit the holder to fly any airplane under any circumstances. A pilot who wishes, for example, to fly in bad weather or at night must take additional training and pass additional tests.)

What if a woman who lacked a parent's license got pregnant? She would have to participate in an expedited licensing program that would begin with a crash course in prenatal care and would go on to do everything the normal licensing program does, checking the applicant's physical and mental health, financial status and living situation, and providing child-rearing instruction. If the pregnant woman refused to participate in the expedited program or did not pass it, we would stop her from acting as parent: we would let her give birth to the child, but turn her newborn over to a man and woman who have parent's licenses and wish to adopt.[2] If we let the woman keep her baby, we would effectively undermine the licensing scheme: women everywhere could become parents without the hassle of getting a license by simply staging a "surprise pregnancy."

In the same way as a pilot can lose his license for flying in a reckless manner, parents could lose their license for parenting in a manner that endangers their child; and when parents lost their license, they would simultaneously lose custody of their child. This, by the way, is pretty much the same as currently happens, only we don't refer to the loss of a child as a loss of a parent's license. Where the licensing proposal differs from our current system is not with respect to how children are removed from parents, but with respect to which people are allowed to parent in the first place.

The above proposal describes just one of the ways a parent's license could work. I present it in detail not because I think licensing requires these exact features, but because I want to give the reader something concrete to think about. Readers who dislike various features of my licensing proposal are encouraged to modify it to their own liking. The issue that concerns us here is not whether *this exact* licensing program is desirable, but whether *some* licensing program—which may differ significantly from the one I have proposed—is desirable.

Licensing and Adoption

Many will find the licensing proposal to be morally repugnant. These same individuals probably see nothing wrong, however, with the state placing restrictions on who can and who cannot adopt children. These views are arguably inconsistent.

The state does not allow just anyone to adopt a baby. If you wish to adopt, there are a number of requirements the state will make you meet, requirements much like those described in my licensing proposal. If you wish to adopt, the state will investigate you, visit your home, and talk to your neighbors. It usually won't let people who are unmarried, unemployed, impoverished, or addicted to drugs adopt; nor will it let teenagers adopt. At the same time, if an unmarried, unemployed, impoverished, crack-addicted teenager—the sort of person the state would *never* let adopt—possesses the biological ability to make a baby, and if she goes ahead and makes one, the state will staunchly defend her right to attempt to raise the child she has brought into the world.

On the face of it, the state is engaged in a blatant double standard. If children are precious enough for the state to block unqualified *adoptive* parents from raising them, shouldn't it also block—by means of a parental licensing program like the one I proposed—unqualified *biological* parents from raising them?

Professor Bartholet Adopts

For a concrete example of what is involved in the adoption process, consider the case of Harvard Law professor Elizabeth Bartholet, who discovered in herself a desire to mother a child. Bartholet—as she tells us in her autobiographical *Family Bonds: Adoption and the Politics of Parenting*—found a willing male and tried to get pregnant in the natural way, but failed. She also tried in vitro fertilization but in the end was forced to give up the idea of making a baby. Her only remaining option was to adopt.

Bartholet assumed that adoption agencies would not question her fitness as a parent. After all, she had already successfully raised one child, the product of a former marriage. But from the agencies' point of view, she was marginally fit to parent. She was, after all, over forty (strike one) and single (strike two). She discovered, much to her astonishment, that agencies also discriminate on the basis of race, religion, physical handicaps, and sexual orientation, and that the discrimination in question isn't just *allowed* by law, it is *required*.

In order to determine her fitness to parent, the adoption agency Bartholet went to put her through a home study process. They inquired into her childhood, her relationship with her parents, her former marriage (which ended in divorce), and her current love life. They inquired into her finances: would her bank account and work situation leave her free to be a full-time parent during the first six months of the adoption and to play the role of parent after that? They inquired into her sex life: was she heterosexual but not promiscuous? They told Bartholet that they needed a letter from a minister certifying that she was of good character. This presented a problem since she didn't have a minister. Fortunately for her, Harvard University did have one. She visited him for an hour, and he wrote a letter testifying to her suitability as a parent.

The home study process Bartholet endured was of moderate rigor because she attempted a *private* agency adoption. Had she instead pursued a *public* agency adoption, she would, because of her age and marital status, have found herself excluded from adopting anything but "undesirable" children—for example, seriously disabled teenagers. On the other hand, if she had bypassed *agency* adoptions in favor of an *independent* adoption—in which birth parents place their children with adoptive parents either directly or through an intermediary—she could have avoided home study altogether. Which type of adoption prospective parents pursue depends in large part on how much money they have: private agency adoptions and independent adoptions are considerably more expensive than public agency adoptions.

In the end, Bartholet's quest for a child was successful. She adopted a Peruvian child and a short time later went back to Peru and adopted a second one.

The Adoption Process

The screening process Bartholet went through was not unusual. Prospective adoptive parents typically need to satisfy an adoption agency in numerous respects.

Would-be adoptive parents have to provide various documents, including their marriage license, tax returns, and photographs of themselves and possibly of their home. It helps if an applicant—especially an adoptive father—has a college diploma. Agencies also check to see whether applicants have a criminal record and in particular whether they have been accused or convicted of child abuse.

Agencies want applicants who are in good health. Being overweight counts against an applicant, as does having a physical handicap[3] or a potentially fatal disease like cancer. Even if an applicant has been cured of cancer, agencies will think twice before turning over a child to him. Agencies frown on applicants who are alcoholics as well as those who are "recovered" alcoholics. They might require these applicants to undergo a psychological evaluation.

While adoption agencies want applicants to be healthy, they don't want them to be *too* healthy. To the contrary, most agencies require adoptive parents to have one significant health problem—infertility.

Age is also a factor in adoptions. Agencies rarely allow people under age twenty-one to adopt, and some even require adoptive parents to be over twenty-five. Furthermore, many agencies want there to be not more than a forty-year age difference between parents and their adopted children.

If an adoptive couple already has two or more children, their chances of adopting will be hurt unless an agency thinks a child would benefit from being placed in a large family.

An applicant's religion can be an issue. Some agencies will reject outright those who don't attend church. Other agencies will consider nonchurchgoers but ask how, in the absence of religion, these applicants plan to teach their child a set of values. And even if a person is an active churchgoer, some agencies will hold it against him if his religion is opposed to the medical treatment of illnesses. Finally, in some states there are laws that block adoptions across religious lines.

It goes without saying that agencies prefer married couples over unmarried couples or single parents. Even if you are married, it helps to have been married for a few years before you attempt to adopt. (This allows adoptive parents to establish the existence of an infertility problem.) If an applicant is on his second marriage, it will hurt his chances of adopting. A past divorce, many agencies reason, increases the likelihood of a future divorce and might indicate that a person is not deeply committed to family life. Along similar lines, the fact that a divorced person failed to meet his child support obligations will be held against him.

This is not to say that it is impossible for single parents to adopt. A black single parent, for example, will find it easier to adopt than a white single parent will. Agencies favor same-race adoptions, and there is (relatively speaking) a shortage of adoptive black parents; this means that the standards for adoption are lowered for blacks. Also, a single woman might have a good chance of adopting a child who was sexually abused by a male and is having trouble recovering from the abuse.

When they are allowed to adopt, single parents are often given "difficult" children. This is ironic, since a couple would probably have an easier time handling the needs of such a child than a single parent would.

Until recently it was difficult if not impossible for homosexuals or homosexual couples to adopt. One exception was cases in which agencies were trying to place a troubled gay teenager. Another was if a pregnant woman sympathized with the plight of a gay couple and agreed to let them adopt her baby.

In conclusion, adoption agencies are quite careful about whom they will let adopt. They operate on the theory that not everyone is equally suited to parenthood and that certain characteristics—for example, good physical and mental health, a certain degree of affluence, a certain educational level, and being part of a committed relationship—are desirable in parents. They set their adoption requirements with these characteristics in mind. We might quibble about the exact requirements they set, but there can be no doubt, I think, that in setting requirements, agencies have the interests of children squarely in mind.

The Double Standard

Elizabeth Bartholet was affluent, articulate, responsible, mature, gainfully employed, and free of addictions. She possessed a good "track record" as a parent, having successfully raised one son. Despite all this, adoption agencies, backed by the state, felt the need to investigate her thoroughly before allowing her to adopt a child. If, on the other hand, Bartholet had been an unemployed, illiterate, alcoholic with no experience at parenting, *but had possessed the biological ability to make a baby*, the state would not have questioned her right to raise any children she produced. Indeed, the state would have used its powers to prevent anyone from taking her child. By all appearances this is a double standard, and it isn't the only double standard that exists with regard to the state's views on who should and who shouldn't be allowed to parent.

Consider, for example, the transition that takes place when an adoption is finalized. We have seen how careful an agency is to screen potential adoptive parents. Even after an agency has placed a child with a couple (but before the adoption has been finalized) the agency will monitor that couple's fitness as parents. Should their marriage become unstable, the child might be taken from them. But the day the adoption is finalized, all this changes. The agency, in most cases, will stop caring about how the adoptive parents live their life. If they file for divorce or quit their job, the child will not be taken from them. If it was so important that they possess the characteristics of a good parent before the adoption and in the months immediately after the adoption, isn't it also important that they possess them, say, a year after the adoption?

Or consider the situation of foster parents. They are not attempting to adopt a child, but are merely asking for permission temporarily to act as parent for a child in need. Does the state let just anyone perform this valuable service? Of course not. To become a foster parent, a person must go through a screening process and be licensed by the state. (Prospective foster parents are inspected in much the same way as prospective adoptive parents.) But if the state feels compelled to license people who are going to act as a child's parents for a matter of days or weeks, then why doesn't it likewise feel compelled to license biological parents who are going to raise a child for eighteen years?

Consider, finally, the situation of day-care providers. In many states, not just anyone can run a day-care center; you must first be licensed by the state. The idea is that not everyone is fit to act as "parent" for a few hours a day. At the same time, someone who was unable to get licensed as a day-care provider would be allowed by the state to act as parent to his or her own children for twenty-four hours a day. Strange logic indeed.

If we "license" adoptive parents, foster parents, and day-care providers, why not license biological parents as well? Why do we presume—in many cases, not only wrongly, but with tragic consequences for children—that all biological parents deserve a chance to raise the children they create? Why do we allow this apparent double standard to go unchallenged?

Significant Differences

Someone can respond to the charge of a double standard by arguing that there are significant differences between adopting children and giving birth to them—differences that justify our licensing adoptive parents but not biological parents.

Someone might argue, to begin with, that a biological mother will by nature love her child. She carried it in her womb for nine months, endured the pain of childbirth, and witnessed the child's emergence into the world. The same cannot be said of an adoptive mother. To the contrary, the adoptive mother is (usually) a complete stranger to the baby she adopts. She must learn to love it. The problem is that not all women can learn to love a strange baby; and if a woman doesn't love a child, she is unlikely to lavish it with the care and attention it needs. It is for this reason—the argument goes—that the state has to be careful about whom it allows to adopt.[4]

The suggestion that biological parents love their children immediately and intensely while adoptive parents either don't love their children or do so belatedly and halfheartedly is a sweeping generalization. It is entirely possible for biological mothers not to love their children—witness the growing tendency in the 1990s for biological mothers to murder their unwanted newborn babies. At the same time, it is possible for adoptive parents to love their adopted children at or even before first sight.

Indeed, we might even go so far as to argue that adoptive parents will typically be *more* loving than biological parents. It is far easier and a lot more fun to have sex than it is to go through the adoption process. Because of this, there are many biological parents who became parents as the result of an accident and might therefore feel indifferent or even hostile toward their accidental child. No one adopts by accident, though. You have to be intensely committed to parenthood to have a chance at successfully adopting. Who, then, is more likely to be a loving parent, the woman who just had her third reproductive accident, or the man and woman who have endured months of agency investigation and spent thousands of dollars in their efforts to gain parenthood? Following this line of reasoning, someone might argue that there is, if anything, *less* reason to license adoptive parents than there is to license biological parents.

Another difference between adoptive and biological parents is that biological parents *created* their child. The process of creation, some might suggest, gives biological parents various rights with respect to their child, including the right to raise it. Stated bluntly, the suggestion is this: biological parents create their children and therefore own them. Licensing such parents would be wrong, inasmuch as it would deprive some (unfit) parents of their ownership rights. Adoptive parents, by way of contrast, did not create the child they seek to adopt and thus have no rights with respect to it. The only way they will come to have rights is if the state chooses to grant them.

The problem with this line of argument is that it assumes creating a child is like creating a vase. If a man and woman dig the clay for a vase and then shape and fire the clay, the resulting vase will be theirs, and it will be theirs *because they created it.* And because it is theirs, they can do with it as they please. They can put it on a shelf or sell it or smash it with a hammer; the state will not interfere. The ownership rights a man and woman gain in creating a child are different, however, than the ownership rights they gain in creating a vase. This is because the child, unlike the vase, can experience pain and joy and has rights and interests. Parents may be able to smash a vase because they created it, but they cannot likewise smash a child because they created it. The state—all but the most radical defenders of the ownership model of parenting will admit—can legitimately interfere with the "ownership rights" of biological parents. (In Chapter 9, I will consider cases in which the state not only interferes with the rights of biological parents, but strips them of these rights.)

It is clear that the government has the interests of children in mind when it prohibits child abuse. But why wait until abuse actually takes place before stepping in to protect children? Why not act to prevent potentially abusive parents from having access to children? Why not protect all children to the same extent as we protect adopted children? These questions, of course, are uppermost in the minds of those who advocate that we license parents.

Resolving the Double Standard

Suppose, for the sake of argument, we admit that there are no significant differences between biological parents and adoptive parents, and therefore that we are inconsistent in being quite careful about whom we allow to adopt children while allowing all biological parents to raise the children they create. We will then be faced with an interesting choice.

There are, after all, two ways in which the inconsistency can be resolved. On the one hand, we can argue that biological parents should be treated the same as adoptive parents. We should screen biological parents, allowing only those who would be fit parents to raise the children they create. This, of course, is what the parental licensing program advocates. On the other hand, we can argue that adoptive parents should be treated in the same way as we treat biological parents. In other words, we should allow anyone at all to adopt children—or, equivalently, we should stop "licensing" adoptive parents.

Elizabeth Bartholet leans toward this last solution. She wants to make it much easier for people to adopt. She would require that adoptive parents be "minimally fit" and would base her standards of what constitutes minimal fitness on the standards that now exist for removing a child from its biological parents. In particular she would disqualify serious and persistent drug or alcohol abusers, child abusers, and those seriously ill or of advanced age. Beyond that, adoption agencies would operate on a first-come, first-served basis.

Bartholet's proposal has certain advantages over the current adoption system. It would, for one thing, be fairer. Rich and poor people would be on an equal footing, and the rich would not be allowed to buy their way out of being screened. Her proposed system would also have the advantage of finding children homes quickly. In America there are hundreds of thousands of children in foster care, and abroad there are millions of children who need homes. This is not, Bartholet argues, the time to be picky about who gets to adopt and who does not.

Bartholet also points to various defects in the current screening process. Because the process is so involved, adoption agencies are forced to rely on poorly paid social workers to carry it out, and these individuals often have heavy caseloads. Under such circumstances, it can be difficult to assess a person's capacity to love and raise children. It is also relatively easy for prospective adoptive parents to "cheat" during the home study and say things the social worker wants to hear; because of this, the home study can produce a candidate analysis that, despite its impressive detail, is largely illusory. And finally, there is no evidence that the factors relied on by the screening process are good predictors of parental ability. In particular, there is no evidence, Bartholet claims, that those who become adoptive parents as a result of the agency screening process are any better as parents than those who become adoptive parents as a result of the relatively unscreened independent-adoption process.

Whatever its merits may be, Bartholet's proposal does not eliminate the double standard in our treatment of adoptive and biological parents. Under her proposal, after all, we would still screen—albeit minimally—adoptive parents but not biological parents. Why not eliminate screening for both groups of parents? Why not, in other words, allow *anyone at all* to adopt, the way we currently allow *all* biological parents to raise the children they create? Such a proposal would have the same advantages as her proposal: when it came to adoption, poor people would be treated the same as the rich; it would be the quickest way to handle the glut of adoptable children; and, by eliminating the current screening process, it would obviously eliminate the various defects of this process.

Bartholet would presumably respond to such a suggestion by pointing out that under an unrestricted adoption system, the rights of children would be trampled. Children's best interests, she tells us, "require nurturing homes and parenting relationships." Furthermore, some level of screening is necessary "to assure people that adoption would not result in the kinds of abuses that occurred in the nineteenth century, when some children were turned over to families who saw them as a form of cheap labor."

Such a response would have some obvious problems, though. For one thing, not all biological parents will provide children with the level of nurturing that, according to Bartholet, their best interests require. Furthermore, biological parents are capable of making children for all the wrong reasons—for example, as a source of cheap labor. Aren't the rights of biological children as important as the rights of adopted children? Bartholet hints at the possibility of licensing biological parents but does not directly address the issue.

Other Criticisms of the Licensing Proposal

Now let us turn to some of the other criticisms that might be leveled against the licensing proposal. These criticisms focus not on the existence of a double standard in our treatment of biological and adoptive parents, but instead on defects in the licensing proposal and the rationale behind it.

Criticism. The licensing program will sometimes make mistakes. In particular, it will sometimes allow people who are not competent to parent to slip through the screening process and get a parent's license.

Reply. I concede that programs to license parents will make mistakes. The licensing process, after all, will have to deal with millions of applicants yearly and will therefore have to rely on "faceless bureaucrats" to make decisions about who gets licenses and who doesn't. Having made this concession, let me hasten to add that just because a governmental program sometimes makes mistakes it does not follow that we should reject the program in question. If it did, we would have no governmental programs at all. When we are considering governmental programs, the question is not whether they sometimes make mistakes, but whether they are better than the alternatives. We live in an imperfect world and so must settle for imperfect governmental programs.

Furthermore, although a program to license parents will *sometimes* mistakenly allow incompetent individuals to become parents, this flaw seems insignificant when we realize that our current system, in allowing anyone with the biological ability to make a baby to act as its parent, *always* allows incompetent individuals to become parents. It deprives them of parenthood only if their incompetence turns into outright abuse. Thus, when it comes to the mistake of allowing incompetent people to parent, the licensing proposal, though flawed, is far less flawed than the current system.

Criticism. There is another, more serious mistake that a licensing program will make: it will sometimes fail to grant a parent's license to an individual who is perfectly competent to parent. Our current unlicensed system, by way of contrast, never prevents someone from becoming a parent and therefore never makes this mistake.

Reply. Again, it is true that a licensing program will sometimes mistakenly fail to issue parent's licenses, but this isn't tantamount to telling people they can never become a parent. To the contrary, most rejections will be conditional: "You cannot become a parent until you get a job, or get married, or stay off drugs for a year." The conditions would be ones that most people could satisfy if they were seriously interested in parenting. And by the way, if they weren't seriously interested in parenting, why should they be allowed to try to raise a child? Why should we allow someone's whimsical desire to act as parent to outweigh the very real interests of the child that will be under his care?

A thoughtful person, besides considering the harm done by a licensing program, will consider the harm done in the absence of such a program—that is, the harm done when we allow anyone with the biological ability to create a child to act as parent for that child. There is abundant evidence that in America today this latter harm is significant. There are many woefully incompetent people who not only become parents, but become parents many times over. They are indifferent to the children they have. On good days they ignore them, and on bad days they abuse them. They are parents that no child in his right mind would want. The harm done by a licensing program pales in comparison.

Criticism. People have a right to procreate. The licensing proposal would violate this right.

Reply. It is doubtful, as we saw in Part One of this book, that people have an absolute right to procreate, but even if they do, this doesn't count against the licensing proposal. Remember, after all, that the licensing proposal does not prevent unlicensed people from procreating; it instead prevents them from raising the children they produce. Their children are instead turned over to (licensed) adoptive parents shortly after birth.

Criticism. You can't really teach someone to be a good parent, so licensing parents would be a waste of time.

Reply. The licensing program described above is only partly concerned with teaching people to be good parents. It is also concerned with screening out people who almost certainly would be bad parents. Even if it failed in the first of these functions, the licensing program would still, in carrying out the second function, significantly reduce the amount of harm done to children. Furthermore, although it admittedly will be difficult to teach some people to be a good parent—for example, people who are stupid, lack patience, or are by nature cold and uncaring—most people's parenting skills can be improved by training. In the training in question, we would pass along objective information about children's nutritional, medical, emotional, and physical needs; we would describe the advantages and disadvantages of the various techniques that can be used to discipline children; and we can make them aware that the way they were raised—which they might otherwise take as the model of how to raise a child—is not necessarily the best way and is certainly not the only way to raise a child.

Most people voluntarily engage in self-education programs when confronted with parenthood. They take classes on parenting. They read books and magazines on child care. They talk to people who have had babies. The licensing proposal would require such behavior of all potential parents, the theory being that a parent who was unwilling to learn about the needs of children probably wouldn't make a good parent.

Criticism. Under the licensing proposal, there will be a sharp increase in the number of children who are put up for adoption, since we will be taking away the babies of parents who had them without a license.

Reply. There are two reasons why this prospect is not as worrisome as it might seem. In the first place, notice that the criticism assumes that if the licensing proposal were implemented, "unqualified" women would continue producing children at the same rate as they now do. It is far from clear that this would happen. Perhaps licensing would result in a sharp decline in the number of children produced by "unqualified" women. Why have children if you are going to lose them? Why go through pregnancy if there will be nothing to show for it but stretch marks? If the licensing proposal were implemented, "unqualified" women would soon come to realize that without a license, getting pregnant had many costs but few benefits. In the second place, notice that even if such a decline did not take place, the babies taken at birth would be just the sort of children—newborns—for whom there is the greatest demand among adoptive parents. These children, unlike older children, would have little trouble getting adopted.

Criticism. The licensing proposal violates a central principle of American justice—namely, that a person is innocent until proven guilty. The law does not allow us to jail someone because we think it likely that he will steal a car; we must wait until he has stolen or tried to steal one before we jail him. Along these same lines, it is one thing to take away the children of parents who have abused them and quite another thing to prevent people from becoming parents simply because we think it likely that they will abuse children. The licensing proposal, instead of assuming that everyone is fit to parent until proven otherwise, assumes that everyone is unfit to parent until they prove otherwise by taking classes, passing exams, and so forth.

Reply. To begin with, it is not really true that in America people are innocent until proven guilty. If the state suspects that a person stole a car, it will jail him and not let him out until he comes up with bail, it will search his home, and it will question him. This is not how we treat "innocent" people. Furthermore, the innocent-until-proven-guilty principle applies primarily to activities like burglary, in which a person intends to harm others. It does not apply to activities in which a person does not intend to harm others, but might do so accidentally. Thus, we don't apply the innocent-until-proven-guilty principle to would-be pilots: we don't allow everyone to attempt to fly and then take away the flying privileges of only those who crash. Such a policy would, after all, have disastrous consequences for people on the ground.

Parenting is not (for most people) an activity in which parents intend to harm their children. It is, however, an activity in which parents can inadvertently harm their children. Thus, it seems as inappropriate for us to apply the innocent-until-proven-guilty principle to parenting as it does to apply this principle to piloting.

Criticism. The government could use its licensing power to punish people it regarded as enemies. Imagine living in a country in which, if you belonged to a certain political party, you would lose your chance at becoming a parent.

Reply. It is indeed conceivable that our government could abuse its power to license parents, but it is arguably unlikely that it would. After all, it does not abuse the licensing powers it presently possesses. One doesn't hear of cases in which someone is denied, say, a driver's license or a license to practice medicine because of his political views. Notice, more significantly, that one doesn't hear of cases in which someone is denied a "license" to adopt because of his political views. If we can live with the danger that the government will abuse the "licensing" of adoptive parents, why can't we also live with the danger that the government might abuse the licensing of biological parents?

Conclusions

So much for the licensing proposal. If I have established anything in the above discussions, it is this: the argument for licensing parents is much more plausible than one might initially have thought. At the same time, I suspect that many people, after hearing the argument, will remain reluctant to advocate such licensing.

Their reluctance is, I think, the result of their being haunted by two images. The first is the image of newborn babies being torn from the arms of unlicensed mothers. If we license parents, such heartbreaking seizures will necessarily occur. The second image is that of an Orwellian Big Brother government that has the right to determine who is allowed to act as parent. An advocate of parent's licenses must concede the psychological power of these images and somehow counteract them.

Perhaps the best way to accomplish this is to place before us images of childhood when parents *aren't* licensed. The image of a newborn baby being taken from its mother's arms is indeed heartbreaking, but if we let an unfit woman keep the baby she has made, we are faced with a second heartbreaking image—that of a child who spends his formative years being alternately ignored and abused by his mother. Similarly, the image of a Big Brother bureaucrat maliciously withholding a parent's license from a woman who would make a wonderful mother is disturbing, but so is the image of the present-day American government that defends an unmarried, teenage, drug-addicted prostitute's attempt to raise the child she thoughtlessly brought into the world.

CHAPTER 8

ADOPTION

In the preceding chapter I argued that we should license biological parents in much the same way as we "license" adoptive parents. Let us now take a closer look at the adoption process itself. In this chapter I will first relate the history of adoption in America and then describe some of the ways the current adoption process might be improved. In particular, I will argue that under certain circumstances we should allow biological parents to sell their children to adoptive parents.

Adoption in America

These days there is a shortage of "desirable" adoptable children, and as a result couples must go to great lengths to adopt. There was a time, however, when the opposite was true—when relatively few people wanted to adopt children, and those who did often had less-than-noble motives for wanting to do so.

To have been orphaned in America before 1800 meant a very insecure existence. An orphan was likely taken care of in a makeshift manner. If young, he might be taken in by relatives or neighbors in a so-called informal adoption. If older, he might be apprenticed to a trade, in which case his master would take care of him. But if no one wanted a child, his plight was dire. He might end up in the almshouse, or he might be taken in by someone who wanted not to parent him lovingly but to exploit him.

Today, a young woman who gives birth to a baby she doesn't want can put it up for adoption—indeed, might even be paid for doing so. In the 1800s, putting an unwanted child up for adoption wasn't really an option; instead, a woman found herself with a baby-disposal problem. She might have solved this problem by simply throwing the baby away, or she might have paid ten dollars to place it with a so-called baby-farmer. Although baby-farmers promised to find homes for the babies they took in, their promises were rarely fulfilled. More often the babies in their care met an early death.

Why were our ancestors indifferent to the plight of orphans? In part because they were (particularly before the nineteenth century) indifferent to the plight of *all* children, viewing them, in many cases, as exploitable property. Such adults did not view adoption as a chance to form a loving relationship with a child. Instead, they regarded it as the assumption of an odious duty—something to be avoided, if possible. Furthermore, the absence of effective means of contraception meant that parents probably had (or soon would have) more children than they could handle and were therefore less than thrilled by the prospect of taking in an orphan.

Why weren't orphans sent to orphanages? Because until the second half of the nineteenth century, orphanages were a rarity in America. The first American orphanage opened its doors in Louisiana in 1729, but they were slow to catch on. By 1825, New York State had only four orphanages, and by 1866 it had sixty. Americans today tend to think of orphanages as evil institutions, but at one time their construction represented a bold reform in the treatment of children.

Even when orphanages were an option, many orphans failed to benefit from their existence. Thus, by the middle of the nineteenth century an estimated ten thousand orphans lived in the streets of New York City. Many of them made a living stealing. It was not unusual for these street-dwelling orphans to end up in jail.

Around this time, America's farmlands experienced a labor shortage. It dawned on Charles Loring Brace that the nation could simultaneously take care of its urban orphans and relieve the labor shortage: it could send the orphans to rural farms, where they would find homes—and be put to work. Thus began the "orphan trains," which continued to operate until the 1920s.

In the twentieth century, orphanages were displaced by foster care. The children in foster care were a mix of those who had been orphaned, those who had been taken from their parents, and those whose biological parents had "given them up" but not yet signed away their parental rights. Because parents are reluctant to admit that they are unfit or unwilling to raise their children, and because American courts are reluctant to terminate the rights of biological parents, the children in these last two groups tended to linger in foster care for years and thereby—because most adoptive parents prefer babies or at least young children—become unadoptable. The growing number of children "trapped" in foster care led some observers in the mid-1990s to call for a revival of orphanages in America.

At the beginning of the twenty-first century the outlook for children in foster care remains bleak, but there are two rays of hope. One is the end of the ban on transracial adoptions—more on this in a moment. Another (possibly illusory) ray of hope is what looks like an increased willingness on the part of courts to sever the rights of biological parents who have essentially abandoned their children but are reluctant to admit as much to themselves and the world. Thus, the courts allowed Gregory Kingsley to "divorce" his mother, who had allowed Gregory to languish in foster care for years while she tried to make up her mind whether or not to keep him. I will save the details of Gregory's story for the next chapter.

Modern Adoption

In Chapter 7, I described the screening process that adoption agencies put potential adoptive parents through. A primary goal of agencies is to screen out incompetent parents. Another important goal of agencies, until recently, was to match adoptive parents with children—that is, to place children with adults who look like they could have been their biological parents. Ideally, adoptive parents should not be too old or too young to have had the child themselves; they should be of the same race as the child; and if the child had blue eyes and blond hair, it would be absolutely wonderful, as far as agencies were concerned, if the adoptive parents did as well. In matching parents and children, agencies made it possible for adoptive parents to conceal from both their child and the world at large the fact that he had been adopted and simultaneously to conceal their own reproductive shortcomings.

In the closing decades of the twentieth century, the dynamics of adoption changed. In the aftermath of *Roe v. Wade*, fetuses that in the past would have been delivered and put up for adoption were instead aborted. In 1970 there were 89,200 adoptions by unrelated petitioners; by 1975 that number had declined to 47,700; and by 1986 it had recovered only to 51,000. At the same time as the supply of babies was declining, the desire to adopt was increasing. Liberated women started putting their careers ahead of motherhood, but by waiting until they were in their late twenties or their thirties to get pregnant, they increased the chance of fertility problems. What had been a glut of adoptable babies became a shortage.

Because of this shortage, the costs associated with adopting a "desirable" child—that is, a white, newborn baby—rose, and the time couples spent waiting to adopt grew longer. Parents wishing to adopt became less choosy than the adoptive parents of the previous generation had been. In particular, they were willing to adopt across racial lines and to adopt children from other countries.

In one respect, the shortage of adoptable children was paradoxical, for in the final decades of the century there was a sharp and disturbing rise in the number of children born out of wedlock. In the past most of these children would have been put up for adoption. By 1990, though, unwed motherhood had lost much of its stigma. Many of the women who had babies out of wedlock chose to keep them, and their decision contributed to the shortage of adoptable infants.

In the 1990s, changes in America's political environment meant changes in the adoption process. In a nation eager to embrace diversity, the goal of matching adoptive parents and children started to seem misguided. If a child needed a home, it should get one as quickly as possible, even if it would be obvious to everyone that this child could not be the biological offspring of these parents. By the end of the century, only a clueless individual would have asked a white couple why they had a black or Asian child.

The ban on whites adopting blacks has a curious history. In the first half of the twentieth century it was primarily whites opposed to "race mixing" who objected to such adoptions. By the 1970s, blacks had become the leading opponents of transracial adoption. They feared that black children raised by whites would be "raised white" and that the end result would be a kind of cultural genocide. The problem with this point of view was that there simply weren't enough blacks willing and able to adopt the relatively large number of black children who needed homes. By the early 1990s it was clear to virtually everyone that the harm done to black children by being kept in foster care in the hope that black parents would adopt them was far worse than any harm that might be done to them by being raised by white parents.

Another consequence of the changed political environment was a growing willingness on the part of adoption agencies to let single parents adopt and to let gay and lesbian couples adopt. Agencies used to argue that single parents were unfit to adopt, inasmuch as it takes two people to parent a child properly. They also used to argue that gay and lesbian couples were unfit to adopt because of their illegal behavior; and when homosexuality was decriminalized, agencies argued that homosexual behavior, although legal, was immoral and therefore set a bad example for children, or that it takes a man and a woman to parent a child properly. By the end of the 1990s these arguments were losing their force.

Should we be reluctant to let single parents and gay and lesbian couples adopt? I think so—not because of any moral qualms about single-parenthood or homosexuality, but for the same reasons as I argued, in the previous chapter, that parent's licenses should generally be issued to married men and women. Nevertheless, there are circumstances under which single parents or gay and lesbian couples should be allowed to adopt. To be raised by a highly motivated single parent or homosexual couple is better for a child than being bounced around in foster care. Likewise, a girl who has been sexually abused by a man might be better off placed with a single woman than with a couple, and homosexual teenagers might be better off placed with homosexual couples than with heterosexual couples.

Buying Children

Although American law allows adoptive parents to pay a birth mother, it places strict limits on the transaction. The payment in question can cover the birth mother's living expenses for a specified period of time, the medical bills generated by her pregnancy, and perhaps even a "recuperation allowance" to help her recover from the pregnancy—and thereby let her "break even" on the pregnancy. What the payment cannot do is let her profit from the pregnancy. But we can reasonably ask, Why not let a birth mother profit from a pregnancy? If she can find a couple willing to pay, say, a million dollars for the baby she is carrying, why not allow the transaction? Why not, in other words, allow birth mothers to sell their babies?

Let me make it clear from the outset that when I talk about mothers selling their children, I do not mean selling, say, four-year-olds. Such sales would obviously be harmful to the children in question. Instead, I have in mind cases in which mothers sell babies not more than a few weeks old. Furthermore, when I talk about mothers selling their children, I do not mean selling them indiscriminately—selling them to, say, a millionaire pederast.[1] Instead, they can sell them only to adoptive parents who have undergone the home study process and been judged more than adequate as parents—or in a perfect world, to a husband and wife who possess parent's licenses. In other words, when I talk about mothers selling their children, I am describing a procedure like the current adoption procedure but for one thing: the mothers would be allowed not just to break even from a pregnancy, but to profit from it.

By way of illustration, consider the following case. Suppose John and Mary Able are a wealthy young couple whose reproductive efforts have been unfruitful. Mary has a medical condition that prevents her from successfully carrying a fetus to term in her uterus. Her obstetrician suggests that she try in vitro fertilization. Eggs will be removed from Mary, fertilized with John's sperm, and then implanted into the uterus of a surrogate mother. Suppose the Ables put an ad in the paper and are contacted by a woman who is willing to play the role of surrogate mother in exchange for a cash payment of $50,000, with $15,000 going to cover her medical and living costs, and the other $35,000 being her profit. Suppose the deal is struck and that when the baby is born it is turned over to the Ables—who, by the way, underwent the home study process and showed themselves to be fine candidates for parenthood. Why should the state interfere with this voluntary arrangement? What harm is done by it? Let us now consider some possible criticisms of "baby-selling."

Criticisms and Replies

Criticism. It is wrong to sell a human being, so the law should not permit mothers to sell their babies.

Reply. The law already permits mothers to sell their babies: it allows adoptive parents to make "break-even" payments to birth mothers. If we think it wrong to sell a child, we should allow no payments at all to birth mothers. Few of those raising this criticism, however, would advocate the abolition of such payments.

Some will counter this reply by claiming that when adoptive parents make break-even payments to a birth mother in an independent adoption, they aren't really *buying* a child; they are merely compensating the mother for the costs resulting from her pregnancy. This semantical distinction is dubious. If a grocer announced that you could have a banana if and only if you made a certain payment, and if you made the payment in question and walked out with the banana, we would say that you had bought the banana. Indeed, even if the banana was what in the grocery business they call a "loss leader," meaning that the grocer made no profit on the banana, we would still say that you had bought the banana from him. The same is true in transactions involving children in which the adoptive parents have to make a break-even payment to the birth mother. Like it or not, whenever a birth mother says that she will part with a baby if and only if a payment is made to her, she is selling the baby and the adoptive parents are buying it.

The semantical dodge just described shows that when it comes to adoptions, Americans are reluctant to call a spade a spade and say that a certain birth mother had sold her baby and that the adoptive parents had bought it. We are reluctant because we want our children to be priceless; when they are bought and sold, it becomes obvious not only that they have a price, but that their price is less than that of a fine automobile. We also want the adoption process to be motivated by love, not money. We want the birth mother to turn the baby over to the adoptive couple because she loves it and wants to do right by it; and we want the adoptive couple to take the child in because they love it and want it to have a wonderful life. Indeed, it would even be nice if the birth mother and adoptive couple felt love toward each other. This is the ideal. In the real world, though, pecuniary motives play a considerable role. Even under current laws that regulate payments to birth mothers, there exists a "baby market," as adoptive parents will readily confirm. At the time of this writing, a desirable (that is, a healthy white newborn) baby might fetch thirty thousand dollars on the baby market.

What makes the currently existing baby market interesting, from the economic point of view, is that market forces have been distorted by the requirement that women not profit from pregnancies. More precisely, under the current system pregnant women are subject to price controls. For this reason the market price of babies is lower than it would otherwise be, and this in turn means that there is a shortage of babies on the baby market. (If you told grocers that they had to sell their bananas "at cost," many of them would ask, "Then why bother selling them?" A shortage of bananas for sale would soon follow.) If we allowed mothers to profit from pregnancies, economic theory predicts a rise in the market price of adoptable babies as well as an increase in the number of them brought to market.

Criticism. The price rise just described would be undesirable. It is bad enough that adoptive parents have to pay $30,000 for a child. If we allow women to sell babies at a profit, this price might rise to $40,000, $50,000, or—who knows?—maybe even $100,000. By allowing women to profit from their pregnancies, we are, in effect, financially penalizing adoptive parents for bigheartedly taking in a child who needs a home. This is a strange way to show our gratitude.

Reply. The imaginary Ables, described above, were not taking in a homeless child out of the goodness of their heart; they were causing a child to come into existence who would need a home. In other cases—in which the adoptive parents are not causing a child to come into existence but are instead adopting, say, the baby of a woman who accidentally became pregnant—it is also misleading to describe them as selflessly taking in a homeless child. What they are doing is taking in a *desirable* homeless child. If they were less picky in their child preferences, they could probably obtain a child at negligible cost.

There is another way to respond to the above criticism. It is true that by not allowing mothers to profit from pregnancies, we reduce the price adoptive parents have to pay for a baby. They will be (or should be) pleased that profit is prohibited. At the same time, the pregnant woman ends up poorer because of the prohibition. In not letting her profit from her pregnancy, we are, in effect, asking her to subsidize the adoptive couple. Since the adoptive parents are considering shelling out tens of thousands of dollars for a baby, they are presumably more affluent than the pregnant woman—particularly if she is a single woman who got pregnant by accident. This hardly seems fair.

Criticism. Affluent adoptive couples aren't the only ones who will be hurt by a rise in the price of babies. Poor couples that want to adopt will be priced out of the market.

Reply. Poor couples are already priced out of the market, if what they seek to adopt is a "desirable" child. Furthermore, a case can be made—I made it in the previous chapter—that extremely poor people not only shouldn't be allowed to adopt, but shouldn't even be allowed to keep their own biological offspring.

Criticism. If we allow women to profit from their pregnancies, they will have an additional incentive to make babies, and there will soon be a glut of babies on the baby market. Indeed, we can imagine women going into the baby-making business. We can also imagine pregnant women who might otherwise have gotten an abortion instead choosing to have the child and sell it at a profit.

Reply. To begin with, an increase in the number of children available for adoption would not, in the beginning, lead to a glut of adoptable children; instead, it would ameliorate the current shortage of adoptable children, presumably a desirable outcome. After that, a glut of adoptable children is unlikely since as more babies are brought to market, their price will stop rising and may even start to fall. By letting market forces operate, we are likely to end up with a reasonably good match between the supply of babies put up for adoption and the demand to adopt them.

Criticism. If we allow women to profit from pregnancies, the resulting increase in the number of desirable babies put up for adoption will hurt less-desirable children's chances of being adopted.

Reply. It is difficult to predict what would happen if women could profit from pregnancy. It is true that the prices of desirable babies would rise. It is also true that because of this price rise, some women will be induced to make babies for adoption who otherwise would not have. It is hard to say, though, exactly how many "made-for-market" babies would come into existence.

Let us suppose, for the sake of argument, that when women are allowed to profit from pregnancy, a substantial number of women decide to go into the baby-making business. Will this hurt less-desirable children's chances of being adopted? Not necessarily. Notice, after all, that the babies that come into existence because their mothers hope to profit will be expensive to adopt. Presumably the market for such babies is different from the market for less-desirable children, and therefore this increased supply of "high-end" babies will have minimal impact on people's desire to adopt less-desirable children. Notice, by way of economic analogy, that the market for high-end Lexuses is different from the market for low-end Chevys. When Toyota builds more Lexuses, it does not affect the demand for Chevys.

If we are truly concerned about the plight of less-desirable children and want to increase their chances of being adopted, it is clear what we should do: we should take steps to inhibit the production of desirable babies. We should, for example, stop allowing payments that let women break even on their pregnancies. Such payments doubtless encourage some women to have their child and put it up for adoption who otherwise would have aborted it. (Returning to the above car analogy, although increasing the number of high-priced Lexuses that are produced has little impact on the demand for Chevys, a dramatic decrease in the supply of Lexuses—and simultaneously, of other mid- and high-priced cars—would stimulate the demand for Chevys, since car buyers would have nothing else to buy.) Few will advocate, however, that we take steps to restrict the supply of adoptable desirable babies.

In some respects our feelings about women who profit from pregnancy resemble our feelings about women who profit from sex. Realize, to begin with, that women who profit from sex—we call them prostitutes—and women who profit from pregnancy are doing for money what most women do for love. As long as a woman refuses monetary payments for sex or a baby, most people feel that the state has no business interfering with her; but as soon as a woman tries to make her living having sex or being pregnant, many of us are perfectly willing to sic the law on her. It isn't at all clear why.

In much the same way as libertarians have argued that women should be allowed to sell sex, we can argue that women should be allowed to sell babies. Prostitution is a victimless crime.[2] By outlawing prostitution, we prevent prostitutes and their customers from engaging in a transaction that they find to be mutually beneficial, and we thereby hurt them. Likewise, selling newborn babies at a profit (to qualified adoptive parents) is a victimless crime. When we forbid women to profit from pregnancy, we prevent them from entering into transactions that both they and the adoptive parents find beneficial, and we thereby hurt them.

Some feminists argue that prostitution should be outlawed because it exploits women. Someone might likewise argue that if we allow women to profit from pregnancy, some will transform themselves into baby factories, turning out babies for adoption in exchange for money. If we take advantage of the service they provide, we will be exploiting them. As was suggested above, though, there is less to the charge of exploitation than meets the eye. Isn't the woman who profits from her pregnancy considerably better off than the woman who isn't allowed to profit? What sense, then, does it make to claim that the former woman is being exploited while the latter woman is not? More generally, isn't it exploitative to ask impoverished birth mothers to subsidize the adoptive yearnings of affluent couples, as is our current practice?

CHAPTER 9

CONTESTED PARENTAL RIGHTS

Sometimes two or more people independently claim the right to act as parent of a child. The most obvious such case is when, during a divorce, a man and woman each fight for custody of their children, but there are other cases as well.

Consider, for example, cases in which, because of a mistake at the hospital, a couple takes home the wrong baby and raises it for several years. Suppose the mixup is later discovered and the child's biological parents demand their child back. Or consider cases involving a "contract mother"—a woman who agrees to become pregnant and to turn over the baby she makes to adoptive parents. Suppose this woman changes her mind and claims parental rights with respect to the child she brought into the world. Consider, finally, cases in which a man rapes a woman and then seeks custody—or at least joint custody—of the child that results.

Besides cases in which *adults* argue over who should have the right to act as a child's parent, there are cases in which *a child* argues that his current parents should lose parental rights with respect to him. The child in question might be attempting to "divorce" his current parents and replace them with other parents more to his liking or might be asking to be emancipated, in which case no one will have the right to act as his parent.

The cases described above are of particular interest inasmuch as they challenge the common notion that biological parents "own" their children—that by bringing a child into existence you automatically gain the right to act as its parent. In each case the presumptive rights of biological parents are challenged. The cases described above are also useful in focusing our attention on the conflict between the rights of parents and the interests of their children. It is not uncommon, as we shall see, for the interests of a child to be best served by terminating the rights of one or both biological parents.

Parental Rights in America

In America today, if you bring a child into existence, you have a legal right to act as that child's parent. This right to parent encompasses many subsidiary rights, such as the right to determine the child's name, where it lives, whether or not it is sent to day care, whether it is raised in a religion, and where it is educated. It also includes the right to live with the child. Historically, courts have held the right to parent to be one of our most sacred rights.

This is not to say, however, that the right to parent is an absolute right. To the contrary, the state will terminate a couple's parental rights if it believes that their child has been abandoned, neglected, or abused. A child is assumed to have been abandoned if a parent fails to communicate with or provide support for the child for an extended period, in many states a year or more. Child neglect includes such things as keeping a child in an unsanitary home, failing to feed or educate him, failing to provide special care to a child with a mental condition, and attempting to sell a child on the black market. Child abuse involves not only acts that harm a child, but acts that expose him to a substantial risk of harm as well as inaction that results in harm to him. Generally, corporal punishment does not count as child abuse unless it is excessive.

The law, however, tends to be quirky in its decisions about when to terminate parental rights. It sometimes terminates the rights of parents who are arguably fit. In one case, for example, authorities removed the six children of a couple because the children sometimes went out without proper winter clothing and sometimes were late arriving at school. Also—horrors!—dirty dishes and laundry were sometimes allowed to accumulate in the children's home. The parents of these children were still fighting to get them back six years later. In other cases, individuals who many would say were patently unfit to parent have been allowed to retain their parental rights. One striking example of this is Latrena Pixley, who smothered her six-week-old daughter, put her in the trash, and went out for barbecue with her boyfriend. Despite this crime and various other crimes that followed, the state did not think it appropriate, when she was sent back to jail, to take away her (surviving) children. These cases make it clear that the state has considerable discretion in its decisions regarding termination of parental rights. It can let a child-killer keep her children, and it can remove the children of parents who, though not perfect, are loving and competent.

The poor, by the way, are more likely than the rich to have their parental rights interfered with. For one thing, their poverty makes it harder for them to meet the needs of their children. It also typically exposes them to a stream of welfare workers, any of whom can "blow the whistle" on their perceived shortcomings as parents; and poor people whose parental rights are threatened might not be able to afford a lawyer to defend them.

Custody Disputes in Divorce

As long as the biological parents of a child are married, they share custody of him. They both live with him, and they jointly make parental decisions affecting him. If the parents cannot agree—if, for example, the father wants a child raised as a Catholic and the mother wants it raised as a Mormon—the state expects them to come to a compromise. The state gives couples considerable discretion in how they make decisions and in what decisions they make.

When biological parents divorce, all this changes. The state starts making decisions that previously would have been left to the parents. If, for example, the parents cannot agree on where their child will go to school, a judge might decide the matter for them. The state will also, in most cases, interfere with the rights of parents to be with or live with their child. Thus, the state might give the father access to his children on weekends and let the mother have them during the remainder of the week. In many divorces, each parent fights to retain as many parental rights as possible, and when a parent does relinquish rights, it might be done shrewdly, trading one right for another. It becomes the divorce court judge's job to reapportion parental rights and determine which parent gets which right.

The state used to side with mothers in this reapportionment of rights, the reasoning being that the children fared best when raised by their mothers. Only if a father could show that the mother was unfit—that, for example, she was an alcoholic or promiscuous—did he have a chance of retaining the bulk of his parental rights. This thinking changed in the 1970s. Rather than automatically favoring the mother, states became more willing to let fathers retain parental rights. In particular, they became more willing to allow joint-custody arrangements. They did this partly because, thanks to the triumph of the women's movement, courts stopped assuming that only women were fit to parent—if a woman can be an electrician, then a man can be a stay-at-home "mother." Despite these changes, courts still overwhelmingly favor women in custody disputes.

Psychological parenthood became a key concept in post-divorce custody hearings. A child's psychological parent is whomever the child identifies as the person who takes care of him, plays with him, comforts him, and tucks him in. In the old days the mother was typically the psychological parent of her children; it was, after all, her job to spend her days with the children and take care of their needs. These days, however, it might be the father who is the caregiver for the children while the mother travels the world in conjunction with her job; in this case the children will likely identify him as their psychological parent. Indeed, a child's psychological parent could be neither its father nor mother, but instead, say, its grandmother, who raised the child as both its parents traveled the world in conjunction with their jobs.

Steward-parents—whose primary concern is the well-being of their children—will approve of the growing importance of psychological parenthood in divorce-related custody hearings. We harm children when we tear them from their psychological parents, and for this reason steward-parents will typically argue that in a divorce, a child's psychological parent should be granted a disproportional share of parental rights. At the same time, steward-parents will be deeply disturbed by America's high divorce rate. They will point out that although it is nice that courts take an interest in the well-being of children after a divorce has been granted, it is shameful that these same courts are utterly indifferent to the well-being of children when they decide *whether the divorce should be granted in the first place.* A steward-parent might thus argue that America made a big mistake when, in the 1970s, it implemented no-fault divorce laws and thereby opened the divorce floodgates. I will have more to say on this subject in Chapter 11.

The Parental Rights of Biological Fathers

When it comes to parental rights, biological fathers and mothers are not equal. Almost invariably, biological mothers are assumed to have parental rights with respect to their offspring. The same cannot be said of biological fathers. Suppose, for example, that a man gains biological fatherhood by raping a woman. He will, under current law, have no parental rights at all. Or suppose a married man and woman set out to make a baby. She becomes pregnant but after a few months decides that pregnancy is not to her liking and announces her intention to have an abortion. Under current law, her husband would have a hard time stopping her; but in having the abortion, she will, in effect, be terminating his parental rights.

Biological mothers should have considerable say about what happens to their offspring. A biological mother has, after all, a much bigger investment in her baby than its biological father has. She has to undergo nine months of pregnancy with its associated risks and discomforts in order to make the baby. On the other hand, all that is required of the biological father is a few moments of pleasurable sexual activity. Nevertheless, one can reasonably ask whether we have gone too far in letting biological mothers determine the fates of their offspring.

In order to focus our thinking on this issue, let us distinguish between, on the one hand, cases in which the biological mother is pregnant because she and the biological father had consensual sex and, on the other hand, cases in which they did not—cases, that is, in which the woman is pregnant because the man raped her.

Rapists' Rights?

If a woman is pregnant as the result of rape, almost everyone would agree that the biological father of the fetus—the rapist—should have no rights with respect to it and no say in what becomes of it. The question is, How can we justify this refusal to grant parental rights to a biological parent? In our attempt to answer this question, let us consider three separate cases: the case in which the pregnant woman wants to abort the fetus, the case in which she wants to have and raise the child, and the case in which she wants to have the child but put it up for adoption.

Suppose, to begin with, that a woman who is pregnant as the result of rape declares her intention to abort the fetus, and suppose the rapist sues to prevent the abortion.[1] Most will argue that the suit should be dismissed: the rapist has already profoundly interfered with the woman's life, and it would be unconscionable for the state to grant him the right to go on interfering with her life in the rape's aftermath.

Now suppose the raped woman intends not to abort the fetus, but to carry it to term and raise it. Suppose the rapist, on learning this, declares his intention to assert his parental rights when the child is born. In particular, he wants joint custody of the child. What this will mean in practical terms is that he gets a say in what name the baby is given and where it lives. He also wants visitation privileges (which in this case presumably will mean having the child visit him in prison). I am unaware of any case in which a rapist has asserted his parental rights in this manner—indeed, most rapists are anxious to *deny* that they are a rape-child's biological father; to assert fatherhood is, after all, to admit to having raped the child's mother—but suppose one did? How should we react? If we declare that, despite his biological parenthood, he has no parental rights, how can we justify ourselves?

The obvious way, once again, is to invoke the principle that the state should not grant criminals the right to go on interfering with their victims' lives after the crime has been committed. The suggestion that the raped woman should have to consult with the rapist in picking out a name for the child or should have to take the child to visit his "daddy" in prison seems outrageous.

Suppose, finally, that the raped woman plans to have the baby and put it up for adoption, and suppose that the rapist, on hearing this, declares that the baby is as much his as hers and that she therefore has no right to put it up for adoption. Instead—he argues—it should be turned over to him at birth. In this case we cannot say, as we did in the previous two cases, that criminals should have no right to go on interfering with their victims' lives in the aftermath of a crime. Once the raped woman puts the baby up for adoption, it will be out of her life, so the rapist's adoption of the child can hardly count as interference with her life. If we want to deny the rapist the right to "adopt" the child, we will have to invoke new grounds for our denial.

Someone might suggest at this point that the rapist should not be allowed to "adopt" the child because he will be in no position to act as parent. He will, after all, be in prison when the child is born and might remain there in the first decade of the child's life. Prisoners are in no position to raise children. To see the problem with this suggestion, suppose a rapist is sentenced by a lenient judge in a state with lenient rape laws and thereby avoids going to prison. Will we, in such cases, be willing to permit the rapist to "adopt" the child? I think not.

Someone might now suggest that rapists, even if they manage to avoid prison (or can make arrangements for care of a child while they are in prison), should be denied parental rights for the simple reason that they are convicted felons. In other words, the state shouldn't let just anyone act as parent, and among those it should exclude from parenthood are convicted felons. This suggestion is promising. (Indeed, it will delight those who advocate that we license parents.) The problem is that most people, although they will be unwilling to let convicted rapists have the children that result from their rape, are perfectly willing to let other felons—for example, bank robbers—retain their parental rights. Indeed, they are even willing to let rapists retain their parental rights with respect to children that they "legitimately" fathered.

What is it that makes us unwilling to grant parental rights to the "adoptive" rapist? I think it is the fact that in doing so, we allow him to "profit" from his crime: if we let the rapist become parent to the rape-child, he will have profited. Notice that the same cannot be said if we let bank robbers retain their parental rights, or if we let rapists retain any parental rights they might have had before they committed rape. This, I think, is what lies at the heart of our reluctance to turn the child begot by rape over to the rapist in those cases in which the mother wants to give birth to the child and then put it up for adoption.

Now let us turn our attention to cases involving not rape, but consensual sex. Let us first assume that the man and woman having the sex are married.

Husbands' Rights

If a husband impregnates his wife and she chooses to have the baby, it is clear that when the baby is born, the husband will have the full complement of parental rights. The wife cannot unilaterally put the child up for adoption. Important parental decisions regarding the baby—what to name it, whether to get it circumcised, where it will live—must be made by the husband and wife together. And if the wife doesn't like her husband having this degree of control over the child, she has little choice but to divorce him and try to gain sole custody of it.

Now consider those cases in which a husband impregnates his wife and shortly thereafter she declares her intention to get an abortion. Should the husband be able to block the abortion? Most would say he shouldn't. The woman has, after all, a right *not* to reproduce. If she wants an abortion, so be it.

Before giving in to this line of reasoning, we would do well to consider certain other cases involving abortion. Suppose, to begin with, that after a husband impregnates his wife, he declares that he has changed his mind and no longer wants offspring. In saying this, he isn't simply declaring that he doesn't want to play the role of father;

if this were his complaint, the issue could be resolved with a divorce. What he is declaring is that he doesn't want to reproduce—that he doesn't want to bring a child into the world. He is, in other words, exercising *his* right *not* to reproduce. If a woman can exercise her right not to reproduce and abort without the husband's permission, shouldn't he likewise be able to exercise his right not to reproduce and force her to abort?

Alternatively, suppose doctors tell a woman that although she will never be able to become pregnant, she can reproduce by means of in vitro fertilization. Eggs will be removed from her, fertilized with her husband's sperm, and then implanted into the womb of another woman—the womb provider. Suppose the woman finds a willing womb provider and that she is successfully "impregnated."

So far, so good. But suppose that after a few months, the womb provider gets an abortion without the permission of the egg donor. How we respond to this apparent breach of the contract between the egg donor and the womb provider will depend on the circumstances of the abortion. Suppose, to begin with, that she broke the contract because it became clear that continuing the pregnancy would almost certainly result in her death. In this case, the breach of contract can be justified on force majeure grounds and is utterly forgivable. Suppose, on the other hand, the womb provider has an abortion for whimsical reasons—because, say, it dawned on her that if she continued the pregnancy, she would not be able to play (recreational) softball during the coming summer. In this case it is unlikely that the egg donor will be forgiving or that she will respond to the abortion by calmly invoking the feminist maxim that it is the womb provider's body and that she should be able to do what she wants with it. Instead she will complain loud and long. The womb provider knowingly entered into the contract, and in doing so she relinquished the right to control her womb (exceptional circumstances aside). This frivolous breach of the contract between them is unconscionable.

If the egg donor's complaints seem justified, we should realize that they are pretty much the same complaints as a husband would raise if, after voluntarily becoming pregnant by him, his wife had an abortion for whimsical reasons and without his permission. Perhaps, then, the state would be justified, in both the case of the womb provider and the case of the voluntarily pregnant wife, in forcing the pregnancies to continue.

Let us consider one last case. Suppose a wife voluntarily becomes pregnant by her husband *and does so in the knowledge that this is almost certainly her husband's last chance at reproduction.* He has, let us suppose, a medical condition that makes it extraordinarily difficult for him to impregnate anyone, a condition that will worsen in coming months and years. Indeed, for him to have gotten his wife pregnant at all was a medical miracle. Imagine the emotional harm that will be done to this man if his wife has an abortion for reasons as whimsical as those of the above-described womb provider. In this case, the wife's decision to abort will be as big a deal, emotionally and morally speaking, as the womb provider's whimsical decision to abort.

What should the state do, then, when a womb provider or a wife pregnant with her husband's last-chance offspring decides to abort for whimsical reasons? I would like to suggest that it is within the proper bounds of government to block the abortion.

Think again about the nature of reproductive rights. As we saw back in Chapter 2, the right to reproduce is unusual inasmuch as it is a cooperative right. You cannot exercise this right all by yourself, as you can exercise, say, your right to bear arms. To the contrary, it is a right that must be coexercised with someone else. If you are a woman, you need a man who is willing to part with his sperm before you can reproduce; and if you are a man, you need a woman who is willing to have one of her eggs fertilized and a woman who is willing to shelter the developing fetus within her womb. (In the old days the egg donor and the womb provider were invariably the same, but thanks to technological breakthroughs they no longer have to be.) Another thing to keep in mind is that if a woman is to reproduce, she needs a man's cooperation for only a few minutes; but if a man is to reproduce, he needs a woman's cooperation for nine months, and during those months the woman's cooperation is unilaterally retractable. Although it takes two people to get pregnant, it takes only one to have an abortion.

Now think about rights in general. Rights are not "inalienable." To the contrary, they can be relinquished or transferred. Go to work for the CIA or the top-secret research department of a corporation and you relinquish (part of) your freedom of speech. Join the army and you relinquish (a large part of) your right to determine how you will spend your days. Sell your car and you transfer your ownership rights to someone else, usually in return for their transferring ownership rights to a certain amount of money to you. Throw away your old, broken television set, and you relinquish your ownership right to it. Indeed, even your right to life can be relinquished—if, at any rate, the advocates of euthanasia are correct. In asking to die, a terminally ill patient is relinquishing his right to life.

Some might complain that by allowing rights to be transferred or relinquished, we lessen their value. To understand the mistake in this thinking, consider what an inalienable right—one you could never transfer or relinquish—would be like. Suppose your right of car ownership were an inalienable right, meaning that you could never sell or junk the car. It is clear that as the years went by, this "right" would become increasingly burdensome—indeed, it would come to resemble a duty rather than a right. Examples like this make it clear that rights that can be transferred or relinquished are intrinsically more valuable than rights that can't.

Thus, even if we agree that a woman has a right to control what happens in her womb, we are probably doing her a favor if we allow her to transfer or relinquish this right. A womb provider should be allowed to contract away some of her womb rights, as should a wife. By allowing a woman to transfer or relinquish her "womb rights," we arguably increase the value of these rights and simultaneously increase her freedom. When a woman contracts away her womb rights, though, the state should enforce the contract, the way it enforces any number of other contracts. This might mean, in some cases, forcing pregnant women to continue their pregnancies.

Boyfriends' Rights

Let us now consider cases in which a man has had consensual sex with a woman who isn't his wife and has thereby impregnated her. What parental rights, if any, should this man have with respect to the child? Some will suggest that this case should be treated the same as if the man and woman were married—that the parental rights of a boyfriend should be the same as the parental rights of a husband. I will argue to the contrary.

At present in America we do confer parental rights on boy-friends. It is a consequence of our view that biological parenthood is (usually) sacred, even in cases in which a male drifts off shortly after the procreative act and as a consequence doesn't even realize that he is a father. In conferring these rights, however, we create hardship for others. Consider, by way of illustration, the story of Baby Jessica. (Readers should be careful not to confuse this Baby Jessica, whose real name was Jessica DeBoer, with a second Baby Jessica—Jessica McClure—who gained fame by falling down a well in 1987.) Cara Clausen gave birth to Baby Jessica in 1991. Clausen and the man she identified as Baby Jessica's father signed the necessary releases to put the child up for adoption. Jan and Roberta DeBoer adopted Jessica, but shortly thereafter Clausen informed them not only that she wanted her baby back, but that Dan Schmidt, a different man from the one she originally identified, was Baby Jessica's father. This claim, if true, meant that Jessica's biological father had never signed away his parental rights, and this in turn meant that the DeBoer's adoption of Jessica was in legal limbo. In the end, the courts decided that Cara Clausen and Dan Schmidt (who were now married) should get the child. The Schmidts renamed the two-year-old child "Anna" and moved her hundreds of miles away from her former home. Cameras were there to capture Baby Jessica's tears as she was taken from one set of parents and given to the other.

When we grant parental rights to boyfriends, we give them significant power over their girlfriends and offspring—power they can abuse. If, after impregnating his girlfriend, a man takes off to parts unknown, the girlfriend's life and that of her child are in limbo until the boyfriend's intentions with respect to the child are known. Does he wish to exercise his parental rights? Until we find out, the mother won't be able to put the child up for adoption. This delay gives the mother and baby time to grow attached to each other, and what could have been a relatively easy transfer of the baby from its biological mother to adoptive parents might turn into a transfer that is traumatic for both the biological mother and the baby.

In the aftermath of the Baby Jessica story and other contested adoptions, many states set up paternity registries to prevent similar episodes. A boyfriend could register as the father of a child. If a boyfriend failed to register, his parental rights with respect to a child could be terminated without his knowledge. In particular, the child could be given up for adoption without his consent.[2]

The move to paternity registries is well intended but arguably redundant. We already have, after all, a way for men to register their desire to retain their parental rights with respect to any child they may father: they can marry the mother of the child. Why not, one might ask, dispense with paternity registries and instead simply declare that if a man impregnates a woman who is not his wife, he will have no parental rights with respect to the child unless he marries her? Under this plan, a mere boyfriend (as opposed to a husband) will have no say in the baby's name, whether it is baptized, where it will live, and whether it will be put up for adoption. He will not even have the right to visit the child. If this lack of parental rights is distressful to him, the solution is at hand: he need only marry the child's mother, preferably before impregnating her.

If the suggestion that mere boyfriends should have no parental rights seems outlandish, impractical, or old-fashioned, it is because we (usually) hold biological parenthood to be something sacred. As a result, we are willing to confer parental rights even on someone who has clearly demonstrated that he neither seeks nor values these rights. (What else can be said of a man who, after the sexual act is completed, does not even stick around long enough to find out whether it resulted in pregnancy?) But why should an individual who has indicated an unwillingness to shoulder the responsibilities of fatherhood be granted the rights of fatherhood? Indeed, why should we feel compelled to thrust these rights upon him?

Before ending our discussion of boyfriends' rights, let us consider two last questions. First, what should happen if a mother refuses to marry her child's biological father? In doing so she will, if we deny parental rights to mere boyfriends, be depriving him of his parental rights. Should women have this much power? The answer to this question is that men can easily avoid giving women this power over their lives: they can either avoid having sex with women they aren't married to or take precautionary measures when having sex with them. A second question is whether the boyfriend should automatically be given custody of the child if the mother doesn't wish to keep it. In this case, we aren't interfering with the life of the mother by allowing the father to gain parental rights. Nor are we allowing a father maliciously or thoughtlessly to delay the adoption of his child. Someone might argue, in other words, that no one is harmed if we give the boyfriend a "right of first refusal" in the event that the baby is put up for adoption.

This granting of paternal rights to boyfriends is less objectionable than the ones described above. At the same time, if we started licensing parents (see Chapter 7), it is unlikely that boyfriends—or their girlfriends, for that matter—would be granted parental rights. If effective parenting requires two people, and if it requires that those two people remain on the job as parents for two decades, we will want only married couples to act as parents, and hence will issue parent's licenses only to them. The question of boyfriends' parental rights is one of many troubling questions that will vanish if, instead of assuming that all biological parents have a right to try to raise the child they brought into existence, we allow only licensed parents to gain parental rights.

Wrongly Gained Rights

Sometimes people gain parental rights improperly. This can happen when an adoption takes place without the biological parents having given up their parental rights, when children are accidentally switched at birth, when children are put up for adoption in the mistaken belief that they have been orphaned, and when adults gain parental rights by kidnapping a child. Let us take a closer look at such cases.

Adoptions usually do not involve disputes over parental rights. It is quite clear, at any given moment, who has the right to parent a child. At first it is his biological parents, his foster parents, or some state agency; then, when the adoption is finalized, it is his adoptive parents. The adoptive parents, in asking to adopt, are not arguing that the child's biological mother has no right to parent the child; instead, they are humbly requesting that her fully acknowledged right to parent the child be transferred to them.

Sometimes the adoption process goes awry. Above I described the case of Baby Jessica. A less publicized adoption-reversal occurred in Connecticut. In June of 1991, Gina Pellegrino went to a hospital, learned that she was pregnant, gave birth to a baby, and walked out of the hospital without making clear her intentions with respect to the baby. In October of that year, the state, which assumed that the Pellegrino baby had been abandoned, placed it with adoptive parents. Shortly thereafter, Ms. Pellegrino asserted her parental rights. Even though Ms. Pellegrino had all the appearances of a person who did not value parental rights, and even though some would question her fitness to parent, a judge returned her baby.

In another case that made national headlines in the early 1990s, Daniela Janikova became pregnant (out of wedlock) by Otakar Kirchner. Late in the pregnancy Ms. Janikova thought Mr. Kirchner had run off with another woman, when in fact he had gone to Czechoslovakia to care for his grandmother. Ms. Janikova gave birth to Baby Richard and gave the child up for adoption, refusing all the while to name the baby's father. When Mr. Kirchner returned to America and located Ms. Janikova, she told him that the baby had died. She later revealed the truth to him. They got married and fought to get their baby back. At first the courts held the adoption to be legal. The biological father had not, after all, shown any interest in the child in the days after its birth. In the end, though, the courts reversed the adoption and returned Baby Richard to the Kirchners. Their reasoning was that the father would have asserted his parental rights if he had not been deceived into thinking that Baby Richard was dead. Because of the time it took to settle the custody issue, Baby Richard was nearly four years old when he was returned to his biological parents.

One can also imagine cases in which adoptions of children older than this are contested. Suppose the state, acting in the belief that a ten-year-old child's parents are dead, grants custody of the child to new parents. Suppose that five years later, it turns out that the parents were not dead but had instead been held captive by terrorists. When these parents return home, they will likely want their now-fifteen-year-old child back. If the adoptive parents balk, what should the state do? (I state this question hypothetically because I am unaware of any actual cases in which this sort of thing has happened.)

The cases described above all involve "defective" adoptions, but this isn't the only way people can improperly gain parental rights. In 1978, for example, an apparent hospital error resulted in Kimberly Mays and Arlena Twigg being switched at birth. When Arlena Twigg died years later, the Twiggs discovered (as a result of tissue tests) that Arlena was not their biological child. The Twiggs investigated and ultimately concluded that the child being raised by Robert Mays (his wife, Barbara Mays, had died in 1981) was in fact their biological child. They fought to get her back or at least be allowed to communicate with her, but Kimberly Mays wanted nothing to do with them. In 1993 a Florida court sided with her and allowed her to stay with her psychological parent, Robert Mays.

In the past it was difficult to prove that babies had been switched at birth. Even if a child didn't look like its parents, it could still be their biological offspring, given the semirandom nature of genetics. Advances in DNA testing, however, have changed all this. In coming years America might witness a miniboom in the detection of switched births, and with these discoveries will come disputes regarding parental rights.

Thus, consider the plight of Paula Johnson, who tried, by means of a DNA test, to show that her ex-boyfriend was the father of her three-year-old child. The test revealed that he wasn't the father—and that she wasn't the mother! There had apparently been a mixup at the hospital, and she had been given the wrong baby. She tracked down her biological baby. She and this baby's "parents"[3] agreed not to correct the mixup, but to keep their "current" children.

Medical advances have also made it possible for babies to be switched *before* birth. In the cases in question, women undergoing in vitro fertilization are implanted with the wrong eggs. An egg mixup resulted in Donna Fasano being implanted with one egg fertilized by her husband and a second egg that belonged to a black couple. She gave birth to two boys, one white and one black. The other couple demanded custody of the black baby, and the Fasanos reluctantly turned him over.

Sometimes parental rights disputes arise because someone knowingly violates the parental rights of someone else. Thus in the late 1970s the military dictators of Argentina engaged in a "dirty war" against Argentine citizens who were suspected of leftist tendencies. The police routinely rounded up, questioned, and killed such citizens, who subsequently became known as the *desaparecidos* (the "disappeared"). Sometimes pregnant women were among those rounded up, and in more than 140 such cases they were allowed to give birth before being killed. There were also at least sixty infants who were abducted along with their parents and not subsequently returned to relatives. Some of these kidnapped children were adopted by police and military officers—sometimes, it is suspected, by the same officers who killed the children's parents—and other kidnapped children were given to adoptive parents who were unaware of their history.

After the dirty war ended the kidnappings came to light, and relatives of the adopted children demanded that these fraudulent adoptions be reversed. Genetic tests were used to match adopted children with relatives. By 1993, twenty-five of the adoptions had been reversed, and children were turned over to blood relatives. In another thirteen cases, blood relatives consented to allow the children to stay with their adoptive families.

In another case here in America, John E. Robinson Sr. is accused of killing Lisa Stasi and then arranging for his brother and sister-in-law to adopt Lisa's infant daughter Tiffany. The adoptive couple was apparently unaware of the illegal nature of the adoption. When the alleged kidnapping of Tiffany came to light in 2000, the girl was fifteen years old. Her biological father, Carl Stasi, has sought to communicate with his daughter but did not seek custody of her.

In yet another case, children were "kidnapped" *before* being born. Dr. Ricardo Asch is alleged to have "played God" with the fertilized embryos entrusted to him by patients undergoing in vitro fertilization. He is accused of taking eggs from one couple (without their knowledge or consent) and implanting them in another. A blizzard of lawsuits resulted.

When people improperly gain parental rights with respect to a child, it is tempting to say that the biological parents should get their child back—tempting until we think about the situation from the child's point of view. Suppose that when you were nine years old, someone came to your front door and announced that because of a mixup at your birth, you were not the child of your "current" parents but of two strangers in a distant city. (Suppose, in other words, that you experienced Kimberly Mays's fate.) It is true that we would be righting a wrong if we returned you to your biological parents. But your current parents—the people who have cared for you for the last nine years—even though they are not your *biological* parents and even though they became your parents as the result of a mixup, are your *psychological* parents. Your original, biological parents, on the other hand, are perfect strangers. To make you leave your current parents will therefore cause you considerable psychological harm.

With this in mind, we might be tempted to reverse ourselves and conclude that when people improperly gain parental rights, we should settle any rights disputes that arise by considering the interests of the child. This, typically, will entail favoring the child's current parents over its biological parents. Again, this is arguably an overly simplistic answer to a complex question. Let us, therefore, examine the issue in greater detail.

What to Do?

In any dispute involving wrongly gained parental rights, there will be three parties: the people (usually the child's biological parents) whose parental rights were wrongly terminated, the people who wrongly gained parental rights over the child, and the child itself. Each of these parties has interests and will be affected, perhaps profoundly, by any resolution to the dispute over parental rights.

Let us consider first those cases in which the parents who wrongly gained parental rights did so innocently. This was true of the DeBoers (who did not realize that their adoption of Baby Jessica was defective), the Mayses (who had nothing to do with the mixup at the hospital), and those Argentinians who didn't realize that the children they were adopting had been kidnapped. (It was not true, however, of the Argentinian authorities who *did* know the history of the children they were adopting. We will consider their case in a moment.)

Suppose, then, that a couple gained their parental rights innocently and that the child's biological parents demand their baby back. One key factor in settling such disputes is the amount of time that has passed since the child was removed from his biological parents. If it has been a few months, of course the child should be returned, but if it has been longer than that, we must consider the psychological state of the child. If the child not only remembers his biological parents but wants to be reunited with them (as might be the case if the child's parents had been mistakenly declared dead when he was ten and rescued from terrorists when he was fifteen), it seems clear that he should be reunited with them. The rights of the biological parents and the interests of the child in this case clearly outweigh the interests of the current parents. If, on the other hand, the child has no memory of his biological parents and regards his current parents as his real parents (as was the case with Kimberly Mays), then a strong case can be made for leaving the child with his current parents. It is true that this violates the rights of the biological parents—they have lost their child through no fault of their own—but these rights must be weighed against the well-being of their child. Indeed, it is likely that the biological parents, if they were caring, sensitive people, would not insist on their parental rights. For the sake of "their" child, they would sacrifice these rights.

Now let us turn our attention to cases in which a couple knows that it wrongly gained parental rights. For the sake of concreteness, suppose a couple sneaks into a hospital and kidnaps a newborn baby.

Suppose it is ten years before they are caught, at which time the child's biological parents demand its return. In this case, many will argue that the child should be reunited with its biological parents, even though it wants to stay with its current parents and will be harmed by the change in parents. In justifying this forced reunification, we might find ourselves echoing the rationale given for refusing to grant parental rights to rapists: wrongdoers shouldn't be allowed to profit from their wrongdoing. By taking the child away from the kidnappers, we are sending a message to kidnappers everywhere that even if they can avoid detection for years, they will be deprived of "their" child when they are caught. In this case, we are sacrificing the interests of the kidnapped child in order to prevent future kidnappings and the suffering they would cause.[4]

In the above discussions we have ignored a question that some might think significant in cases of wrongly gained parental rights: who would do a better job of parenting, the biological parents or the current parents? This question was raised by media commentators in the case of Baby Jessica. The baby's then-current parents, the DeBoers, were affluent professionals who had gone to considerable lengths to become adoptive parents. By way of contrast, Baby Jessica's biological mother was unwed at the time of Jessica's birth, and her biological father was a truck driver who was failing to make his child support payments on behalf of two children by a previous marriage. He had abandoned one of these children and never seen the other. It was clear to many that the DeBoers would make better parents for Baby Jessica—that if the child had a say in it, she would favor the DeBoers over the Schmidts.[5]

In cases involving disputed adoptions, courts are extremely reluctant to concern themselves with the best interests of the child in question. They don't care who would do the best job of parenting. They instead focus on the narrow legal issues involved. Their job is to determine who has the legal right to parent (maybe well, maybe poorly) a child.[6] In other words, courts treat the contested "ownership" of a child much the same way as they treat, say, the contested ownership of a car. The question in such cases is not, Who will take better care of this car? Instead it is, Who, given the evidence at hand and given currently existing laws, should be declared the legal owner of this car? Of course, children, unlike cars, have interests and rights themselves. They also have lives that can be damaged, if not ruined, by being turned over to inadequate parents.

It is clear that someone operating on the stewardship model of parenting *will* be concerned with the fitness of the people seeking parental rights with respect to a child. In particular, if one of the parties to a dispute looks unlicensable—as Cara Clausen and Dan Schmidt arguably did—they will not be allowed to gain custody of the child. (Indeed, if parents were licensed, Clausen and Schmidt probably would have been forced to put Baby Jessica up for adoption.) In many cases, though, the rival parties seeking parental rights will all be licensable, meaning that the dispute will have to be settled on the basis of the narrow legal issues involved.

Techno-Babies

When adoptions were contested in the past, there were usually two contesting parties: the child's biological parents and the child's adoptive parents. Medical breakthroughs have changed all this.

At one time, every child had exactly two biological parents. In vitro fertilization makes it possible for a child to have *three* "biological" parents, a biological father, a genetic mother from whose eggs it developed, and a birth mother from whose womb it emerged. The law now has to distinguish between these two biological mothers and determine which should have parental rights with respect to the child. Should it be the child's genetic mother, who initiated the reproductive act, with the birth mother merely serving as an incubator in which the egg grew? Should it be the birth mother, who, during her pregnancy, invested far more of herself into the child than the genetic mother did? Or should both mothers share custody of the child?

In early 2001 this picture became even more confusing when scientists announced the creation of children who had two *genetic* mothers. In making these children, doctors removed an egg from a woman who was infertile because of a cytoplasmic defect in her eggs. They also removed an egg from a second woman, removed the cytoplasm from her egg, and inserted it into the infertile woman's egg along with the sperm of her mate. When this "cytoplasm transplant" was made, though, some of the second woman's mitochondria (which normally float around in the cytoplasm) were inadvertently transferred into the infertile woman's egg. This mitochondria has its own DNA, different from the DNA found in the nucleus of the infertile woman's egg. The baby that resulted thereby came to have genetic material from two different women and therefore can be said to have two genetic mothers. (The babies produced in this fashion, by the way, will pass on their mixed genetic makeup to their offspring, making this arguably the first human germline genetic modification in medical history.)

Because of advances in medicine, disputes concerning parental rights can be dauntingly complex. Suppose, for example, an infertile husband and wife wish to bring into existence a child for them to adopt. Suppose they find a man willing to act as sperm donor, a woman willing to act as egg donor, and another woman willing to act as womb provider. In this case there would be five different adults—two men and three women—who had a hand in the making of the baby and who could conceivably assert parental rights with respect to it once it was born. Now suppose that in the case just described, the egg donor's egg turns out to be defective and that, rather than getting a new egg, doctors "fix" the egg with cytoplasm transplanted from the egg of yet another woman. (Why not just use the egg of the cytoplasm donor? Because—let us assume—her genetic makeup is less desirable than that of the egg donor.) Suppose that during the cytoplasm transplant, some of the cytoplasm donor's mitochondrial DNA is inadvertently transferred. This would raise the number of adults who had a hand in making the baby to six: the two adoptive parents, the womb provider, and three "genetic parents"—the sperm donor, the egg donor (who contributed nuclear DNA), and the cytoplasm donor (who contributed mitochondrial DNA). This crowd of "parents," we should realize, will grow larger still if scientists start blending the *nuclear* DNA of two or more women or of two or more men—in order, perhaps, to correct a genetic defect or to implant a desirable trait.

America has already gotten a taste of the sort of custody fight that can break out when more than two parents have a hand in the making of a child. One of the earliest and most famous cases involved Mary Beth Whitehead. Ms. Whitehead signed a contract with William Stern in which she agreed to be artificially inseminated by Mr. Stern and to turn over to Stern and his wife for adoption any child that might be produced. Ms. Whitehead had Baby M (as the media called it), turned it over to the Sterns, but later took it back. The Sterns sued to regain custody of the child. Authorities seized the baby, and a lower court allowed the Sterns to adopt it. The case finally made it to the New Jersey Supreme Court, which decided that the surrogacy contract between Whitehead and Stern was invalid and unenforceable. Nevertheless, because a strong case could be made that the child's best interests were served by remaining with the Sterns, the Court awarded custody of the child to the Sterns.[7]

Above I suggested that when more than two adults are involved in the creation of a child, the parties in question might fight to gain parental rights with respect to the child. The opposite can also happen: adults might fight to avoid parental responsibilities with respect to a child. Consider, for example, the case of Jaycee Buzzanca. Five people were involved in her creation: Luanne and John Buzzanca (who wanted a baby but could not conceive), Pamela Snell (who was willing to "rent" her womb to the Buzzancas), one anonymous sperm donor, and one anonymous egg donor. A month before Jaycee was born, John Buzzanca filed for divorce. When Luanne sought child support payments from him, he argued that, according to the legal definition of "fatherhood," he wasn't the baby's father. The court not only agreed with him, but also held that as far as the law was concerned, Luanne wasn't the baby's mother—and that Pamela Snell wasn't either. Jaycee thereby became, for a time, the world's first techno-orphan. An appeals court later declared Luanne and John to be Jaycee's legal parents.

In other cases, the people who initiate a contract pregnancy change their mind during the pregnancy—because they don't like the sex of the child the surrogate mother is carrying or because they don't want twins—and disavow the contract in question. What becomes of a child in these circumstances? What right, if any, does the surrogate mother have to sue the adoptive parents for damages? These are interesting questions that will, most likely, be answered on a case-by-case basis in coming years.

We can argue about whether birth mothers should or shouldn't be able to contract away their parental rights. (I suggested earlier that they should.) One thing that is clear, though, is that everyone would benefit from a clarification of the legal issues involved in contract pregnancies. Rather than waiting until techno-babies come into existence and then letting the various parties fight over custody of them, the state should make it clear exactly what parental rights are and aren't transferable by contract. By doing so, the state will prevent any number of custody disputes and their accompanying heartbreak.

Divorcing One's Parents

America has started experimenting with allowing children to divorce their parents. Consider the case of Gregory Kingsley. His parents separated in 1983, when Gregory was three years old. His father had custody of him until 1989, when he was accused of neglect and physical abuse of the child. At that point Gregory was turned over to his mother, who ignored him and subsequently decided to put him up for adoption. In the early 1990s a children's rights attorney who had become Gregory's foster parent tried to adopt him. Gregory's mother, however, refused to give up her parental rights, even though she had spent only a few months with him in the previous eight years and had gone for as long as two years without any attempt to communicate with him. For reasons that are entirely understandable, Gregory favored his foster parents over his natural parents and brought a legal action in his own right—possibly the first time a child had done such a thing. In 1992 a Florida judge granted Gregory a "divorce" from his parents.

Kimberly Mays—the child switched at birth—is also sometimes

described as a child who divorced her parents, but her case is significantly different from that of Kingsley. Mays was fighting to prevent someone (her biological parents) from gaining parental rights with respect to her. She had no problem with those who possessed these rights (her "current" parents) retaining them. Kingsley, on the other hand, was fighting to have parental rights with respect to him taken away from his biological mother and transferred to other adults.

By allowing Kingsley to divorce his parents, the state was clearly looking out for his best interests. Indeed, the only person who would object to the outcome of the Kingsley case would be someone who regards biological parenthood as somehow sacred and is indifferent to the interests of children. Someone favoring the stewardship model of parenting, on the other hand, will not be troubled by the Kingsley case. What happened is that a child initiated a process—termination of parental rights—that arguably should have been initiated long before by state authorities.

Having said this, I should add that steward-parents will not advocate that the state *encourage* children to divorce their parents. Such divorces should be fairly hard to get and be granted only in exceptional cases. Otherwise, the possibility of obtaining them would undermine the role of steward-parents. After all, if it were relatively easy for a child to divorce his parents, many children would be tempted to use the threat of divorce to get what they want. If parents were, in the eyes of a child, too strict or not generous enough at Christmas, he could threaten a divorce. The balance of power would clearly be tipped in favor of children, and this would likely have unfortunate consequences, since children would tend to abuse the power.

Indeed, consider again the case of Kimberly Mays. A year after successfully fighting against a reunification with her biological parents— indeed, after declaring that she wanted nothing to do with them—she ran away to live with these same parents. It is not unreasonable to think that this move was part of a teenage power struggle. By playing off the rival sets of parents against each other, she could win concessions that would otherwise be unavailable. (Much the same thing happens when parents divorce. Their children quickly realize that they can gain power by playing off the parents against each other.)

There is another way in which children can "divorce" their parents. In many states it is possible for children to petition to gain emancipation. In cases of emancipation, parental rights are not *transferred*, as they were in the case of Gregory Kingsley and as they might have been in the case of Kimberly Mays, but instead are *terminated*. After a child is emancipated, no adult has parental rights with respect to him—he is, in short, parentless. As a result the child no longer has to live with or answer to the parents, and the parents no longer have to provide for the child.

Emancipation does not raise the range of issues raised by the Kingsley case. For one thing, most courts will emancipate a child only if it is demonstrably in the child's best interests to be emancipated. For another thing, it usually requires the consent of his parents before the child will be emancipated. Thus, emancipation does not threaten parental rights and does not undermine parental stewardship to the same degree as a true divorce of one's parents does.

This concludes our discussion of who should be allowed to act as parent. As we have seen, it is important that children, rather than being "liberated" or raised by the state, are raised by parents, usually a married man and woman. We have also seen that the view that biological parents should automatically be given a chance to raise the children they bring into the world, although popular, is hardly incontrovertible. And we have seen the extent to which technological breakthroughs have challenged the concept of parenthood and thereby given rise to custody disputes that in the past would have been beyond imagining. Let us now assume that we have determined who should be allowed to parent a given child and turn our attention to the extent to which the government should regulate the behavior of these parents.

PART THREE

HOW SHOULD THE GOVERNMENT REGULATE PARENTAL BEHAVIOR?

CHAPTER 10

REGULATING PARENTAL BEHAVIOR

I will divide my discussion of governmental regulation of parental behavior into two parts. In this chapter I will consider the ways the government can regulate the parent/child relationship. In my discussion I will focus my attention on three specific debates that have arisen with respect to governmental interference with this relationship, one concerning medical care, one concerning education, and one concerning corporal punishment. In the next chapter I will turn my attention to governmental regulation of the relationship not between parents and their children, but between the parents themselves. More precisely, I will consider the circumstances under which parents should be allowed to divorce.

The Range of Governmental Regulations

The positions one can take with respect to governmental regulation of parental behavior can be placed on a continuum. At one endpoint of this continuum we find the laissez-faire view: the government should let parents do what they want with their children. Although this position will seem extreme to modern readers, it was the position that our ancestors took for granted. Thus in 1761, Englishwoman Anne Martin was sentenced to two years in prison for poking out the eyes of children. She did it so they would be more effective props when they went out begging. The thing to realize is that the courts were angry at Anne Martin because the children she mutilated *were not her own children.* Had they been her children, she would have been within her rights as a parent to poke their eyes out and no crime would have been committed. At the same time as some English children were having their eyes poked out, others were forced to climb up the insides of chimneys and clean them with a brush—dirty and dangerous work, to say the least. And when these "climbing boys" weren't climbing, they were likely living, with the masters to whom they were apprenticed, in filth. They were starved, since a well-fed climbing boy would have a hard time fitting into a chimney. If they complained about their working and living conditions or refused to work, they were beaten. When passers-by chastised one master sweeper for physically abusing his climbing boy, the master made a comment that wonderfully reveals the thinking of the time: he told them that the boy was his own child, and he could do with him as he pleased.

John Stuart Mill, writing in 1859, describes the consensus view on parent/child relations in the following terms: "One would almost think that a man's children were supposed to be literally, and not metaphorically, a part of himself, so jealous is opinion of the smallest interference of law with his absolute and exclusive control over them; more jealous than of almost any interference with his own freedom of action: so much less do the generality of mankind value liberty than power." (Mill, by the way, did not agree with this view; to the contrary, he was an early advocate of the stewardship model of parenting.)

At the other endpoint of the regulation continuum we find the view that the government should micromanage parents, giving them detailed guidelines on how to raise children and punishing them when they fail to adhere to these guidelines. A totalitarian dictator might view micromanagement as a cost-effective alternative to the state-run nurseries we considered back in Chapter 6. He might let children stay with their parents, but tell the parents how the children should be raised, the goal being to turn them into compliant citizens. It would be a mistake, though, to think that only a totalitarian dictator would advocate micromanagement. A more enlightened advocate of governmental control of parental behavior might argue that the best way for the government to raise the overall quality of parenting in America is to establish standards of parenting and require all parents to adhere to these standards. Good parents shouldn't object to the government setting standards, since they are probably already adhering to these, if not even higher standards of parenting. And if inferior parents object to standards, too bad for them: their children deserve a certain level of parenting.

Where people's views fall on the above continuum depends in large part on how much they fear big government and on which model of parenting they favor, the ownership model or the stewardship model. Someone who favors the ownership model of parenting and fears governmental abuse of power will almost certainly be at the laissez-faire end of the regulation continuum. Someone, on the other hand, who favors the stewardship model of parenting and thinks the government trustworthy and competent might advocate extensive governmental regulation of parental behavior.

For most people, though, the issue is rather more complicated than this. To begin with, relatively few people are advocates of pure steward-parenthood or pure owner-parenthood. Instead they favor a "hybrid" model of parenting, with lots of stewardship but some element of ownership mixed in. Furthermore, most people are neither wholly trusting nor utterly fearful of government, but think government can be trusted—to a point. As a result, most people will reject the two endpoints of the regulation continuum and will instead favor positions somewhere in the middle.

In rejecting the laissez-faire position, they might remind us that history shows what happens when the government lets parents do whatever they want with their children. We saw two examples of this above—the Anne Martin case and the plight of climbing boys—but this is only the beginning. Until the last few centuries, virtually all children were abused children. Indeed, at one time it would have been a mistake to say that children were treated like animals, since they were treated *worse than* animals: in America before the 1870s, there were laws against cruelty to animals but not against cruelty to children.

In rejecting governmental micromanagement of parental behavior, people will remind us that most parents (and certainly most steward-parents) have a much better idea of the needs of their children, how to best satisfy these needs, how to get their children to cooperate, and so forth, than any government bureaucrat will—indeed, than any blue-ribbon panel of government experts will. In much the same way as we can argue that government bureaucrats simply don't know enough to manage the economy (if they did know enough, they wouldn't be bureaucrats; they would instead be rich and successful businessmen), we can argue that they don't know enough to manage America's parents.

Raising children is an art, not a science. What works with one child can fail miserably with another, as anyone who has raised multiple children will attest. To be effective as a parent, one needs to spend time with a child, learn how the child's mind works, and tailor one's parenting to that specific child. The government, if it were to tell people how to parent, would probably choose a "one size fits all" approach; this, after all, is how bureaucrats and politicians tend to think, and they will be the ones writing the parenting manuals. But when it comes to parenting, one size definitely doesn't fit all.

America's partiality to the middle of the regulation continuum is also revealed by currently existing laws that deal with parental behavior. The government does not let parents do whatever they want with their children. It does not, for example, let parents beat their children. And if parents ignore these restrictions on parental behavior, government will respond with fines, jail sentences, or even termination of parental rights. At the same time, the government does give parents considerable discretion about how they raise their children. It may prohibit child-beating, but it tolerates a number of punishments that are less abusive, including spanking children, sending them to bed without dinner, and putting them in "time-out." Indeed, if parents want to raise their children without ever punishing them, the government will tolerate that, too.

Let us now explore in more detail the middle of the regulation continuum and consider various parental behaviors and the degree to which government should regulate them.

Some Governmental Regulations Considered

How can we determine the extent to which the government should regulate parental behavior? One way is to start with a list of children's rights and then regulate parental behavior so as to guarantee these rights. The problem with this plan is in coming up with a list of children's rights.

No such list of rights exists in American law; there is no Bill of Rights for Children. We might turn our attention to the Convention on the Rights of the Child drawn up by the United Nations, but when we examine it we find some apparent inconsistencies. Article 3 tells us that "In all actions concerning children, whether undertaken by public or private social welfare institutions, courts of law, administrative authorities or legislative bodies, the best interests of the child shall be a primary consideration." This is curious since Article 16 of the United Nations' Universal Declaration of Human Rights—which lists the rights of all people, old and young alike—tells us that "Men and women of full age, without any limitation due to race, nationality or religion, have the right to marry and to found a family." Might it not sometimes be in the best interests of children not to be born to a certain set of parents or, indeed, not to be born at all? In such cases, by enforcing people's right to have children, governments must ignore the best interests of those children. Article 14 of the Convention on the Rights of the Child tells us that children have the right of religion, a right that is widely ignored within countries that have ratified the Convention. Parents are, after all, routinely allowed to choose the religion that their children are "indoctrinated into." Article 15 gives children freedom of association, but once again parents around the world routinely violate this freedom by determining—as all good parents should—which adults and children their children can and can't associate with.

Why not, in the absence of a satisfactory list of children's rights, begin with a list of adult rights—say, the Bill of Rights of the Constitution—as a starting point and deduce children's rights from it? The problem with this approach is that the rights of children are different from the rights of adults. In particular, parents have rights—for example, the right to enter into contracts—that children don't. In order to pursue this approach, we would need a principle by which we can determine what adult rights do and what rights don't apply to children.

Instead of trying to develop such a principle, I will proceed in a different manner. In *Doing Right by Children*, I gave an argument for the stewardship model of parenting. I would now like to take up the question of where, on the above-described continuum of governmental regulation of parental behavior, steward-parents will fall.

Parents will have many goals with respect to their children. They will want their children, for example, to have a nourishing breakfast, to arrive at school safely, and to learn things while there. But these are merely *intermediate* goals; they are goals that parents want to accomplish in order that they may accomplish certain ultimate goals.

Suppose, then, we ask parents about their *ultimate* goals in parenting. They might suggest that one central goal of parents should be for their children to grow up to be successful adults, but this suggestion is unsatisfactory, inasmuch as different people will have different definitions of adult success. Some will consider a person who grows up to become a highly paid doctor to be a success, while others will argue that it is underpaid teachers, not physicians, who are the successes. Yet others will argue that it doesn't matter what people do as adults as long as they like what they do. The argument will not quickly be settled.

If not success, then what about happiness as the ultimate goal of parenting? The problem with this suggestion is that you can't make someone happy. The best parents can hope to do is remove obstacles to happiness, like hunger and sickness. Removal of these obstacles does not, however, guarantee subsequent happiness; the world is full of healthy, well-fed people who are unhappy. When all is said and done, it will be the children who make themselves happy, largely as a result of the life-affecting choices they make.

What, then, should the ultimate goal of parenting be? In *Doing Right by Children*, I argue for freedom as a central goal—or maybe even *the* central goal—of steward-parenting.[1] By "freedom" I of course mean freedom for the child, not freedom for the steward-parents. Furthermore, in saying that steward-parents should seek freedom for their child, I am not suggesting that they should simply set him free, the way a Children's Liberationist—discussed back in Chapter 6—will. Instead, a steward-parent will place strict limits on his child's childhood freedom in order to increase his child's future (adult) freedom, and thereby maximize his lifetime freedom.

There are two reasons why steward-parents will have freedom as a goal. First of all, freedom is intrinsically valuable. You can harm someone by eliminating choices he would otherwise have, especially if one of the choices you eliminate is the one he would have chosen; but generally speaking, you cannot harm someone by adding to the choices he already has. Furthermore, in raising their child to be free, steward-parents are demonstrating their respect for the child as a person. They aren't raising him to play a role in their grand design, as an owner-parent might. They are raising him so that he can make his own grand design and live his life in accordance with that design. Steward-parents will be acutely aware that the day will come when their stewardship ends and their child takes control of his life. Good steward-parents will raise their child with that day in mind.

Suppose we agree that freedom, in the sense described above, is a central goal of parenting. What conclusions will we then draw about the role of government in regulating parental behavior?

We would, first of all, advocate various restrictions on parental behavior. There will be some things that the government shouldn't let parents do. Certainly the government should stop parents from killing their children. A dead child can't do anything at all and therefore isn't free to do what he wants. Similarly, the government should stop parents from doing things that risk their children's lives—like letting them play with guns.

We can also extend this reasoning to parental behavior that, although it is unlikely to result in the death of a child, is certain or likely to diminish that child's future freedom. Consider again, by way of example, child-blinder Anne Martin. The children she mutilated did not die, but it is clear that by blinding them she impaired their future freedom. Mental and emotional abuse will also impair a child's future freedom, inasmuch as it will seriously undermine his self-esteem. He will in many cases find it impossible to make the transition to genuine autonomy.

Besides restricting what parents do *to* children, a government that cares about the future freedom of children will require parents to do things *for* them. It will, for example, require parents not just to feed their children, but to nourish them adequately, since a child's mental and physical capabilities—and therefore his freedom—can be diminished by malnutrition.

Let us now consider three specific areas—forcing parents to provide medical care for children, forcing parents to educate children, and allowing parents to spank children—in which Americans disagree about what role, if any, the government should play in regulating parental behavior. For each area, I will first describe the ongoing debate concerning governmental regulation and then ask what kind of regulation we would favor if we advocated the stewardship model of parenting—if, that is, our primary concern was the future freedom of children.

Medical Care

Let us divide our examination of parents' role in protecting and promoting the health of their children into four questions: Should the government force parents to get medical care for sick or injured children? Should the government force parents to take medical steps (for example, getting them vaccinated against contagious illnesses) to reduce the chance of their children getting sick in the future? Should the government stop parental behavior (like drug use by pregnant women) that can jeopardize the health of their children? and, Should the government allow children to make important medical decisions without the advice and consent of their parents?

Four Debates

Most Americans think that if children are sick or injured, it is their parents' duty to get medical care for them. Christian Scientists don't agree with this viewpoint, for the simple reason that they don't really believe in medical science. They instead believe that sickness can be cured through prayer—supplemented, perhaps, by changes in lifestyle and diet. As long as their children have simple ailments like colds or the flu, the failure of Christian Scientist parents to seek medical help is inconsequential, but when their children have more serious ailments, the result can be disastrous.

In 1992, Andrew Wantland was a twelve-year-old in the custody of a Christian Scientist father. Andrew became seriously ill, but his father did not seek medical treatment for Andrew until his condition was critical. Andrew died shortly thereafter. Subsequent investigation revealed that Andrew had died of diabetes and suggested that if his father had been quicker about getting medical treatment for Andrew, his life might have been saved or at least prolonged.

Other children who—it has been argued—paid a price for their Christian Scientist parents' beliefs include Ian Lundman, who also died of diabetes; Robyn Twitchell, who died at age two of a bowel obstruction; and Harrison Johnson, who died at age two after being stung hundreds of times by wasps. In each of these cases the parents prayed for the child but were slow to seek medical help; and in each of these cases it was argued that if medical help had been sought promptly, it would have made a difference. For the most part, the government condoned these parents' behavior.[2]

Most Americans are outraged by cases like these. They argue that the government should not allow such things to happen—that it should require parents to get medical care for a sick child and should punish parents who fail to do so. Christian Scientists might reply that the parents described above are failing to get medical care for their children not because they are lazy or because they want their children to suffer. Rather, their medical inaction is motivated by their religious beliefs. It is pointless to save your child's body (by getting medical care for him) if in doing so you doom his soul. Developing this argument further, they might suggest that the Constitution of the United States *requires* the government to accept and defend the religious views of parents, even though doing so jeopardizes the medical well-being of their children. In particular, they might point out that the First Amendment to the Constitution states unequivocally that "Congress shall make no law respecting an establishment of religion, or prohibiting the free exercise thereof."

As is the case with much of the Constitution, though, Congress and the courts have played fast and loose in their interpretation of seemingly unequivocal clauses. Courts have, most significantly, distinguished between religious *beliefs* and religious *practices*. What the Constitution guarantees (the Supreme Court has subsequently revealed) is the right to hold any religious belief you want. It does not likewise guarantee your right to put your beliefs into practice. Thus, in banning certain religious practices, the government is not prohibiting the free exercise of religion—or so the argument goes.

There is, however, less to this argument than meets the eye. In the absence of a technology that enables us to read people's minds, it is not in the power of the government to prohibit religious belief. Thus, there is no meaningful way for the government to prohibit, say, belief in the existence of God: as long as people keep their belief in God to themselves, the government has no way of knowing who does and who doesn't believe in God, so any prohibition would be ineffectual. What the government *can* meaningfully prohibit is people putting their religious beliefs into practice, by sharing them with others or acting on them. So when the government says that it prohibits religious practices but not religious beliefs, we should not take this as a sign of liberality on its part.

An examination of court cases reveals a government at war with itself over which religious practices will be tolerated and which will not.

In 1878, in *Reynolds v. United States*, the Supreme Court considered the Mormon practice of polygamy. According to Mormon religious doctrine, men have not merely a right, but a duty to enter into polygamous marriages, circumstances permitting. The Court decided that laws against polygamy did not violate Mormons' freedom of religion. They reasoned that "Laws are made for the government of actions, and while they cannot interfere with mere religious belief and opinions, they may with practices." (The Supreme Court, in other words, was willing to allow Mormons to believe that polygamous marriages are what God wants, but not to fulfill God's will by entering into such marriages.) The Court also argued that if the government allowed polygamous marriages, it would have to allow other, even more odious practices: "Suppose one believed that human sacrifices were a necessary part of religious worship, would it be seriously contended that the civil government under which he lived could not interfere to prevent a sacrifice?"

In response to this last question, we can point out that of course if the person being sacrificed doesn't want to be sacrificed, the government has a right to interfere. (In like fashion, it should interfere in those cases in which women are forced into polygamous marriages against their will.) Suppose, however, that the person being sacrificed, *wants* (because of his religious beliefs) to be sacrificed. The government stands back and watches men sacrifice their lives in time of war—indeed, it even encourages them to do so. If you can sacrifice your life for your country, why not for your God? This, unfortunately, is a question the Court did not entertain.

The Court mentioned the "evil consequences" that flow from polygamous marriages but spent little time describing these consequences. At one point it reminded us that "polygamy leads to the patriarchal principle…which, when applied to large communities, fetters the people in stationary despotism, while that principle cannot long exist in connection with monogamy," but it also admits that "An exceptional colony of polygamists under an exceptional leadership may sometimes exist for a time without appearing to disturb the social condition of the people who surround it." Many thoughtful individuals will question whether these "evil consequences" are worrisome enough to justify governmental interference.

The government's condemnation of polygamy, by the way, seems hypocritical. In 2001, Mormon Tom Green was sentenced to prison for marrying too many women. At the same time, the government turned a blind eye to the millions of men who had married no women at all but nevertheless fathered children out of wedlock. The harm done to children and the community at large by these single men is, however, arguably far worse than the harm done by polygamist fathers. It also seems hypocritical for the government to condemn the Mormon religious practice of taking multiple wives and not likewise condemn the Christian Scientist practice of not getting medical treatment for sick children: it is presumably far worse for a child to die of untreated diabetes than to live with multiple mothers.

In the late twentieth century, courts were still trying to deter- mine just what religious practices were and weren't allowed by the Constitution. Among other things, they considered whether Native Americans can use peyote in connection with their religious worship and whether practitioners of the Santeria religion can engage in ani- mal sacrifice.

In the cases described above, parents refused to get medical care for sick or hurt children. Let us now turn our attention to cases in which parents refuse to take steps that will prevent their children from becoming sick in the future. Consider, in particular, cases in which parents refuse to allow their children to be vaccinated against contagious diseases. Some of these parents have religious grounds for their refusal. Others have medical grounds: they believe that the medical risk posed by such vaccinations outweighs the medical benefit to be derived from them. Although the government has been reluctant to force parents to get medical treatment for sick children, it almost universally requires parents to get their children vaccinated against contagious diseases: across America, children are not allowed to attend school if they have not been vaccinated (although, as we shall see, the requirement is one that can easily be got around).

When the government forces parents to get medical care for a child suffering from diabetes, it can justify doing so by pointing out that the child will benefit from such care. When, on the other hand, the government forces parents to get their child vaccinated against a contagious disease, it can justify doing so not only by pointing out that *the child* will benefit from the vaccination (since, having been vaccinated, he cannot catch the contagious disease),[3] but by pointing out that *the child's fellow citizens* will also benefit (since by getting vaccinated, he makes it harder for the disease to spread to them). In other words, in its defense of forced vaccinations, the government can invoke the universalizability principle, which we encountered in earlier chapters. Here is how the government's argument might go.

My not getting vaccinated against a contagious disease will not, in and of itself, undermine the government's efforts to block the spread of that disease. Indeed, if I am the *only* one who is not vaccinated, there can be no outbreak of the disease: those who have been vaccinated cannot get it, and since none of them can get it, I cannot catch it from them, meaning that I, too, am protected. Likewise, if a relatively small percentage of the population shuns vaccination against a contagious disease, it will be nearly impossible for the disease to spread, since there won't exist a "critical mass" of susceptible people. For these reasons, some citizens will be tempted to forgo vaccination. They can—as long as most other people get vaccinated—enjoy the benefits of vaccination without getting vaccinated themselves; they can, in other words, get a free ride. The problem is that if enough people reason along these lines, the result will be an underimmunized population in which the disease can spread. (This isn't just a theoretical possibility: underimmunization has recently resulted in outbreaks of whooping cough in both America and Australia.) According to the universalizability principle, though, the government is justified in banning behavior (like dumping used motor oil in one's backyard) that is not harmful if done by one person, but would be harmful if done by many people; thus, the government is justified in forcing people to vaccinate their children.

Although Americans are required to vaccinate their children—both for the good of their children and for the good of their fellow citizens—the degree of compulsion is minimal. State governments allow people to get an exemption from mandatory vaccinations, and one of the grounds for exemption is a declaration that such vaccinations are against one's religious beliefs. In allowing these exemptions, the government avoids provoking those who are opposed to vaccination on religious grounds; and as long as relatively few people apply for exemptions, this allowance does not seriously undermine the efficacy of the vaccination program. Thus, the government can simultaneously "compel" people to get vaccinated and not have to deal with the question of whether by doing so it is violating people's freedom of religion; politically speaking, it gets to have its cake and eat it too.

It is one thing if a parent refuses to get medical care for a sick child or refuses a vaccination that might prevent his child from getting sick; it is another thing if the parent engages in behavior that directly causes his child to become sick. Suppose, for example, a woman abuses drugs while pregnant. This behavior on the part of the mother might mean that her baby's first experience on entering the world is the agony of drug withdrawal. After that, the physical, mental, and emotional health of her child may be damaged for the rest of its life. The harm done can be far worse than if the child had been physically abused at birth.

The 1980s saw a dramatic upsurge in the number of babies born to women who had used crack cocaine while pregnant. In response to this phenomenon, police started arresting women who were caught using drugs while pregnant, charging them with child endangerment or with distributing drugs to children. Many of these women appealed their convictions, with mixed results. In the early 1990s, for example, Cornelia Whitner was sentenced to eight years in prison for using cocaine while pregnant. Her case made it to the South Carolina Supreme Court, which upheld the sentence, reasoning that the fetus was a child, so that by endangering the fetus Ms. Whitner was guilty of child endangerment. Elsewhere, prosecutors have had less luck prosecuting women who abused drugs while pregnant: courts have been skeptical of the prosecutorial argument that lawmakers had fetuses in mind when they wrote statutes against child endangerment and distributing drugs to children.[4]

In 2001, a case involving drug abuse by pregnant women (*Ferguson v. Charleston*) made headlines by reaching the United States Supreme Court. In the late 1980s the staff members at a public hospital in Charleston, South Carolina, grew alarmed by the increase in the number of crack babies. At first they tried a noncoercive response to the situation: when a pregnant woman tested positive for cocaine use, the hospital referred her for counseling and treatment. When it became clear that this wasn't stopping women from continuing to use cocaine while pregnant, the hospital decided that coercive measures were called for. It volunteered to turn over to city police the results of urine tests of women who had just given birth, whenever these tests indicated that a woman had been using drugs. Because the women in question had not been informed that the results of their urine tests could be turned over to the police, the Supreme Court declared that this use of urine tests constituted an unreasonable search.

When courts declared that currently existing laws against child endangerment or against distributing drugs to children were not written with fetuses in mind and therefore did not apply to pregnant drug abusers, it fell to legislators to write new laws if they wanted to punish pregnant drug abusers. In many states, though, legislators were reluctant to write such laws. Their reasoning: when we threaten to punish pregnant women for their fetus-affecting behavior, we give them reason to hide this behavior. And what better way to hide it than by not seeking medical care until a few days after a child has been born, when evidence of drug abuse will hopefully be out of the mother's system? This delay, however, will only compound the harm done to the children of drug-abusing mothers. A more enlightened course of action, some argued, is to encourage women to get prenatal care, and if we discover that they are using drugs, encourage them to stop doing so for the sake of their fetus. We will take a closer look at this argument in a moment.

Who gets to decide what medical treatments a child will undergo? The rule used to be that, other than in emergency situations in which they weren't present, parents had a right to make health decisions for their children. The reasoning was that children were not mature or knowledgeable enough to make these decisions for themselves. In recent decades, though, states have started allowing exceptions to this rule. In many states, children can now get prescription contraceptives, abortions, or treatment for drug abuse without the knowledge of their parents.

The theory behind this gutting of parental notification is simple. If girls have to obtain their parents' permission to get oral contraception, many will (in an attempt to conceal their sexual activities from their parents) forgo contraception and therefore run an increased risk of pregnancy. If girls have to obtain their parents' permission to have an abortion, many will (again, in an attempt to conceal their sexual activities) seek a back-alley abortion or try to hide the pregnancy and thereby endanger their and the fetus's health. If kids have to obtain their parents' permission before they can get drug treatment, many will (in an attempt to conceal their drug use from their parents) delay getting help for their addiction, which again can endanger their health. The claim, in other words, is that by not involving parents in health-care decisions affecting their children, we have the health of their children in mind. This claim is questionable for a pair of reasons.

To begin with, by allowing children to hide their sexual or drug-using activities from their parents, we inadvertently encourage them to engage in such activities. A girl who thinks she can have sex without getting caught is more likely to have sex than a girl who fears both pregnancy and parental disapprobation. Likewise, a boy who thinks he can use drugs without getting caught is more likely to use drugs than a boy who fears parental disapprobation. Thus, it may be true that by allowing girls to obtain prescription contraceptives without the permission of their parents we make it more likely that they will use contraception, but we also make it more likely that the child will be sexually active and will therefore need contraception. Likewise, it may be true that by allowing boys to hide treatment for drug addiction from their parents we make it more likely that they will seek drug therapy, but we also make it more likely that they will use drugs and therefore need drug therapy. This hardly sounds like progress.

Furthermore, and quite significantly, by not requiring doctors to keep parents informed of the medicines and treatments their children have received, the state seriously undermines parental stewardship. To be an effective steward, a parent must be knowledgeable about what is going on in a child's life. This doesn't mean having a detailed knowledge of *all* of the child's activities—such knowledge would require twenty-four-hour surveillance—but it does mean knowing the major events of a child's life. Getting an abortion or getting treatment for drug addiction would certainly count as major events.

Imagine, then, the predicament of parents trying to understand and deal with the behavior of a daughter who, without their knowledge, has recently had an abortion, or a son who, again without their knowledge, is being treated for drug addiction. Because they are deprived of important information about their children's lives, these parents' efforts to help their children will likely be inappropriate and therefore counterproductive. The parent/child relationship will be further undermined.

Those who are opposed to parental notification laws tend to assume that lots of parents have terrible relationships with their children and that because of this, we needn't fear undermining the parent/child relationship. (There isn't much there to undermine.) They also tend to assume that lots of parents reject the role of steward-parent and as a result are relatively indifferent to the well-being of their children. Unfortunately, both assumptions are probably correct, in large part because of the increased selfishness of parents in recent decades. At the same time, by building these assumptions into the law, the government makes it that much harder for parents to have good relationships with their children and play the role of steward successfully.

Steward-Parents' Response

Steward-parents will have little difficulty taking sides in the above medical debates. One of the central goals of steward-parents is that their children be free (in the sense described above) when they enter adulthood. They will therefore be willing to advocate governmental interference with parental behavior if there is reason to think that such interference will dramatically increase the freedom of children.

Should the government force parents to get medical care for sick and injured children? Of course it should, the steward-parent will tell us. If a child has been seriously injured and does not get first aid, he might die; dead children do not develop into free adults. Or suppose, less dramatically, that a child has an ear infection that his parents let go untreated. The child could lose his hearing as a result, and this loss of hearing would have an obvious impact on his future freedom: there will be things he can't do that he could have done if his parents had treated the infection.

In making the above claims, steward-parents are not advocating that doctors be given carte blanche to do whatever they want with children. After all, doctors sometimes are mistaken in their diagnoses and treatments of illnesses, and one very important job of the steward-parent is to protect his child from the mistakes of other adults. Nor are steward-parents advocating that *parents* be given carte blanche to do with their children as they will, particularly if the parents in question have unorthodox, unscientific beliefs about medicine.

It is clear that the government should stop people from acting on false medical beliefs that are *not* justified by religion. Thus, suppose a parent forcefully shakes his child to put him to sleep and does so not because his religion tells him to do so, but because he sincerely (but wrongly) believes that it is a safe and effective way to comfort a child. All but the staunchest owner-parents will agree that the government should stop him; and if he refuses to change his ways, the government should take the child from him. Suppose, however, that someone offers a religious justification for acting on false medical beliefs. We have already seen that the government feels justified in forbidding certain religious practices with the public good in mind. But if the government is justified in forbidding members of certain religions to practice polygamy or to use drugs, isn't it even more justified in forcing Christian Scientist parents to get medical attention for their sick and injured children?

Some would argue that the government, if it forced Christian Scientist parents to get medical attention for their children, would be violating the parents' freedom of religion. Even if this were true, it doesn't settle the issue; for what about *their children's* freedom of religion? When they are young, children cannot meaningfully be said to have chosen a religion. It is only when they are in their teens—and probably even their late teens—that children know enough about themselves and the world for the choice of a religion to be a genuine choice. This in turn means that if we respect a child's freedom of religion, we will do what we can to ensure that he makes it out of childhood alive—at which time he can declare his religious preference. Parents who cause the death of a child by imposing their religious values on him may be acting in their own best interests or in the interests of their religion, but they are not acting in the best interests of their child. They are not respecting the child's freedom of religion, and they certainly are not acting as steward-parents.

Should the government force parents to have their children vaccinated against contagious diseases? Steward-parents will say it should, if the vaccines in question are safe and effective. (I think the vaccines American children are currently required to get are safe and effective, but it would carry me beyond the scope of this work to present evidence in support of this view.) Once again, a child who dies of a contagious illness will be deprived of all his freedom. On the other hand, if there are solid, medical grounds for thinking that a vaccination is unsafe, a steward-parent will refuse to have his child vaccinated.

Should the government punish women who use drugs while pregnant or incarcerate them to prevent continued drug use during pregnancy? The steward-parent would probably see little difference between a woman who gives a fetus drugs by taking drugs herself while pregnant and a woman who gives drugs to a newborn baby by injecting them into it. If children deserve a drug-free existence at age one day, why not during the months before they emerge from the womb? But if we agree that the state should act to prevent pregnant women from using drugs, it follows that the state might, under some circumstances, have to incarcerate pregnant women if that is the only way to prevent them from taking drugs while pregnant.

What about the suggestion that instead of punishing or incarcerating these women, we need to encourage them to get counseling and treatment? The Charleston hospital described above tried this approach, but found it ineffective: the pull of crack cocaine was just too strong. What about the argument that if we punish or incarcerate women who use drugs while pregnant, we give them an incentive to hide their pregnancy—and thereby not avail themselves of prenatal care? Anyone impressed by this line of reasoning should realize that a similar argument can be given to show that we shouldn't punish women who abuse their babies: if we do so, we give them an incentive to hide their abusive activities, to the detriment of their babies; better that such women, when caught, are encouraged to seek help. Not too many people, I think, will advocate this way of dealing with women who abuse babies.

Should the government let minors make important medical decisions without the advice and consent of their parents? Of course not, steward-parents will argue. Children in general lack the judgment to make these decisions, and children who use drugs or are sexually promiscuous at an early age arguably have even worse judgment than children in general. Furthermore, as was argued above, by allowing minors to make important medical decisions, we undermine the role of the steward-parent, something steward-parents will obviously be reluctant to see happen.

Education

Children receive two sorts of education. The first is the formal education that a child receives in the classroom, primarily by means of books, lectures, and tests. The other—arguably even more important—is the informal education a child receives, mostly as a result of interacting with his parents, his siblings, and the world around him. In the course of this informal education, he will acquire his first language; he will learn about "how the world works," both physically and socially; he will discover his likes and dislikes as well as his talents; and he will acquire many of the values that will carry him through life. An education is valuable because it contributes enormously to a child's lifetime freedom. Someone who enters early adulthood with a complete education—in both the formal and informal senses of the word—will have a wider range of options open to him, a better idea of what these options are, and a greater ability to attain the goals he sets for himself.

The government requires Americans to educate their children formally: it requires that they send their children to school at least until they have reached high school. The government is not quite so demanding when it comes to the informal educations parents provide. If parents invest little time or money helping their children explore their world and their talents, acquire values, and shape themselves, the state will not object. In America today it is perfectly legal for parents to ignore their children: they can make little or no effort to try to establish a loving relationship with a child, play with and teach the child, or help the child explore his talents. What they can't do is neglect (say, by not feeding him) or abuse a child.

One suspects that many of the parents who ignore their children do so because they didn't really want to become parents in the first place. Some became parents because of a reproductive accident. Others became parents voluntarily, but whimsically: without doing much research and without ever having spent much time around children, they decided that they would become parents, thinking that parenting would be both fun and rewarding. They quickly found out that not everyone is cut out to be a parent or to enjoy the rewards that parenting has to offer.

It would, of course, be difficult for the government to force parents to invest more time and money in their children's informal educations. It would require a degree of snooping that most would find objectionable. (Did you read to your child today? Did you share a meal with your child today? Why aren't you getting ballet lessons for your child?) There is one way, however, that the government could improve children's informal educations without having to become a snoop: it could adopt the licensing proposal described back in Chapter 7. Licensing would make it impossible for people to become parents by accident or on a whim. (A woman could, of course, accidentally get pregnant, but unless she had a parent's license, she wouldn't be allowed to act as parent for the child to whom she gave birth.) I will have more to say about licensing and governmental regulation of parental behavior later in this chapter.

While most Americans understand and defend the government's requirement that parents formally educate their children, there have been some dissenters. Consider, for example, the Amish who, in the 1972 court case *Wisconsin v. Yoder*, challenged the state requirement that their children attend school until they were sixteen years old. They had no objection to sending their children to school through eighth grade but argued that their children had little to gain and a lot to lose by attending high school. They had little to gain because after eighth grade (wrote Justice Warren Burger in delivering the opinion of the Supreme Court), "the children must acquire Amish attitudes favoring manual work and self-reliance and the specific skills needed to perform the adult role of an Amish farmer or housewife. They must learn to enjoy physical labor. Once a child has learned basic reading, writing, and elementary mathematics, these traits, skills, and attitudes admittedly fall within the category of those best learned through example and 'doing' rather than in a classroom." And they had a lot to lose because a high school education would place Amish children "in an environment hostile to Amish beliefs with increasing emphasis on competition in class work and sports and with pressure to conform to the styles, manners, and ways of the peer group, but also because it takes them away from their community, physically and emotionally, during the crucial and formative adolescent period of life." Indeed, some of the Amish feared that mandatory high school for Amish children would mean the end of the Amish way of life. The Court ended up siding with the Amish: it would be a violation of their religious freedom to force them to send their children to high school.

This decision should trouble anyone who values the religious freedom of children. It is one thing for parents to encourage their children to follow in their religious footsteps by setting an example for them or by persuading them, when they are older, by means of rational argumentation. In allowing Amish parents not to send their children to high school, the Court is letting the parents "encourage" their children to retain the Amish faith by keeping them in the dark about alternative religions and lifestyles. As a consequence, the choices these children make hardly seem free, and the government, by backing the Amish elders, seems to be undermining the children's freedom of religion.

Supreme Court Justice William O. Douglas realized as much. In *Wisconsin v. Yoder* he argued that "a child who expresses a desire to attend public high school in conflict with the wishes of his parents should not be prevented from doing so." According to Justice Douglas, "If the parents in this case are allowed a religious exemption, the inevitable effect is to impose the parents' notions of religious duty upon their children. Where the child is mature enough to express potentially conflicting desires, it would be an invasion of the child's rights to permit such an imposition without canvassing his views."

It is, by the way, ironic that the Amish would seek to control their children's religious views. If the ancestors of the Amish had successfully controlled *their* children's religious views, the Amish wouldn't exist: the Amish sect, after all, was founded by Jakob Ammann, whose own unwillingness to follow the directives of his elders caused a schism in the Mennonite Church.

In behaving as they do, Amish parents seem to be operating not on the stewardship model of parenting—which places, as we have seen, a high value on raising children to be free—but on what might be called the religious model of parenting: they are raising their children not so the children can form their own life plan, but so their children will conform to what the parents believe is God's plan for them.

In advocating compulsory education *through* high school, I am not likewise advocating compulsory education *in* American high schools. In many of these schools, after all, it is possible to obtain a high school diploma without having learned much of anything since eighth grade. Most steward-parents will respond to America's educational crisis by going above and beyond the government's current educational requirements. Rather than send their child to the local "free" high school, they might move to a different school district or enroll their child in a private school, even though it is inconvenient and expensive to do so. Indeed, most steward-parents will do what they can to enable their children to attend college, even though the government does not require them to do so.

Corporal Punishment

For most of the history of mankind, child-beating was not only legal, but commonplace. Until the nineteenth century, growing up meant getting spanked, hit, thrown, whipped, cudgeled, and pummeled, not just by your parents, but by your schoolmaster (if you were lucky enough to go to school), your master (if you were an apprentice), your neighbors—indeed, almost any adult you happened to offend. The "child psychology experts" of the past thought it obvious that corporal punishment was the best way to make a child obey. For them the question was not whether to beat children, but how to beat them without killing them. And if you challenged them to defend corporal punishment, they might have cited the proverb, "Spare the rod, spoil the child."

Since the campaigns against child abuse in the 1870s, child-beating has become uncommon; and since the publication of Benjamin Spock's *Common Sense Book of Baby and Child Care* in the 1940s, even spanking of children has declined in popularity as a method of child discipline. (Between 1962 and 1992, the percentage of American parents who spanked their children fell from 59 to 19. By the 1990s the favorite disciplinary technique of parents was nonviolent "time-outs.")

In America today the law allows parents to hit their children as long as the hitting doesn't leave marks, welts, cuts, or bruises—that is, as long as the hitting doesn't leave physical evidence. This means that Americans are free to spank and perhaps even slap their children, which in turn means that Americans can do something to their two-year-old which, if they did it to an adult, would get them jailed for battery. It is indeed curious: when our fellow adults displease us, we are expected to reason with them, but the law allows us to resort to violence to make a point with our children.

Some think America should follow the lead of certain other countries and ban spanking. Others think we have already gone too far in coddling our children and argue that teachers should be allowed to spank students and that parents should be allowed to engage in more aggressive forms of discipline than spanking. Let us, then, examine the debate over corporal punishment and inquire into the extent to which government should regulate the disciplinary techniques used by parents.

For many people, whether the government should allow parents to spank their children depends on how we answer the following question: is spanking an effective disciplinary technique? If it is, then the government should allow or even encourage parents to spank; otherwise, it should not. The problem with this question—more precisely, the *first* problem with this question—is that before we can answer it, we need to come to an agreement about what counts as a disciplined child.

Consider, then, a pair of children, Alphonse and Bob. Alphonse has exceptionally good manners; indeed, some characterize him as painfully polite. He doesn't speak unless spoken to. His behavior is "responsible" to the point of being compulsive; for example, he not only does his homework without being told but does it days ahead of when it is due. Alphonse never gets into trouble. He is very respectful of adults, always addressing them as Mr. and Ms. and never talking back to them. He does as he is told in school and as a result has made a very good impression on his teachers. Bob, on the other hand, has good manners but not the exceptionally good manners of Alphonse. He lets adults know when something is bothering him but isn't a whiner. He is pretty good about doing what he is asked to do but sometimes forgets. Although he is respectful to adults, he sometimes jokes with them and on occasion even makes fun of their foibles. He sometimes gets into trouble but accepts the punishment when he gets caught. In school, he is a solid but not spectacular student.

Who is the better behaved child, Alphonse or Bob? In one common sense of "behaved," Alphonse is obviously better behaved than Bob. In fact, some would describe Alphonse as being *perfectly* well behaved. The problem is that lots of parents will sense that Alphonse is, if anything, *too* well behaved and that it is a mistake to expect perfect behavior in children. Alphonse should lighten up and have some fun, the way Bob does. He is only going to be a child once, after all.

This thought raises a new question: what is the point of being well behaved? Is it valuable (in a child) for its own sake or as a means to some other end?

Owner-parents will tend to think that good behavior is valuable for its own sake. The job of parenting Alphonse will, after all, be significantly easier than the job of parenting Bob. Alphonse will be very helpful, will do as he is told, and won't make trouble. Furthermore, Alphonse will never say things to undermine his parents' self-esteem: he won't point out their failings or comment on their foibles. Bob, on the other hand, will require active parenting and will sometimes pop his parents' bubble of self-esteem. From the owner-parent's point of view, the less effort involved in parenting the better, and since perfectly behaved children will require the least parental effort, these are the sorts of children owner-parents will want.

Steward-parents, on the other hand, will value good behavior in a child not for its own sake, but as a means to some other end. Their point is not to raise a child in a way that makes the parents' life pleasant, but to raise a child in a way that makes it likely that the child has a good life, both as a child and as an adult. If you asked steward-parents who was better behaved, Alphonse or Bob, they might admit that in the usual sense of "well behaved," Alphonse was, but go on to suggest that Alphonse's good behavior benefited Alphonse's parents *at Alphonse's expense.* Indeed they might criticize Alphonse's parents for their selfishness in raising Alphonse to be so well behaved.

What sort of behavior will steward-parents encourage in a child? Since a primary goal of steward-parents is the freedom of their child, they will seek in their child behavior that increases the child's chances of becoming a free individual. They will therefore encourage their child to be well mannered and to obey rules, inasmuch as people who are ill mannered generally have far fewer opportunities open to them in life (and are therefore less free than they might have been), and people who are incapable of following rules often end up in jail (and are likewise less free than they might have been). They will encourage their child to respect his parents, his teachers, and adults in general. After all, if the child does not respect the adults who are raising him, he is unlikely to take their advice seriously or obey their commands, perhaps with disastrous results to the child. And steward-parents, because they value their child's freedom, will want to help him develop self-control. If he has self-control, *he* controls himself and is therefore free to do what he wants to do. If he lacks self-control, it isn't he, but other people or external forces that decide what he does, and he therefore won't really be free. Finally, steward-parents will want their child to be reasonable and to connect actions with consequences.

But besides teaching their child to behave, steward-parents will want to give him plenty of opportunity to explore himself and his world. They will encourage him to have lots of conversations with them, conversations in which he can relate his hopes and fears, the events of his life, and the "experiments in living" he is tempted to undertake. The parents can then respond to his comments and offer guidance. (Responsive comments are probably the best way to shape the behavior of an adolescent and at any rate are arguably better than periodic lectures.) These conversations are likely to take place only if the child has a close, trusting relationship with his parents, one in which the lines of communication are wide open. A child who has been taught to speak only when spoken to is not likely to turn to his parents for help in his investigation of life.

In short, steward-parents will seek a child who is well behaved but not too well behaved. Their goal will be to produce a Bob, not an Alphonse. Alphonse's parents might enjoy having such a self-restrained child, but is this degree of self-restraint compatible with the child's freedom, either now or later?

If we can settle the question of what counts as *appropriately* good behavior—behavior that is good but not too good—in a child, we will encounter the second problem with the question, Is spanking an effective disciplinary technique? It is arguably the wrong question for us to be asking. Our concern should not be with whether spanking is *an* effective disciplinary technique but whether it is *the most* effective disciplinary technique. To better understand this distinction, consider the following medical analogy. Is amputation an effective way to treat athlete's foot? In one sense of "effective," it is: if you amputate, you not only get rid of a person's athlete's foot, but eliminate the possibility of him ever getting it again. In another, more obvious sense of "effective," though, amputation is a foolish way to treat athlete's foot, since there exist other treatments that are more effective—that accomplish the same goal at a lower "cost" to the patient.

Thus, in one sense of "effective," spanking is an effective disciplinary technique: it does make a child mind his behavior, and a child who is spanked will certainly be better behaved than a child whose parents never discipline him in any way. The question we should be concerned with, though, is not whether spanking is an effective disciplinary technique, but whether it is more effective than alternative disciplinary techniques; and in order to answer this last question, we must compare the effectiveness of spanking with that of other disciplinary techniques.

Allow me, then, to describe an alternative disciplinary technique, one to which many steward-parents will instinctively be drawn.

Steward-parents will do what they can to establish an intense, loving relationship with their children. They will make it clear to their children that they are loved unconditionally. Because their children realize the extent of their parents' love, they will experience mental anguish when they disappoint their parents. It will be this sense of anguish, more than anything, that will make their children toe the line and try to live up to their parents' expectations.

Steward-parents will be reluctant to spank or slap their children for the simple reason that hitting someone will usually destroy any chance of having a loving relationship with that person. Children who are routinely spanked do not relate to their parents the same as children whose parents treat them with respect. If a child is routinely spanked, what motivates him to behave is not a sense of anguish at the possibility of disappointing his parents, but a sense of fear—fear of being spanked.

Most adults realize that if you go around hitting other adults, it dramatically changes your relationship with them. If a man hits his wife, it seriously undermines their relationship. If a man repeatedly hits his wife, it will destroy the loving relationship between them. Even if an abused wife says she still loves her husband, we will suspect that what she is experiencing isn't truly love but is instead a symptom of low self-esteem. Notice, too, that the motivations of a wife who is routinely hit will differ from those of a wife whose husband treats her with love and respect. Both wives might want to keep their husband happy, but the former will be motivated by fear—she might get hit if she disappoints her husband—while the latter will be motivated by a sense of anguish, by an intense desire not to let down this person who has shown her love and respect.

The loving relationship between steward-parents and their children lies at the heart of the child-discipline strategies of steward-parents. It isn't that these parents will threaten to withhold their love from their children unless they behave—steward-parents would never do such a thing. They will, however, be perfectly willing to "use" the above-described feelings of anguish (which feelings exist because of the loving relationship between child and parents) in their attempt to raise a disciplined child.

Steward-parents will not, however, rely solely on their child's sense of anguish to make him behave. They will supplement it with various nonviolent behavior modification techniques. Steward-parents will spend a great deal of time studying their children and trying behavior modification experiments on them. They will realize that behavior modification techniques that work well on one child don't work at all on another and that what works on a child at one stage of his development might not work on him later. They will develop a good idea of how their child thinks and what it takes to get him to change his ways for the better.

Positive reinforcement will be at the top of steward-parents' list of nonviolent behavior modification techniques. Steward-parents will praise and reward their children for good behavior. When their children misbehave (as they inevitably will), steward-parents' initial disciplinary technique will be conversational: they will explain to a child why his behavior is unacceptable and how it affects others. Steward-parents want to raise their child to be a reasonable person, and the best way to accomplish this is to expose the child to the reasoning process whenever possible. If reasoning fails (as it often will) steward-parents' next disciplinary technique will involve nonviolent punishments, like time-outs or the loss of privileges.

In a perfect world, steward-parents will never "get physical" with their children. Unfortunately, this ideal is probably impossible to attain. It is, first of all, necessary for parents to sometimes physically restrain their children. If a child starts hitting his playmates, for example, a parent shouldn't stand there talking to the child while he flails away; he should instead physically restrain him, calm him, and then start talking to him. Likewise, a parent may be forced to "incarcerate" a child who will not stay put in his time-out zone. And finally—regrettably—a steward-parent is only human and might, in a flash of anger, reflexively swat a child who has, say, just pinched him at the end of a long, exhausting day. The steward-parent will, however, quickly apologize for such lapses and work hard not to let them happen.

The disciplinary techniques employed by steward-parents will take time and energy. Spanking, on the other hand, requires zero mental effort and only minimal physical effort (as long as the person being spanked is small). A parent who spanks does not have to think through possible behavior modification strategies, go to the trouble of trying to reason with a child, or spend the hour of vigilance required to enforce an hour-long time-out. Indeed, one suspects that many parents spank, not because they are convinced that spanking is the most effective way to discipline a child, but because they are lazy and spanking is a "cheap" (in terms of physical and mental effort) way to discipline a child. Steward-parents, on the other hand, will not mind the time and effort spent employing nonviolent behavior modification techniques, if that is what it takes to raise their children properly.

Are the nonviolent behavior modification techniques favored by steward-parents more effective than spanking? I think so, especially if our goal is not to produce a *perfectly* behaved child, but one who is *properly* behaved.[5] Does it follow from this that spanking should be banned? I think not.

What worries me about a ban on spanking are the practical consequences such a ban could have. If the government told parents they could no longer spank children and did not teach them alternative disciplinary techniques (in particular, the kind of nonviolent behavior modification techniques described above), the results could be disastrous. Some of the parents who spank their children might interpret the ban as a sign that the government simply wants them to stop disciplining their children—wants them, that is, to let their children run wild. Other parents might realize that what the government wants is for them to substitute nonviolent behavior modification techniques for spanking, but might find that these techniques require too much time and energy and might therefore respond to the spanking ban by ceasing to discipline their children. Thus, as far as the interests of children are concerned, a ban on spanking could backfire: spanking may be a relatively ineffective way to discipline children, but it is better (for children) than no discipline at all.

A ban on spanking would also be difficult to enforce. Because spanking does not leave marks, it would be difficult for authorities to know when parents had violated the ban on spanking, as long as the spanking was done in the privacy of their home. It would be the child's word against the parents'. If the authorities made a practice of accepting the child's word, children would gain considerable leverage over their parents: whenever a parent displeased a child, the child could accuse the parent of spanking. And if the authorities refused to accept children's claims that they had been spanked, the ban on spanking would be ineffectual.

Some readers might agree that the government has an important role to play in regulating parental behavior but might, at the same time, reject the suggestion that the government, in order to play this role, should spend its time snooping into family life. Is there a way, we might ask, for the government to ensure (to the extent possible) that parents look out for the interests of their children without constantly having to poke its nose into the affairs of parents? Indeed there is: the government can license parents—license them in such a way that only those individuals who are genuinely concerned about the well-being of children will be able to get a license and thus play the role of parent. A person who didn't see the need to rush a multiply-wasp-stung child to the hospital simply wouldn't get a license; nor would a person who didn't see the need to send a child to high school; nor would a person who thought spanking was the only possible response to misbehavior in a child. If parents were licensed, there would be much less need for the government to intrude into family life.

In the absence of licensing, anyone who possesses the biological ability to create a child is given the chance to raise it. This means (as we saw back in Chapter 7) that lots of people find themselves with a child to parent but lack the desire or competence to parent it. Despite this, the government is willing to let them have a try at parenting, and as long as their parenting isn't manifestly injurious to the child, they will be allowed to keep trying. It is largely because so many unmotivated and marginally competent people are allowed to parent that the issue of governmental regulation of parental behavior arises. If, however, we take steps to see that only qualified individuals are given the opportunity to act as parent, there will be much less need for the government to interfere with the behavior of parents.

Abortion

It would be remiss of me in this, a book about parent/child relations, to ignore the topic of abortion. When a woman gets an abortion, she is clearly engaging in behavior that affects the well-being of the child within her. It is also parental behavior that many people think the government should regulate or ban entirely. I nevertheless find myself reluctant to discuss abortion. My reluctance is not because it is a controversial subject. (Indeed, it is rather innocuous compared to some of the subjects I have taken on in this text.) I am reluctant simply because I don't have anything new to add to the ongoing debate over abortion. I have been thinking about the morality of abortion for thirty years, and there is still much about which I have not yet made up my mind. Let me take this opportunity, though, to share with the reader some of the conclusions that I have drawn about abortion.

First, I think that a significant portion of the debate over abortion is seriously misguided. Lots of people think that the debate turns on the question of whether fetuses are *persons*, in the moral sense of the word. They think that if fetuses are persons, then it is wrong to abort them. This is clearly a non sequitur: it is, after all, sometimes permissible to kill persons. There is nothing morally objectionable, for example, in me killing in self-defense a person who is attacking me, if that is the only way I can save my life.

Let us, for the sake of argument, assume that the fetus is a person—a full-fledged person with the full complement of human rights—from the moment of conception. Even if we make this assumption, abortion will sometimes be morally permissible. Consider, for example, an ectopic pregnancy—that is, a pregnancy in which the fetus is growing outside a woman's womb. In many such pregnancies, the fetus and the mother both will die if the pregnancy is allowed to continue. An abortion will end the life of the fetus but let the mother live.

It is important to realize that in this case, we are not presented with a choice of saving *either* the life of the mother *or* the life of the fetus. To the contrary, *the fetus will die no matter what we do*. The choice instead is whether the mother lives or dies. In such a case, I think that the mother is doing nothing immoral to have the abortion. More precisely, I think her getting an abortion is morally equivalent to killing in self-defense. I also think that the government, if it values human life, should allow (but not force) the mother in question to get an abortion.

Thus, there are cases in which women should be allowed to get abortions. There are also cases in which they shouldn't. Suppose, for example, that a woman voluntarily gets pregnant and carries the child for seven months, at which time she wins a prize: a one-month-long, all-expenses-paid tour of Africa. The only hitch is that she must begin the tour in one month's time (in other words, during her last month of pregnancy). The woman considers her options. She could, to begin with, go to Africa while she is pregnant. She rejects this option since it would be no fun—and in fact would be medically dangerous—to tour Africa while she is in her last month of pregnancy. Alternatively, she could have a cesarean section and leave the child with someone else while she goes to Africa. She also rejects this option, reasoning that she would still be recovering from the operation while on the trip—which, once again, would be no fun as well as medically dangerous. Her final option is to abort the child now. She reasons that a partial-birth abortion—in which the baby, after its head has been collapsed, is delivered via the birth canal—will be far easier to recover from than a cesarean section, and she will consequently be able to enjoy her trip to Africa.

If abortion in the case of a life-threatening ectopic pregnancy is the moral equivalent of killing in self-defense, then the partial-birth abortion just considered is, I think, the moral equivalent of infanticide. The government should not allow such abortions.

According to the stewardship model of parenting, in creating a child you take on an obligation to care for it and look out for its best interests. A woman acting on the stewardship model of parenting will not wait until a child is born before she begins caring for it; while it is still in the womb, she will try to eat right; will refrain from using alcohol, tobacco, and other drugs; and will seek prenatal care. She will, both before and after the child is born, make many sacrifices on behalf of the child: that is what steward-parenthood calls for. The woman described above, who aborts a fetus that she suddenly finds inconvenient, is clearly not operating on the stewardship model of parenting.

To be sure, the cases I have dealt with above—the ectopic pregnancy and the prize-winning woman—are two fairly easy cases to deal with. (That is why I chose them for discussion.) In other cases (for example, women who are pregnant as the result of rape, women who are pregnant despite using effective contraception, and women who didn't use contraception, but are still in the very early stages of pregnancy), I am much less certain what to say. Presumably, I am not alone in this predicament.

CHAPTER 11

DIVORCE

It is obvious that by regulating what parents do to their children, the state can improve the quality of life of these children. But by regulating what parents do *to each other*, the state can also have an impact on the well-being of children. In particular, if the state allows parents to divorce on a whim, it undermines families, and weakened families are not in the best interests of children.

In my discussion of divorce back in Chapter 9, I assumed that couples should be allowed to divorce for less-than-compelling reasons and went on to ask which parent should be allowed to raise their children in the aftermath of their divorce. In this chapter I will no longer make this assumption. To the contrary, I will argue that the American government has gone too far in liberalizing divorce laws.

A Brief History of Divorce

The divorce procedure is described—and approved of, in a qualified way—in Deuteronomy. The grounds for divorce are that a husband find "something shameful" in his wife. In the Middle Ages the grounds for divorce were tightened considerably, making divorces almost impossible to obtain. People could get divorces of bed and board—what we today would call a separation. They would live apart but could not remarry.

The tribulations of King Henry VIII led the English, in 1534, to allow individuals to appeal to the House of Lords for a divorce. This procedure was cumbersome, though, and it wasn't until 1801 that a woman petitioned for a divorce. In 1857, England allowed courts to grant divorces, but this did not open the divorce floodgates: by 1886, British courts were granting only 400 divorces per year. (By way of contrast, in 1890, U.S. courts granted 33,461 divorces.)

In the United States, divorce has been around since the Puritans. In 1639, James Luxford's wife asked for a divorce because Luxford already had a wife. The Puritans had what were, for the time, rather liberal divorce laws. Acceptable grounds for divorce included female adultery, male cruelty, bigamy, desertion, failure to provide, and impotence. Divorce hearings, besides deciding whether a divorce would be granted, determined which party to the divorce had been responsible for the breakup of the marriage. The guilty party was fined, whipped, or put in the stocks. Puritans were also likely to forbid remarriage by the guilty party. Such a person had, after all, shown incompetence in matters matrimonial and had no business trying to form another family.

In the early 1700s, Connecticut accepted the notion that when divorces happened, someone was to blame and should be punished, but added a unique twist: if *both* marriage partners were guilty, then no divorce would be granted. The implication is that in such cases, the appropriate punishment was for the partners to be forced to live with each other.

By the 1830s, divorce was easier to get in America than in Europe, with some states having more liberal divorce laws than others. In Virginia in 1827, acceptable grounds for divorce included adultery, cruelty, and just cause of bodily fear. In South Carolina, on the other hand, divorce was impossible until after the Civil War.

In the course of the nineteenth century, states kept adding to the list of acceptable grounds for divorce, sometimes with unintended results. Indiana accidentally turned itself into a divorce mecca when, in 1852, it allowed judges to grant divorces on grounds they found "proper." This alone would have made Indiana a desirable place to get a divorce, but what really did the trick were three other features of Indiana law. First, Indiana had a minimal residency requirement. Indeed, your own affidavit was regarded as sufficient proof of residency, so that an unscrupulous person might establish his residency in Indiana without actually residing there. Second, Indiana law allowed notification of divorce proceedings to be served through publication. This meant that you could, by putting an ad in an Indiana newspaper—which people in other states and certainly in other countries would be unlikely to read—satisfy the law's requirement that you inform all relevant parties of your intent to divorce. Third, under Indiana law, divorce decrees were irrevocable. In theory, a person could go to Indiana, declare residency, put an ad in a paper, and in short order be divorced. The spouse might not even find out about it until months later, and protests of unfairness would be met with the reply that the divorce was irrevocable. In 1873, Indiana tightened its divorce laws and thereby closed the Pandora's box it had inadvertently opened. This was America's first encounter with "migratory divorces" on a grand scale.

Indiana is not the only place to gain infamy for its divorce practices. Thereafter, Utah gained a reputation as a divorce mill, followed by the Dakotas, Oklahoma Territory, and of course Nevada.

Migratory Divorce

By the beginning of the twentieth century, politicians were up in arms about interstate differences in divorce laws. One state, believing that marriages should be terminated only in extraordinary cases, might enact restrictive divorce laws only to see its citizens slip across the state line to obtain an easy divorce in the neighboring state. And then, adding insult to injury, the citizens in question might cross back, flaunt their divorce, and perhaps even remarry in their original state.

Here in a nutshell is the (political) problem with migratory divorce. If people are allowed to migrate to obtain divorces, the divorce standards of the entire country will effectively be set by the state that is most liberal with respect to divorce. This state will tend to drag down the standards of the other states: they can either maintain their restrictive divorce laws and see them circumvented, or they can weaken them. This might be thought of as Gresham's Law of Divorce. According to the original version of Gresham's Law—found in economics texts—bad money will drive good money out of circulation. (If you had two dimes in your pocket, one of which you knew to be 100 percent silver and the other of which you knew to be only 50 percent silver, you would spend the one with less silver and hoard the other. Others would reason similarly. The debased coin would circulate, the undebased coin would not.) In much the same way, Gresham's Law of Divorce declares that liberal divorce laws in one state will tend to drive restrictive divorce laws out of the law books of surrounding states.

Notice, too, that states that liberalize their divorce laws and become divorce meccas usually profit from doing so. Their hotels will be full, their tourist industry will thrive, and their divorce lawyers will enjoy boom times. The lobbying money spent by these pro-divorce forces is unlikely to be matched by groups opposed to easy divorce. Thus, economic factors bring divorce meccas into existence and help them endure.

There are two fairly obvious ways in which migratory divorces could be blocked, but both raise constitutional issues. The first is for the federal government to enact divorce laws, so that all states have the same standards for divorce. Then no advantage could be gained by crossing state lines to obtain a divorce. It is generally agreed that such laws would be an unconstitutional infringement by the federal government on the rights of states. Some attempts have been made to amend the Constitution in this respect, but to no avail.

A second way to block migratory divorce is for states with restrictive divorce laws simply to refuse to accept divorces granted in states with more liberal laws. When states tried this, chaos resulted, with some states regarding a "divorced" couple as still legally married. In 1906 the Supreme Court settled the issue by ruling, in the case of *Haddock v. Haddock*, that a state could reject a divorce decree issued by a state that was not the couple's marital domicile. In 1942 the Supreme Court modified this view in the case of *Williams et al. v. North Carolina,* which involved a man and woman from North Carolina who were married—but not to each other—and who ran off to Nevada to obtain divorces from their respective spouses. They subsequently got married and returned to North Carolina, where they found themselves charged with bigamy. The Supreme Court ruled that North Carolina had to accept the Nevada divorce, thus overturning *Haddock v. Haddock*. North Carolina kept pestering the couple, though, and questioned whether the couple's six-week residence at the Alamo Auto Court (in Nevada) counted as a valid residence. The Supreme Court concluded that it did not. In short, states were required by the full faith and credit clause of the Constitution to accept the divorces granted in other states—but not always.

The No-Fault Divorce Revolution

After World War II, divorces became easier to obtain. By the mid-1960s, several states included "living apart" among the acceptable grounds for divorce and specified the amount of time that a couple must live apart. Finally, in the late 1960s, even this almost groundless ground was dropped when California became the first state—indeed, the first place in the Western world—to adopt "no-fault" divorce. The "grounds" for a divorce became "irreconcilable differences" causing the "irremediable breakdown" of a marriage. What proof was required that irreconcilable differences existed or that a marriage had broken down irremediably? None, other than the declared opinion of one party to the marriage that they did and it had.

Notice that I said the opinion of *one* party to the marriage. This was the most breathtakingly revolutionary feature of California's no-fault law: it allowed unilateral divorce. The wife of a man seeking a divorce could claim that the differences were not irreconcilable or that the marriage could be saved, but these claims counted for nothing in a court of law. If the husband wanted to go, there was nothing she could do to stop him. There was, in short, no right to remain married.

Unilateral divorce tips the balance of power in favor of the person who wants out of a marriage. The person who is happy in the marriage must beg and compromise in an attempt to get the other to stay. Under traditional divorce laws, it was the person who wished to depart who needed the consent of the spouse and who therefore had to beg or compromise. By tipping the balance of power in favor of the person who wants out of the marriage, the unilateral nature of no-fault divorce laws increases the chance that a divorce will occur.

Many people don't understand this feature of no-fault divorce. When sociologist Lenore Weitzman interviewed divorce lawyers nearly fifteen years after the passage of no-fault, she found that they were still having to explain to their clients that it didn't matter how rotten their ex-spouse had been. From the legal point of view, their spouse's behavior was irrelevant to determining whether or not a divorce should be granted; and if a divorce was granted, the spouse's behavior was irrelevant to determining how the couple's property should be divided and whether the wife should get alimony. Under no-fault divorce laws, marital property is divided equally, and alimony is granted on the basis of need rather than on the basis of marital guilt.

Thus, under no-fault divorce laws, you can violate your marriage vows and pay no price—or, at any rate, pay a far lower price than you would have had to pay under traditional divorce laws. Having an extramarital affair used to be an expensive undertaking: your ex-spouse could get revenge when it came time to divide the property or award alimony. Under no-fault divorce laws, you can be a blatantly unfaithful spouse and fare as well in a divorce as if you had been a perfect spouse.

Not only were the grounds for divorce trivialized, but the divorce process itself was streamlined. A divorce might require only a few pages of paperwork and two minutes of court time—unless, that is, one chose the divorce-by-mail option, in which case no court appearances were necessary. Thus, in its most liberal form, no-fault divorce wasn't that much different from the process used in the Middle East, where to obtain a divorce the man simply declares, "I divorce you."

How, one wonders, did no-fault come to happen? Where were the guardians of the family? Where were the political conservatives?

One of the leading political conservatives, Ronald Reagan, was governor of California when that state triggered the no-fault revolution. Reagan and other conservatives backed the law because as originally proposed, the no-fault divorce law would have created a Family Court that would have attempted to reconcile marriages before granting a divorce. Conservatives liked this aspect of the law and thought it would help preserve the family and reduce California's high divorce rate. At the last minute, though, the Family Court feature was removed from the law. What California ended up with was a law that made it easy for people to separate without first pushing them to reconcile.

No-fault divorce did accomplish one of its original goals: it made the divorce process less acrimonious. In a traditional divorce the two parties typically battled each other, dragging out their spouse's every fault, both real and imagined, for all the world to see. They declared emotional war on each other, and the legal system aided and abetted their acts of war. Under no-fault, though, it didn't matter what your spouse had done to you. The courts no longer wanted to hear about it.

California was not alone in making the move to no-fault. In 1971 the Supreme Court, in *Boddie v. Connecticut*, ruled that divorce is a citizen's fundamental right. By 1980 all but two states had no-fault divorce laws. To be fair, not all these states went as far as California in liberalizing their divorce laws. By the mid-1980s about a quarter of the states still required mutual consent in divorces. States also differed in whether property divisions and alimony awards could be affected by "guilt" on the part of one of the married persons.

This, then, is no-fault divorce. Could divorce laws be liberalized any further? Perhaps. Some have suggested, for example, that marriages have built-in divorces—that marriage contracts have a time limit, after which the contract could be renewed if both parties are willing and terminated at the wish of either party. One suspects, though, that further liberalization of divorce laws is unlikely: it is difficult to imagine the pendulum swinging much farther.

The result of making divorces easier to obtain was—predictably—a sharp rise in divorce rates. Between 1950 and 1965, divorce rates held steady at between 2.2 and 2.6 per thousand. In 1970 the rate rose to 3.5 per thousand, in 1975 to 4.9 per thousand, and in 1980 to 5.2 per thousand. Since 1980 the divorce rate has been fairly constant at between 4.7 and 5.3 per thousand, with a slight downward trend during that period. What do these numbers mean? Put into a historical context, we find that today's divorce rate is nearly eight times the rate that prevailed in 1900. The divorce rate is now half as high as the marriage rate—which, by the way, stayed fairly constant throughout the twentieth century.

Looking around the world, we find that America has one of the highest divorce rates—twice that of Australia, four times that of Japan, eight times that of Mexico, and ten times that of Turkey. To find higher rates, we must turn to exotic cultures like the Kanuri of Nigeria, whose divorce rate is said to be nearly 100 percent.

America's fondness for divorce becomes obvious in other ways. You might think that the religiously ultraconservative Mennonites living in America and Canada would share the same values about marriage, divorce, and life in general, but Mennonites in America divorce four times as often as those in Canada. The American culture of divorce is apparently capable of overwhelming even deeply held value systems.

Why the Revolution?

Why did America switch to no-fault divorce laws? Our ancestors could tolerate traditional restrictions on divorce, as could our contemporaries in most of the rest of the world. Why couldn't we?

It would be nice to be able to answer this question by saying that we were more thoughtful than our ancestors or the rest of the world and that we had made some important discovery in science, psychology, or ethics that justified our move to no-fault divorce laws—it would be nice, in other words, to be able to say that we switched to no-fault divorce laws because we were enlightened in a way that our ancestors and the rest of the world were not. Unfortunately, our reasons for the switch were not quite so high-minded.

We became more tolerant of divorce in part because our religious beliefs changed. This is not to say that we stopped believing in God or going to church. We did become much less willing, however, to let God or our church tell us how to live our lives. Thus, consider the Bible's declaration that a man or woman who remarries after a divorce will be committing adultery—will, that is, be violating the seventh commandment. This alone was sufficient reason for our Christian ancestors to treat divorce as a very serious thing: in getting a divorce, you weren't just abandoning *a* marriage, you were abandoning *marriage itself.* By 1970 many Americans, although still "religious," were perfectly willing to overlook this part of the Bible—to regard it as a curious historical artifact.

And why did Americans become unwilling to let the church tell them how to live their lives? Because we became selfish—that is, we came to value "the self" in a way and to a degree that our ancestors couldn't have imagined. Our ancestors typically thought that lots of things were "bigger than" they were, including their religion, their country, and their family. Because their religion was bigger, they might have to curb their behavior in order to live within its precepts; because their country was bigger, they might have to sacrifice their life in time of war; and because their family was bigger, they might have to stay in a loveless marriage "for the sake of the children." In the 1960s, though, people came to believe that nothing was bigger than they were, and hence that nothing was worth sacrificing for. It is not an accident that the decade that gave us no-fault divorce laws—the 1970s—was christened the Me Decade.

Many of the early opponents of divorce realized that marriage was incompatible with selfishness—or individualism, as they tended to call it. Thus in 1852 we find editor Horace Greeley disparaging the individualistic age in which he lived, an age in which it is "the right of every man to do pretty nearly as he pleases." According to Greeley, the most destructive manifestation of individualism was the rise in divorce rates. In 1880 writer Nathan Allen likewise argued that American individualism was the culprit in the rise in divorces. And in 1909 we find writer Anna B. Rogers claiming that shaky marriages were founded on "the latter-day cult of individualism." Rogers, by the way, characterized the individualism she saw in her time as "the worship of the brazen calf of Self." What might she have thought if she had lived to witness modern individualism?

The Changed Nature of Marriage

It used to make financial sense for a wife to stay home and take care of the needs of her husband and children. In the (unlikely) event of a divorce, she would be compensated for her years of effort. She might be awarded alimony payments for the rest of her life. If her spouse were the "guilty" party in the divorce, she might be awarded an over-sized property settlement. The state saw to it that she would not, as a result of having spent years taking care of her family, subsequently find herself impoverished.

No-fault divorce changed all this. It turned full-time motherhood into a financially hazardous occupation. In the no-fault era, a woman can devote two decades—indeed, arguably the *best* two decades—of her life to her family only to be dumped when her services are no longer required. In most cases the best she can hope for is temporary alimony payments and an equal division of the marital property. She will have to support herself, but thanks to her two-decade layoff, her employment prospects will be bleak.

Suppose a woman tried to protect herself from this financial risk by entering into a premarital agreement with her fiancé stipulating that if she stayed at home and raised the kids, he would, in the event of a divorce, have to support her financially for the rest of her life. In most states this sort of contract will have no legal standing.

Women quickly came to realize that the best way to protect themselves against the risks of stay-at-home motherhood was to combine motherhood with a career. In 1970—the beginning of the no-fault divorce revolution—only 30 percent of married women with children under six years old were in the workforce. By the early 1990s this percentage had doubled.

In pushing mothers into the job market, no-fault divorce pushed their children off their laps. In many cases these children were placed in day-care centers in which the level of care was not nearly as high as a stay-at-home mother might have provided. Instead of countless hours of companionship with their mother, children had to content themselves with their daily quota of "quality time."

Besides changing the relationship between mothers and their children, no-fault divorce laws changed the relationship between husbands and wives. In particular, these laws had the effect of un-dermining people's commitment to marriage. In making it easier for couples that wanted divorces to get them, no-fault laws arguably made it likelier that people *would* want divorces.

In support of this claim, consider the surge in the divorce rate after the enactment of no-fault divorce laws. The surge itself is easily explainable: there was a backlog of people who wanted divorces but couldn't get them until the passage of no-fault laws. Once this backlog had been taken care of, though, something curious happened. The divorce rate did not return to its pre-no-fault rate, and the reason it didn't is arguably because the existence of no-fault divorce laws made marriages more fragile.

Let me resort to an analogy to explain the nature of this change. Suppose you were told (by some authority) that you would have to live in a certain house for the rest of your life. If you were sensible, you would take good care of the house assigned to you. You would maintain it. You might remodel it. You would realize that to abuse the house was, in the long run, to abuse yourself. Suppose, on the other hand, you were told (again, by some authority) that you could live in a certain house but move to another house whenever you wanted and pay no penalty for doing so. In this case you would probably find yourself much less inclined to maintain your house or remodel it. You might instead enjoy wild parties in which windows were smashed and doors were punched through. And why not? You could, when the mess became too great, simply walk away.

Much the same can be said of marriage. If it is difficult to get out of a marriage, there will be more incentive to expend effort in an attempt to make the marriage work. It would be foolish to declare war on your spouse if you knew that "the enemy" was going to be around to retaliate for the next few decades. On the other hand, if you can waltz out of a marriage on a whim—or equally important, if you know that your spouse can waltz out—there will be less incentive to engage in the sort of self-repression and compromise that is typically necessary if a relationship is to endure. The old proverb "Marry in haste, repent at leisure" has, thanks to no-fault divorce, been turned on its head: now the appropriate proverb would be "Marry in haste, divorce in haste."

In short, I am suggesting that in passing no-fault laws, states not only helped people in unhappy marriages escape those marriages, but inadvertently undermined marriages that might otherwise have been happy and thereby brought about divorces that would not otherwise have taken place.

Why Get Married?

Before 1960, Americans had lots of reasons for getting married. Marriage allowed a man and woman to have sex without risking social opprobrium, and if children resulted from their sexual activities, it spared everyone involved the stigma of illegitimacy. Marriage also offered men and women "betrayal insurance": betray your boyfriend or girlfriend and the state turned a blind eye, but betray your spouse and the state made you pay.

In the closing decades of the twentieth century, though, these rationales for getting married became obsolete. Society stopped frowning on sex outside of marriage, illegitimacy lost much of its stigma, and no-fault divorce laws put an end to sanctions against people who broke their wedding vows. Despite this obsolescence, Americans continued to marry with as much zeal as ever. Why? What did marriage offer them?

In seeking an answer to this question, I turned to two acquaintances who had (separately) gotten married after living with someone for years. The first acquaintance married his long-term cohabitant because she was changing jobs and the only way he could get her on his health insurance was to marry her. His motivation, in other words, was financial. The second acquaintance married her cohabitant not because she thought it would change their relationship and not to gain someone health-care benefits, but because it had always been her dream to have a fancy wedding.

The truth of the matter is that in America today, there is little reason to get married. In agreeing to marry someone, you are no longer agreeing—as you were before no-fault divorce—to keep your wedding vows until death parted you and to be punished if you broke them. What we are left with might be called "marriage lite"— all of the wedding gifts but none of the commitment. Marriage is to adult couples what going steady is to high school students: you want people to know that you hold this person to be special, but you want to keep the escape hatch readily available.

Lovers fall into two categories—those who are willing to undertake a lifelong commitment to the person they love and to be "punished" for violating this commitment, and those who are not. Under traditional divorce laws, both groups could be satisfied: those willing to undertake lifelong commitments got married; those unwilling had a relationship outside of marriage. No-fault divorce laws, however, satisfied only one category of lovers, those unwilling to undertake a lifelong commitment. To them, no-fault divorce laws were a godsend, since these laws allowed them to be "married," but without the level of commitment that traditional marriage entailed. On the other hand, those willing to undertake a lifelong commitment found that, thanks to no-fault divorce laws, there no longer existed an institution in which they could make this commitment. As far as they were concerned, marriage had been abolished.

In the late 1990s, America witnessed a backlash against no-fault divorce laws. In 1997, Louisiana attempted to put some meaning back into marriage by recognizing "covenant marriages." Couples wishing to enter into a covenant marriage have to undergo premarital counseling and agree to undergo further counseling if conflicts arise in their marriage. In covenant marriages it is impossible to divorce on a whim. Even when a divorce is mutually agreeable, a couple must wait two years before the divorce will be granted; and if the divorce is not mutually agreeable, the person seeking the divorce must prove that the spouse committed a serious breach of the marriage contract—for example, by committing adultery or being physically abusive. Louisiana also gave people the option of converting their "regular" marriages to covenant marriages. (Significantly, Louisiana did not try to impose covenant marriages on all its citizens, but retained "regular" marriage—that is, marriage dissolvable under no-fault divorce laws—as an option.) By allowing people to enter into covenant marriages, Louisiana lawmakers hoped to reduce the divorce rate.

Other states have been slow to follow in Louisiana's footsteps. At first this seems puzzling. As long as covenant marriage is an *option—*

as long as it isn't forced on everyone—why would anyone oppose it? Isn't it good for citizens to have the freedom to choose the form they want their marriage to take? Those who prefer covenant marriages can have them; those who do not can stick with "regular" marriages. No one is harmed, so why would anyone object?

One source of opposition to covenant marriage is lawmakers who worry that people entering into these marriages will regret having done so. By refusing to recognize covenant marriages, these lawmakers think they are protecting citizens from doing something foolish—protecting them, that is, from themselves. A second source of opposition is citizens who would *not* themselves choose a covenant marriage but nevertheless feel threatened by the covenant marriage option. If a state recognizes covenant marriages, then people getting married in that state will have to declare to their future spouse which sort of marriage they prefer, regular or covenant. This could lead to some awkward situations in which, say, a man had to admit to his fiancée that he didn't feel confident enough of their future life together to ask for a covenant marriage. If covenant marriage isn't an option, this source of awkwardness can be avoided. Thanks to this opposition, it seems unlikely that covenant marriage is going to take America by storm.

The Dark Side of Divorce

In the early 1960s, to file for divorce was to trigger a scandal. Most Americans believed that divorces hurt not only the adults who got them, but—more important—their children. The conventional wisdom was that broken homes produced juvenile delinquents. Couples that got divorced found themselves stigmatized. To avoid this stigma and to avoid harming their children, many people felt compelled to remain in less-than-loving marriages.

These views changed in the late 1960s and early 1970s, when sociologists informed us that children weren't really hurt by divorce—or at any rate that the harm done was less than the harm done when parents stayed together "for the sake of the children." It was true, sociologists argued, that divorces were painful, but most people—adults and children alike—recovered quickly and fully. Much of America found this message wonderfully reassuring: "You are having a midlife crisis and wonder that perhaps you might be happier with someone else? Go ahead, get a divorce. You worry that this would cause grief to those in your family? This is true, but the grief you speak of is nothing compared to the grief that you and your spouse will experience if you continue in a loveless marriage. You worry about the kids? Relax, they'll be fine."

Before long, evidence demonstrating the destructive nature of divorce began to mount. Sociologist Judith Wallerstein, for example, undertook a study of the aftereffects of divorce. At first her plan was to do a one-year study of divorce, figuring this was plenty of time for the wounds of divorce to heal, but she quickly discovered that even after a year, the wounds caused by divorce were open and painful. Her conclusion: adults in general and children in particular did not bounce back quickly after a divorce.

America was not pleased by these findings. Therapists, parents, and lawyers sent angry letters assuring Wallerstein that divorce was innocuous. America, she concluded, was extraordinarily reluctant to admit the harm done by divorce. There were two reasons for this reluctance. First, admitting that divorce had a dark side would mean admitting that we had made a mistake in our hasty passage of no-fault divorce laws—that we were guilty of leaping before we looked. Second, people feared that acknowledgment of the harmful aftereffects of divorce would trigger a return to traditional divorce laws—which in turn would mean that people would have to give up their freedom to divorce on a whim. This was a sacrifice lots of adults were reluctant to make.

Wallerstein extended her study of the children of divorce and found that even decades after a divorce, children remained emotionally scarred.

Who loses in a divorce? Almost everyone involved. Consider first the fate of divorced women. Feminists were early advocates of liberalized divorce laws: they believed that these laws would allow women to escape from oppressive marriages. What they soon discovered, though, is that women tend to fare poorly in no-fault divorces.[1]

Most no-fault divorce laws are based on the assumption that men and women are equal—an assumption feminists heartily endorse. But if they are truly equal, then—divorce-court judges reasoned—they should be equally able to find employment in the aftermath of a divorce and therefore don't need financial support in the form of alimony from their ex-husbands. Judges also tended to think that women benefited from going to work after a divorce: it was a form of postdivorce rehabilitation.

Of course, as much as we might wish it, women were not and are not the economic equals of men. Women who got married before, say, 1960 often lacked job skills: it had been their goal in life to be a good wife, period. (Why gain job skills when the deal you made with your husband is that he will take care of you for life if you take care of him and his children?) Even those women who had once had marketable job skills saw the value of these skills diminish during the years they spent at home acting as mother. After a divorce, these women found themselves marginally employable. And even women who were employed throughout their marriage were likely to be paid less than a man with the same job skills. When all is said and done, most women emerging from a no-fault divorce experience a significant decline in their standard of living.

Men arguably fare better, financially speaking, in a no-fault divorce, but of course money isn't everything. Consider, for example, the matter of child custody. Although it is increasingly possible for divorced fathers to be awarded joint custody of their children, women are still awarded sole custody in the majority of cases. Not only do women get the children, but they typically also get the children's affections. One survey found that only one-third of children from divorced homes had a close relationship with their fathers, as compared with 57 percent who had a close relationship with their mothers. Another study found that 77 percent of divorced fathers said that missing their children was one of the worst consequences of divorce.

How much do men and women suffer as the result of divorce? One study examined the events that do most to shatter a person's equilibrium. The death of a spouse came in number one. Numbers two and three in terms of stress were marital separation and divorce. For many people, getting a divorce is a hellish undertaking.

We might at this point suggest that if men and women suffer from a divorce, they have only themselves to blame. The same cannot be said, however, about the children of divorce. They are given no say at all in whether a divorce takes place and yet are profoundly affected by it.

Before the advent of no-fault divorce, the woman usually got the family home and lived there with her children. Under no-fault laws, however, the family home often must be sold so that its monetary value can be divided equally between the man and woman. This sale typically causes a double disruption in the lives of the children of divorce. First, it tears them from friends in their old neighborhood. Second, they are likely to find that their new home is not nearly as nice as their former dwelling: divorced women are often forced to live in a house or apartment (and neighborhood) that reflects their reduced standard of living.

Divorce undermines parents' ability to parent. It distracts parents and saps their energy, and for this reason parents undergoing a divorce grow more likely to ignore their children and less likely to discipline them. The children feel this change in parental standards and might respond with rebellious behavior.

The children of divorce will typically find that their maternal relationship changes. The divorce might transform their stay-at-home "mommy" into a woman who not only is forced to go to work but who, because of the years she spent at home, can find only employment that is low-paying and stressful. Her children will see her less, and when they do see her, she is likely to be tired and crabby.

The children of divorce are also likely to find that their relationship with their father changes for the worse. He might be attentive to their needs while the divorce is being processed. Indeed, he might even ask for custody of them. But in many cases—and the children might be perceptive enough to realize this—his interest in them is a ploy. He might, for example, be requesting custody of them as a bargaining tactic or in an attempt to punish his spouse. Once his children have served their purpose, the father might show markedly less interest in them—or even no interest at all. According to one survey, more than half the children of divorce haven't seen their father in a year.

Children quickly discover that divorce changes the nature of family gatherings. After a divorce these gatherings tend to be populated by strangers and semistrangers who have been thrust into the children's lives: step-siblings, half-siblings, brothers of stepmothers, and so forth. They may also find that their own mother and father use the gatherings as opportunities to continue the bickering that began with the breakdown of their marriage. According to one study of divorced couples with children, divorce doesn't end parental hostility: even five years after a divorce, one-third of children are routinely exposed to parental acrimony.

What is the net effect of all this stress on children? Here is a partial list of what children can look forward to when their parents divorce: sadness and depression, fatigue, withdrawal from friends, embarrassment (which may last for years and brings loss of self-esteem), intense anger, guilt because of a conflict in loyalty, difficulty concentrating, regression, and somatic symptoms, typically stomachaches or headaches. The question a father and mother contemplating divorce must ask, as psychologist Diane Medved eloquently puts it, is this: "Is the emotional strain of your marriage so bad that you would knowingly inflict these problems on your innocent children?"

Some will react to the above discussion by arguing that I have overstated the harm done to children by divorce. One prominent spokesperson for the "divorce isn't that bad" side of the debate is E. Mavis Hetherington. Her research calls into question many of the conclusions reached, for example, by Judith Wallerstein. Even Hetherington's results, however, make it clear that divorce, while perhaps not as bad as some critics suggest, is rarely a blessing to the individuals who live through it. She argues that within two years after a divorce, most children are beginning to function reasonably well again. The same can be said, one supposes, of Afghan children who step on a land mine: after two years, they have adjusted to their changed circumstances. Wouldn't it be far better, though, for the child not to have been injured at all? She also points out that only 20 percent of children of divorce have significant social, emotional, or psychological problems. *Only* 20 percent? To advocates of the stewardship model of parenting, this percentage will be disturbingly high.

Others will react to my discussion by pointing out that children are harmed when their parents *don't* divorce but instead stay together in a loveless and possibly bitter marriage. They will remind us that we must weigh the harm done to children by a divorce against the harm done to them by such a marriage.

This argument is based on what might be called the Trickle-Down Theory of Happiness: if the state makes parents unhappy by requiring them to stay married, their unhappiness will trickle down to their children; but if the state makes parents happy by letting them divorce, their happiness will also trickle down to their children. As far as happiness is concerned, as the parents go, so go the children—or so the Trickle-Down Theory would have us believe.

If only this were true. According to sociologist Wallerstein, there is no necessary connection between the happiness of parents and the happiness of children. The children may be relatively happy when the parents are miserable but still married, and they may be relatively miserable when the parents are happily divorced.

When a quarrelsome couple gets a divorce, does it help their children? It depends on what the alternative to the dysfunctional family is. If the divorce removes children from an environment awash in hatred and lets them spend their childhoods playing happily with one of their parents, then divorce almost certainly benefits them. The problem, of course, is that in America today, the alternative to living in a dysfunctional family is all too often living with a dysfunctional single parent—typically a mother who is embittered, depressed, impoverished, and stressed out by an unsatisfying job. If you are a child, you might prefer life with two squabbling parents to life with this one parent.

Rethinking Divorce

Our ancestors could have enacted no-fault divorce laws but didn't.

Why not? Why did they insist on allowing divorce only when stringent conditions were met? Let us try to recapture the thinking that went into pre-no-fault divorce laws.

Marriage traditionally involved a contract. The contract in question was rarely written but was nevertheless real. It consisted of a series of promises made (explicitly or implicitly) by a man and woman, including (typically) a promise to be partners for life, to be sexually faithful to one another, to help each other in times of sickness and hardship, and to share worldly goods. Furthermore, the promises made in a traditional marriage were serious promises, the breaking of which could significantly hurt a spouse. How would you like to care for a sickly spouse for years, only to have him turn his back on you in your time of need? Or pass up many potentially pleasurable extramarital affairs only to discover that your spouse has not likewise been passing them up?

Most people agree, however, that one of the most important roles of government is the enforcement of contracts that citizens enter into. If you and I enter into a sales agreement in which you give me your car today and I give you ten thousand dollars next week, and if I subsequently refuse to pay, the government clearly has a role in making me either pay you or return the car to you. If people were allowed to break contracts with impunity, economic and moral chaos would result.

But if marriage involves contracts and if the government has a role in enforcing contracts, it follows that the government has a role in determining the conditions under which marriage contracts are nullified—that is, the conditions under which people are allowed to get divorces. In refusing to grant a divorce, the government is, in effect, forcing the parties to the marriage contract to keep the promises they made. The marriage contract is arguably far more serious than, say, a contract to buy a car; and the harm done to a spouse when someone violates his marriage contract is generally far more serious than the harm done, say, to a car dealer when someone refuses to make payments on a car he has purchased. If we think that the government is justified in enforcing car-purchase contracts, it is even more justified in enforcing marriage contracts.

If we accept the argument so far, we are faced with a new question: what should count as proper grounds for a divorce? Before attempting to answer this question, it will be useful to consider the moral nature of promises.

Promises are not morally sacred: there are times when it is permissible—indeed, when it is morally obligatory—to break a promise. Suppose, for example, you promise to meet me for lunch but break this promise in order to render first aid to an accident victim who would otherwise die. Or suppose a promise is "reciprocal": I promise to pay you rent each month for the next twelve months, and you promise to let me live in your apartment for the next twelve months. Suppose that after the first month you kick me out. Must I, under these circumstances, keep my promise to pay rent each month for the next eleven months? Certainly not. If one party to a reciprocal promise breaks his promise, the other party is no longer (in most cases) morally obligated to keep his promise.

Along similar lines, suppose someone makes a fraudulent reciprocal promise. Suppose that after signing a lease to rent—sight unseen—your apartment for the next twelve months (in return for monthly payments), I discover that the apartment you rented me has no running water, no electricity, no roof, and walls that are only two feet high. Must I, under these circumstances, keep my promise to pay rent each month? Clearly not. More precisely, notice that if I had been told the condition of the "apartment," I would never have agreed to sign the lease. I contracted for an apartment, and what you are leasing me is something very much less than an apartment. I have been misled and because of this, my promise to pay you each month should no longer bind me.

In the same way as there are circumstances under which it is permissible to break a promise, there will be circumstances under which it is permissible to break a marriage contract. Before no-fault divorce laws were implemented, one of the basic tasks of judges in divorce cases was to determine which spouse had failed to live up to his or her marital promises. Thus, if a man deserted his wife, he hadn't kept his promise to be her lifelong partner. If a man had an affair, he hadn't kept his promise to be faithful. Similarly, if a man was impotent, he was (presumably) unable to provide what his end of the marital contract called for. (And if he knew he was impotent and kept it a secret from his wife until they were married, he engaged in a form of fraud.)

This brings us to the question of what, if anything, should happen to the "guilty" party in a divorce. It is useful, in attempting to answer this question, to think about contracts in general. When someone breaks a contract, the government typically responds in one of two ways. It either forces the person to perform—that is, to do whatever the contract obligated him to do—or forces him to compensate the other party to the contract for harm done by the breach of contract. Before no-fault divorce, when someone broke his marital contract, the government typically responded in one of these two ways. When a divorce court forced a man to pay his wife alimony for the rest of her life (or until she remarried, whichever came first), the court was simply forcing him to do what he had promised to do in the marriage contract—namely, provide for her until death parted them. And when the divorce court punished a philandering husband by making him turn over more than half the couple's assets to his spouse, it was attempting to compensate her for the harm done by his breach of the marital contract.

Those on the religious right are fond of appealing to the Bible in their attacks on no-fault divorce. The above discussion, however, shows that such appeals are superfluous. The Bible was never invoked; instead, I invoked the utterly nonreligious and widely accepted principle that the government should make people fulfill their promises, particularly when breaking these promises will seriously harm someone. Anyone who accepts this principle should have serious misgivings about our acceptance of no-fault divorce laws.

In saying this, I don't mean to suggest that pre-no-fault divorce laws were perfect. Indeed, I can think of two respects in which they were defective.

The first involves cases in which a divorce is mutually agreeable to a man and woman *who have no children.* Such a divorce would be "groundless," in the sense that the man and woman seeking it are not claiming that the other party has broken the marriage contract. For this reason, this divorce would not have been granted in many states before the no-fault revolution. I would like to argue, though, that if a divorce is mutually agreeable, then the man and woman are in essence releasing each other from the marital promises they made. The case is like that in which, although a tenant has agreed to rent an apartment for a year, the landlord gives him permission to move out and stop making payments after only six months. When the parties to a contract agree to nullify that contract, the government should not stand in their way—not in real estate transactions and not in childless marriages.

The second defect of traditional divorce laws becomes apparent when we look at what happened to children in a divorce. Before a divorce was granted, the interests of the children counted for nothing at all in a divorce hearing. In particular, it didn't matter that the divorce would devastate them emotionally and financially. *After* granting a divorce, however, the court became quite concerned about the interests of the children. In particular, it was careful to grant custody of them to the parent who would do the best job of parenting. This belated interest in the well-being of children seems odd. Why allow a divorce that might be ruinous to children and only then, after most of the damage has been done, grow concerned about their well-being? A cynic might argue that this belated concern for the children is nothing more than an attempt to assuage the guilt feelings we have (or should have) over allowing their world to be turned upside down.

In the same way as a man and woman have a marriage contract with each other, parents have an unwritten contract with the children they bring into existence. (I have described the nature of this contract in detail in *Doing Right by Children.*) In having children, parents—according to the stewardship model of parenting—create a profound obligation to care for the children in question. Fulfilling this obligation might mean sacrificing many of their own desires in order to meet the needs of their children. A steward-parent will have children only within the context of a marriage and work hard to preserve that marriage. This might mean repressing a number of desires. It might mean not just staying together "for the sake of the children," but trying to look happy doing so.

If the idea of putting the interests of one's children ahead of one's own sexual freedom sounds absurd, chances are that the reader is an advocate not of the stewardship model of parenting, but the rival ownership model. Children are found way down on their owner-parents' list of priorities. If the needs of the children block satisfaction of a parental whim, so much the worse for the children. The parents come first.

Thus, advocates of the stewardship model of parenting might favor divorce laws that in some respects are even stricter than those that existed before the no-fault revolution. Those laws, as we have seen, ignored the needs of children until after a divorce was granted. Advocates of steward-parenthood might argue that courts should be very interested in the needs of children when they determine whether or not a divorce should be granted. It should be quite difficult—but not impossible—for a couple with children to get a divorce, particularly if their children are young. Even if the divorce is mutually agreeable to them, the state should be hesitant to grant it if doing so would harm their children.

Some will be appalled by the suggestion that we make divorces even harder to get than they used to be. They might remind us that in the days before no-fault divorce laws, divorces were messy affairs, with the two sides fighting each other tooth and nail in court. In order to "win" the divorce, the two sides were not averse to telling the whole world of their spouse's shortcomings; and if their spouse lacked any real shortcomings, they were not averse to making some up. Do we really want to return to all this unpleasantness?

I agree that no-fault divorce cuts legal wrangling to a minimum and that my proposed tightening of divorce laws would resurrect the old scenes in which married people use the courtroom as a forum for mudslinging. And while these are not pretty scenes, I must remind the reader that scenes like these are part and parcel of legal practice. In criminal trials the prosecuting attorney makes the defendant out to be the worst monster on the face of the earth, while the defense attorney makes him out to be an angel. Similarly, in civil cases the sides will do as much as they can to make the other side's life miserable. A good attorney will take endless depositions, and in them he will ask questions calculated to make the opposition squirm. His hope is that the opposition will throw in the towel just to avoid the agonies involved in the legal process.

If our goal is to minimize legal wrangling, then no-fault divorce laws are just the beginning. We could go on, for example, to implement no-fault laws with respect to commercial contracts. If I make and then break a contract with you, we can spare everyone involved the bitterness of a court battle if I am in no way penalized for the breach. And if this seems absurd, realize that it is precisely what no-fault divorce laws allow someone to do after he has broken a marriage contract. If commercial contracts are sufficiently important that we are willing to endure legal unpleasantness to protect them, shouldn't we also be willing to endure legal unpleasantness to protect marital contracts? Aren't these latter contracts, after all, at least as important to the functioning of our society as commercial contracts?

Finally, someone might react to my advocacy of strict divorce laws by complaining that under these laws, marriage would become a burdensome undertaking. This, of course, is true. At the same time, it is a burden that can easily be avoided—one need only avoid marriage. What no-fault divorce laws have brought about is a world—covenant marriages aside—in which *no one* is allowed to undertake the burden of "real" marriage. In America today, marriage has been abolished in all but name. And as far as America's children are concerned, this is a pity indeed.

EPILOGUE

While I was writing this book, I taught a college course on the moral and political aspects of parenting. In class discussions I routinely played the role of devil's advocate and challenged consensus views on parenting. In other words, I put my students in the position of having to defend "common sense." In the process of defending it, students not only got a chance to sharpen their logical skills, but they also got to see how hard it is to defend the viewpoints that their culture takes for granted.

One of the better students in the class was always quick to rise to my provocations, always willing to try to persuade me that the views I was expressing were wrong and that the consensus view was right. Late in the course, after one prolonged discussion, he summarized his feelings in the following terms: "The arguments you give are perfectly logical, but I find myself unable to accept your conclusions." I not only understand his feelings but to some extent share them.

In the forgoing pages, I have argued, among other things, that dysgenic parents should be prohibited from reproducing and that only licensed parents should be allowed to raise children. Suppose I somehow managed to gain vast power and could implement any laws I wanted. Suppose, for example, America decided that what it needed was a philosopher king (fat chance) and that I was the philosopher who could best do the job (fatter chance still). Would I really use this power to engage in eugenics or to license parents? I don't know. It is one thing to play devil's advocate and reveal to my society the inconsistencies in its views on children; it is quite another to take action to resolve these inconsistencies.

One thing I do know, though, is that most of the improvement in the quality of childhood between 1700 and 1950 came about because reformers were willing to resort to law to force parents to do right by their children. For the longest time, parents were in the grip of the ownership model of parenting and were simply unable to think of children as beings with needs of their own—needs that sometimes parents had to make sacrifices to meet. Thus, our ancestors thought it was an infringement on their rights to be told that they could no longer beat their children or send them off to the coal mines for twelve hours a day. Today we regard these reformers—these early advocates of the stewardship model of parenting—as moral pioneers. In their time, though, their fellow citizens regarded them as radicals whose proposals flew in the face of "common sense."

Why are we reluctant to resort to government to curb the reproductive activities of dysgenic individuals or to license parents? It is in part because we remain in the grip of the ownership model of parenting. Parents, we tell ourselves, have a very basic right to make and raise children, even though it is a right, the exercise of which can have terrible consequences for the children in question. Only if we can break free of the ownership model and view parenting as involving not a series of rights but a series of responsibilities will we be ready to take the next step toward making sure that all children have a childhood worth living. It is only because I have spent years reflecting on the stewardship model of parenting that I am willing to make the bold proposals I have made in this book. As I said at the outset of this book, I am a libertarian who fears government, but I am also a person who loves children. This book has attempted to reconcile these two viewpoints.

Readers might admit that it may someday be necessary to engage in eugenic measures or license parents, but argue that things aren't yet bad enough to warrant such interference—that the harm parents do to their children is far outweighed by the risks we run by initiating eugenic or licensing programs. This assessment of the current state of affairs may be right—and to tell the truth, I would be delighted if I could get readers to admit *this* much—but it may also be naive. For a good many children, life in America is wretched; for many others, childhood is a pale imitation of what it could and should be.

Consider reporter Rick Bragg's description of a walk through the streets of Miami: "On another mattress, two teenage girls in their underwear, both pregnant, motioned to you, beckoned, offering." These girls are almost certainly victims of our willingness to let anyone with the biological ability to make a baby attempt to raise it. And we can only wonder, What will become of the children of *these* children? As biological parents, these girls will have a government-guaranteed right to try to raise their babies.

This is admittedly an extreme case, but I worry that it is also a case that gives us a glimpse of the future of parenthood in America. To understand why I say this, suppose you could go back in time and describe to a 1950s parent what America would be like in the year 2000: a country in which first graders shoot their classmates, high school students randomly shoot dozens of their classmates, and police must patrol school halls; in which children don't just experiment with sex at an early age, but cycle through sexual partners or engage in sexual acts with multiple partners; in which children experiment not with tobacco and alcohol, but with heroin and cocaine; in which out-of-wedlock pregnancy is not only commonplace, but is regarded as a perfectly acceptable alternative to in-wedlock pregnancy; in which children not only use profanity in the presence of adults, but don't even realize that they are using profanity; and in which many inner-city children's career ambition is to become a drug dealer or pimp. The parents of the 1950s would be shocked by this future. To them, it would be a nightmare world. "How did this come about?" they would ask. "Why do people stand for it?"

The questions the parents of the early twenty-first century should ask themselves are these: Is there any reason to think that the descent into nightmare will stop with us? Is there any reason to think that our children's children won't end up inhabiting a world that *for us* would be a nightmare world? It is difficult to be optimistic about the future of the parent/child relationship.

When the parents of my generation turned their back on the 1950s model of parenting, they knew the model existed but found it inconvenient to adopt. (It was too much trouble to wait until marriage to have sexual relations, to stay at home and raise the children, or to stay in a loveless marriage for the sake of the children.) Many of *our* children, however, won't be turning their back on this model; to the contrary, *they won't even know it exists.* They will be baffled by the idea of sacrificing in order to meet the needs of a child for the simple reason that they have never witnessed anyone making such a sacrifice.

It took hundreds of years of incremental improvement to transform childhood from the wretched thing it once was into the wonderful thing it had become by the 1950s. It took only half a century for us to reverse many of these improvements, and as far as I can tell, the downward spiral of childhood will, if anything, accelerate in coming years. I hope I am wrong about this, but if I am right, the day may come when the proposals in this book no longer seem radical.

NOTES

Prologue

1. When, in the following pages, I speak of "the government" or "the state," I mean the government at any level, federal, state, or local.

2. In *Doing Right by Children*, I explain in great detail the ownership and stewardship models of parenting and describe the rise and subsequent fall of the stewardship model.

Chapter 1: A Brief History of Eugenics

1. The idea of allowing someone else to choose your mate might seem outlandish in our culture, but in other cultures, arranged marriages are commonplace. Such marriages, of course, are motivated more by social than by eugenic considerations.

2. Or perhaps it is slightly dysgenic: some would argue that various welfare programs unintentionally give genetically defective people an incentive to reproduce. I will have more to say about this below.

3. We should not read too much into this support for eugenics, since what *really* bothers people about incest is not, it would seem, the production of defective offspring, but the sexual act itself. Thus, people generally find sexual acts between *sterile* siblings to be as repugnant as sexual acts between fertile siblings, even though there is no chance of their producing offspring, defective or otherwise.

Chapter 2: The Case Against Eugenics

1. From the fact that we have a strong biological urge to reproduce, does it follow that we have a right to act on the urge and therefore that we have a right to reproduce? Clearly not. The mistake in this line of reasoning becomes apparent when we consider, for example, that men sometimes have strong biological urges to have sex with women to whom they have not yet been introduced and that from this it

does not follow that they have a right to act on these urges. Indeed, to a significant extent, morality is *about* suppression of biological urges.

2. It is difficult for men who have cystic fibrosis to reproduce, inasmuch as 90 percent of them lack vasa deferentia—difficult but not impossible, as we shall see in the following chapter.

3. The child's fate, in other words, will be like that of a child who has inherited two copies of the gene for Tay-Sachs disease. Such a child looks normal for the first few months of life, but then things take a turn for the worse. The baby becomes irritable, and its development plateaus. It loses muscle strength to the point of complete helplessness. It slowly goes blind. It suffers from muscular twitches, weight loss, convulsions, and repeated respiratory infections. Such babies typically don't make it out of infancy alive.

4. It has been suggested, by the way, that some of the eugenic measures taken by the Nazis were driven not by the logic of eugenics, but the pressures of war; in particular, it has been suggested that Nazis killed the insane not because they wished to avoid polluting the gene pool, but simply to free up hospital beds for wounded soldiers. Similar wartime pressures drove the United States to do what would otherwise be unthinkable—namely, drop atomic bombs on cities inhabited largely by civilians.

Chapter 3: Designing Children

1. We can imagine motives even more bizarre than these. In her novel *Geek Love*, Katherine Dunn describes a woman who ingests pesticides, radioactive materials, and various drugs in order to enhance her offsprings' desirability as carnival freaks.

Chapter 4: Population Control

1. Even though the earth's population has increased dramatically in the last ten thousand years, there have been periods during which the principal population problem facing humanity was underpopulation rather than overpopulation. Outbreaks of plague, for example, severely depleted the population of Europe. Some epidemics killed 95 percent of the people in affected regions.

2. One can argue that Ehrlich's timing may have been wrong, but that his basic idea was correct. Indeed, Ehrlich offers just such an argument in his and Anne H. Ehrlich's 1990 book, *The Population Explosion*.

3. This argument, it should be noted, applies equally well to parents who, although they do not live in an overpopulated country, are too poor to fulfill their children's needs. In Chapter 7 we will consider the possibility of requiring that people have a certain level of affluence before being allowed to raise children.

Chapter 5: The Population Implosion

1. Some will argue that the right to reproduce *includes* the right not to reproduce, so that by forcing people to reproduce we *are* violating their right to reproduce. I, on the other hand, suspect that these are distinct rights, much like the (First Amendment) right of free speech and the (Fifth Amendment) right to remain silent are, but will not attempt here to resolve this issue.

2. Someone could, at this point, question the morality of bringing new children into the world to protect the interests of currently existing people. In particular, if it is wrong (as I argued in the previous chapter) for parents in an overpopulated country to bring children into existence so they could exploit their labor, isn't it also wrong to bring children into existence to serve as soldiers in a fight against a malevolent dictator? There is, of course, an important difference between these cases. In the overpopulated country, the children brought into existence will almost certainly have miserable lives; in the underpopulated country described above, their lives will probably be worth living—if, at any rate, their creation does in fact preclude an invasion by the dictator. More generally, important moral questions arise *whenever* we have the audacity to bring new children into the world; I explore some of these questions in Chapter 11 of *Doing Right by Children*.

Chapter 6: Children without Parents

1. Reverend Singh's editor, Robert Zingg, himself seems nervous about the blue-glow claim. He offers three pages of footnotes in which a variety of people discuss the possibility of eyes glowing blue. The consensus seems to be that such a thing is not as impossible as one might initially suppose.

2. To be sure, there are questions about whether Plato really espoused the end of the family or whether he was merely engaged, in his description of the ideal city, in a theoretical exercise. Later in the *Republic*, Plato suggests that his city is a "city of words" and adds that "it makes no difference whether it exists anywhere or will exist." And in *The Laws*, a later work, Plato appears to back down from his attack on the family. He allows men and women to choose each other—and even suggests the importance of them seeing each other naked before making their choice.

Chapter 7: Licensing Parents

1. Will the pair have to be a man and a woman? If not, we can't expect them to be married, inasmuch as the law does not recognize same-sex marriages. In Chapter 10 of *Doing Right by Children*, I give my reasons for thinking that parenting is best done by a man and a woman. I also offer a (limited) defense of same-sex marriages.

2. Isn't it cruel to take a newborn baby from its mother? Won't she be heartbroken? She may indeed shed tears, but we should question her sincerity. If her baby meant that much to her, wouldn't she have participated in the expedited licensing program and moved heaven and earth in order to pass it?

3. In special cases, health problems can *benefit* an applicant. A prospective adoptive parent who is confined to a wheelchair and lives in a wheelchair-accessible home might have a better chance of adopting a child confined to a wheelchair: it would spare the adoptive parents the expense of making their home wheelchair accessible. Likewise, a handicapped child who was not adjusting well might benefit from being placed with a handicapped adult who understood the challenges of growing up handicapped.

4. A similar argument can be used to explain why we need to license day-care providers. They are motivated by money, not love. Therefore, there is a far greater chance that they will neglect the children in their care than loving parents would.

Chapter 8: Adoption

1. This possibility is not as outlandish as it may seem. According to the *Wall Street Journal* (January 7, 2002), financier Martin Frankel allegedly brought a female child into existence to serve as a future sex partner. The undertaking—which involved sperm and egg donors, a "womb provider," and an adoptive mother—allegedly cost Mr. Frankel forty thousand dollars. There is no evidence that he abused the resulting child, but if his financial empire had not crumbled while she was still a baby, the child might not have been so lucky.

2. More precisely, if prostitution were decriminalized, it would have no victims; but because we outlaw it, prostitution has plenty of victims including, most notably, the prostitutes themselves. They can't turn to the police for protection as other tradespeople can, but must instead settle for the rough justice of the streets.

Chapter 9: Contested Parental Rights

1. Opponents of abortion might at this point interject that it shouldn't be *the rapist* who stops the woman from having the abortion; it should be *the state.* I will examine the role government should play with respect to abortion in Chapter 10.

2. In considering these cases, it is important to realize that even though a boyfriend chooses not to exercise his rights as a child's biological parent, he will still have obligations with respect to that child. Thus, whether or not a boyfriend registered as the father of a child, the state, if it can prove that he is the father, will require him to make child support payments.

3. The biological parents of the girl Ms. Johnson was raising had died in a car crash before learning of the mixup. "Their" child was therefore being raised by their parents—that is, by the biological grandparents of the child Ms. Johnson was raising.

4. Of course, if the kidnappers, rather than raising the child themselves, turned him over to adoptive parents who had no idea that it had been kidnapped (as sometimes happened in Argentina), the above argument for a forced reunification of the child with its biological parents is weakened considerably. It is unlikely that we will deter future kidnappings if we return these children to their biological parents.

5. Subsequent events confirmed that the Schmidts were less-than-ideal parents: six years after gaining custody of Baby Jessica, they got a divorce, thereby adding one more traumatic event to Baby Jessica's childhood. But before we make too much of this, we should realize that the DeBoers, who successfully adopted a child after losing custody of Baby Jessica, also ended up in divorce court.

6. Although courts are reluctant to consider the interests of children in resolving adoption disputes, these interests are, as we have seen, a primary concern when courts are determining which parent, in the aftermath of a divorce, should get custody of the children. Usually, the children go to the parent who will do the best job of parenting. At first this might seem inconsistent—to care about the interests of children after divorces but not in contested adoptions—but there is an important difference between these cases. In a divorce *both parents* have parental rights with respect to the children; the custody hearings after the divorce are to determine *which* parent will lose which rights. In a disputed adoption, it isn't clear who has parental rights to begin with, and the parties to the dispute are arguing that *they* have parental rights and that rival parties don't.

7. Does this contradict my earlier claim that courts are reluctant to take the interests of children into account when settling adoption disputes? Not really, for

remember that in this case, Mr. Stern is not a stranger trying to gain parental rights with respect to the child, but is instead the child's biological father. Because of this, the court treated the case more like a custody hearing after a divorce than like a typical contested adoption. It also, by the way, awarded Ms. Whitehead the right to visit Baby M.

Chapter 10: Regulating Parental Behavior

1. In saying this, I don't mean to imply that steward-parents don't want their children to be "successful" and happy; they do. What I am saying is that it would, for the reasons given above, be a mistake to identify either "success" or happiness *as a central goal of* steward-parenthood.

2. The cases described had differing legal outcomes. Wantland's mother unsuccessfully sued the Christian Science Church. Lundman's parents were charged with manslaughter, but a judge dismissed the charges; Lundman's father successfully sued members and representatives of the First Church of Christ, Scientists, for negligence. Twitchell's parents were convicted of manslaughter, but the conviction was overturned. Johnson's parents were charged with neglect, but a jury found them not guilty.

3. In saying this I am assuming, unrealistically, that the vaccine is 100 percent effective in those who use it.

4. Indeed, legislators probably *didn't* have these fetuses in mind. Back when the laws against child endangerment were written, no one imagined that a pregnant woman could be so uncaring as to endanger her fetus by using drugs. Times have clearly changed.

5. I am not alone in my rejection of spanking as a disciplinary technique. Murray A. Straus, for example, has compiled an impressive body of evidence showing that spanking isn't an effective way to discipline children, that it harms children, and that society in general ultimately pays a price for the harm done.

Chapter 11: Divorce

1. This is just one area in which the women's movement had unforeseen consequences that harmed women and undermined the interests of their children. For an extended discussion of the harm (inadvertently) done to the family by the women's movement, see my *Doing Right by Children.*

SOURCES

Listed below are sources that I found useful in researching the politics of the parent/child relationship, as well as related writings that might be of interest to readers.

Chapter 1: A Brief History of Eugenics

For a history of eugenics in America, see Mark H. Haller, *Eugenics: Hereditarian Attitudes in American Thought* (New Brunswick, NJ: Rutgers University Press, 1984); and Kenneth M. Ludmerer, *Genetics and American Society: A Historical Appraisal* (Baltimore: Johns Hopkins University Press, 1972). For a discussion of eugenics in light of recent genetic discoveries, see Chapter 21 of Matt Ridley, *Genome: The Autobiography of a Species in 23 Chapters* (New York: HarperCollins, 1999). The Pioneer Fund's eugenic efforts are described in Douglas A. Blackmon, "A Breed Apart...," *Wall Street Journal* (August 17, 1999), p. A1.

Chapter 2: The Case Against Eugenics

The heritability of intelligence and other traits are examined in Richard J. Herrnstein and Charles Murray, *The Bell Curve: Intelligence and Class Structure in American Life* (New York: Free Press, 1994). In *Genome,* Ridley discusses the genetic basis of heredity and Huntington's disease as well as the motivation for Nazi eugenic programs. For a discussion of the dangers of trying to propagate desirable genes, see Ruth Macklin, "Parents and Genetic Counselors: Moral Issues" in William Ruddick and Onora O'Neill, eds., *Having Children: Philosophical and Legal Reflections* (Oxford: Oxford University Press, 1979). Richard Dawkins's views on humans as gene-replication machines can be found in his classic *The Selfish Gene* (Oxford: Oxford University Press, 1976). For information on how medical advances have affected the population of America, see Kevin M. White and Samuel H. Preston, "How Many Americans Are Alive Because of Twentieth-Century Improvements in Mortality?" *Population and Development Review* 22 (3): 415–28 (September 1996). For Garrett Hardin's views on the costs dysgenic reproduction imposes on a couple's fellow citizens, see "The Moral Threat of Personal Medicine" and "Impact on Society: Discussions" in Mack Lipkin Jr. and Peter T. Rowley, eds., *Genetic Responsibility: On Choosing Our Children's Genes* (New York: Plenum Press, 1974). This last article is also the source of the brick-dropping argument that I mention. My discussion of waiving one's rights can be found in my "Basic Rights and Meta-Rights," *Freeman* (December 1989).

Chapter 3: Designing Children

An early examination of the issues that arise when parents design children was Thomas C. Schelling, "Choosing Our Children's Genes" in Lipkin and Rowley, *Genetic Responsibility*; a more recent treatment of this subject can be found in Glenn McGee, *The Perfect Baby: Parenthood in the New World of Cloning and Genetics* (Lanham, MD: Rowman & Littlefield Publishers, 2000). For a description of "cosmetic psychopharmacology," see Peter D. Kramer, *Listening to Prozac* (New York: Viking, 1993).

Chapter 4: Population Control

Paul Ehrlich's predictions of a population explosion can be found in his *Population Bomb* (New York: Ballantine Books, 1968) and in his and Anne H. Ehrlich's *Population Explosion* (New York: Simon & Schuster, 1990). For a skeptical analysis of population explosions, see Joseph L. Bast, Peter J. Hill, and Richard C. Rue, *Eco-Sanity: A Common-Sense Guide to Environmentalism* (Lanham, MD: Madison Books, 1994). Betsy Hartmann's anticapitalist analysis of overpopulation is found in her *Reproductive Rights and Wrongs: The Global Politics of Population Control* (Boston: South End Press, 1995). Onora O'Neill's views on the moral obligations of parenthood can be found in her "Begetting, Bearing, and Rearing" in Onora O'Neill and William Ruddick, eds., *Having Children*.

Chapter 5: The Population Implosion

For a description of the nature and extent of the developed world's population implosion, see Ben Wattenberg, *The Birth Dearth* (New York: Pharos Books, 1987). My discussion of how hard it would be for a single person to manufacture a pencil is based on Leonard Read's classic "I, Pencil: My Family Tree as Told to Leonard E. Read," which first appeared in *Freeman* (December 1958).

Chapter 6: Children without Parents

Farson's defense of Children's Liberation can be found in his *Birthrights* (New York: Macmillan, 1974). For further discussion and criticism of Children's Liberation, see Laurence D. Houlgate "Children, Paternalism, and Rights to Liberty" in O'Neill and Ruddick, eds., *Having Children;* and Laura M. Purdy, *In Their Best Interest?: The Case against Equal Rights for Children* (Ithaca, NY: Cornell University Press, 1992). Two sources of information about feral children are J. A. L. Singh and Robert M. Zingg, *Wolf-Children and Feral Man* (Hamden, CT: Archon Books, 1966); and Douglas Keith Candland, *Feral Children and Clever Animals: Reflections on Human Nature* (New York: Oxford University Press, 1993). For a description of "modern" feral children, see Chapter 9 of Ron Powers, *Tom and Huck Don't Live Here Anymore* (New York: St. Martin's Press, 2001). For descriptions of experiments to raise liberated children, see Purdy, *In*

Their Best Interest?; Christina Hardyment, *Dream Babies: Three Centuries of Good Advice on Child Care* (New York: Harper & Row, 1983); and C. John Sommerville, *The Rise and Fall of Childhood* (Beverly Hills, CA: Sage Publications, 1982).

For descriptions of parent/child relations in ancient Sparta, see Nigel M. Kennell, *Gymnasium of Virtue: Education & Culture in Ancient Sparta* (Chapel Hill: University of North Carolina Press, 1995); Anton Powell, *Athens and Sparta: Constructing Greek Political and Social History from 478 BC* (Portland, OR: Areopagitica Press,1988); and Plutarch, "Lycurgus" in Raymond T. Bond, ed., *Plutarch's Lives* (New York: Tudor Publishing, 1935).

Chapter 7: Licensing Parents

Several people have written articles on licensing parents, including Hugh LaFollett, "Licensing Parents," *Philosophy and Public Affairs* 9 (1980); Roger W. McIntier, "Parenthood Training or Mandatory Birth Control: Take Your Choice," *Psychology Today* 9, no. 5 (October 1973); and Claudia Managel, "Licensing Parents: How Feasible?" *Family Law Quarterly* 22 (1988). Jack C. Westman has written a book on the subject, *Licensing Parents: Can We Prevent Child Abuse and Neglect?* (New York: Insight Books, 1994). For an excellent discussion of the rationale for licensing in general, see Chapter IX of Milton Friedman, *Capitalism and Freedom* (Chicago: University of Chicago Press, 1962). For information on the process people must go through to adopt a child, see Elizabeth Bartholet, *Family Bonds: Adoption and the Politics of Parenting* (Boston: Houghton Mifflin, 1993); Edmund Blair Bolles, *The Penguin Adoption Handbook: A Guide to Creating Your New Family* (New York: Viking Press, 1984); Cynthia D. Martin, *Beating the Adoption Game* (San Diego, CA: Harcourt Brace Jovanovich, 1988); and Arty Elgart with Claire Berman, *Golden Cradle: How the Adoption Establishment Works—and How to Make it Work for You* (New York: Citadel, 1991).

Chapter 8: Adoption

For a history of the treatment of orphans in America, see Viviana A. Zelizer, *Pricing the Priceless Child: The Changing Social Value of Children* (New York: Basic Books, 1985); and Marilyn Irvin Holt, *The Orphan Train: Placing Out in America* (Lincoln: University of Nebraska Press, 1992). For a description of the "baby shortage" of the last decades of the twentieth century, see Martin's *Beating the Adoption Game*. Martin also offers a sympathetic examination of baby-selling, as do Elisabeth M. Landes and Richard A. Posner in "The Economics of the Baby Shortage," 7 *Journal of Legal Studies* 339 (June 1978). Books describing the adoption process are listed in the sources for Chapter 8.

Chapter 9: Contested Parental Rights

Laws on parental rights and their termination vary from state to state. I focused my discussion of the topic on the laws of Ohio, which are described in John Gilchrist,

Kids and the Law (Columbus, OH: Pro Se Publishing Company, 1990). The story of Argentina's *desaparecidos* can be found in John Simpson and Jana Bennett, *The Disappeared and the Mothers of the Plaza: The Story of the 11,000 Argentinians Who Vanished* (New York: St. Martin's Press, 1985). A set of readings on contested adoptions can be found in Andrew Harnack, ed., *Adoption: Opposing Viewpoints* (San Diego, CA: Greenhaven Press, 1995).

Chapter 10: Regulating Parental Behavior

For an in-depth discussion of historical views on the rights of parents and on the goals of steward-parents, see my *Doing Right by Children: Reflections on the Nature of Childhood and the Obligations of Parenthood* (St. Paul, MN: Paragon House, 2001). John Stuart Mill's description of mid-nineteenth-century views on the rights of parents can be found in Chapter V of his *On Liberty*. Henry Bergh's role in ending abuse of children in America is described in Zulma Steele, *Angel in a Top Hat* (New York: Harper & Brothers, 1942). For a discussion of the effectiveness of corporal punishment, see Murray A. Straus, *Beating the Devil Out of Them: Corporal Punishment in American Families and Its Effects on Children* (New Brunswick: Transaction Publishers, 2001).

Chapter 11: Divorce

For a history of divorce in America, see Glenda Riley, *Divorce: An American Tradition* (New York: Oxford University Press, 1991). For an examination of the no-fault divorce revolution and its consequences, see Lenore J. Weitzman, *The Divorce Revolution: The Unexpected Social and Economic Consequences for Women and Children in America* (New York: Free Press, 1985); Diane Medved, *The Case against Divorce* (New York: Donald I. Fine, 1989); Judith S. Wallerstein and Joan Berlin Kelly, *Surviving the Breakup: How Children and Parents Cope with Divorce* (London: Grant McIntyre, 1980); Judith S. Wallerstein and Sandra Blakeslee, *Second Chances: Men, Women, and Children a Decade after Divorce* (New York: Ticknor & Fields, 1989); and Judith Wallerstein, Julia Lewis, and Sandy Blakeslee, *The Unexpected Legacy of Divorce: A 25-Year Landmark Study* (New York: Hyperion, 2000). For divorce practices in other lands, see Paul Bohannan, ed., *Divorce and After* (Garden City, NJ: Doubleday & Company, 1970).

Index

6154

DATE DUE